MW01680251

Two Views of the Millennium

The Apocalypse
A Premillennial Interpretation of the Book of Revelation
by Douglas J. Simpson

The Unsealed Book
An Amillennial View of Revelation
by Wade T. Jernigan

Randall House Publications

114 Bush Road • PO Box 17306
Nashville, Tennessee 37217 USA
phone 615-361-1221 • 1-800-877-7030 fax 615-367-0535
www.randallhouse.com

From the Publisher

There is no subject more talked about than the Book of Revelation or the end times. This comes from preaching, discussions, and Sunday school lessons; all hoping to find the answers about the way things will be as time as we know it is ended.

While many views exist today, we at Randall House decided to present the two most common and recognized teachings on this subject into one volume. *Two Views of the Millennium,* containing *The Apocalypse* (a Premillennial perspective) and *The Unsealed Book* (an Amillennial perspective), will offer readers an opportunity to glean from both viewpoints.

The writers are theologians capable of writing their respected positions, not just from an academic background, but because they have spent years in research and believe what they have written.

This book has 26 studies in Revelation, making it ideal for churches, Sunday schools, Wednesday evenings, and colleges or institutes that want to study this subject in a class setting or individuals who want to satisfy their position on the end times.

Dr. Alton Loveless, President
Randall House Publications

Two Views of the Millennium:
The Apocalypse, The Unsealed Book

All of the Bible quotations in this volume are from the authorized King James Version of the Bible.

Printed in the United States of America.

ISBN: 0-89265-874-6

Preface to the Combined Edition

The Apocalypse or the Book of Revelation is open to a number of different interpretations. Several factors contribute to the differences of interpretation that are found among Bible-believing people. One such factor is the variety of chronological approaches that interpreters take when examining the book. Historically, four chronological schools of thought have surfaced: the preterist, the futurist, the idealist, and the historicist.

The latter two viewpoints are not especially popular today; but a comment about them is still in order. The idealist position usually explains the Book of Revelation as a symbolic presentation of the perennial conflict between the forces of God and the forces of Satan. According to this position, John did not write of any particular period of history; his message was written to challenge, inspire, and encourage believers of all ages to persevere for Christ.

Those who ascribe to the historicist viewpoint believe John presented a view of the Christian Church from the first century through the return of Christ as well as a view of a few events before eternity begins. From this frame of reference, the Apocalypse foretold the conquests of the Romans, Muslims, and Turks as well as of other peoples.

The other two approaches, the preterist and the futurist, are still popular today. The preterist proponents say that the bulk of Revelation treats the problems believers were facing in the Roman Empire during the first century. John, this perspective suggests, wrote to remind believers that God was not unaware of their trials and that He ultimately would bring about the destruction of those forces which were then persecuting them.

The final perspective, the futurist orientation, usually divides the Book of Revelation into two portions: the past (chapters 1-3) and the future (chapters 4-22). As a rule, the chapters dealing with the future are subdivided as follows: (a) The Tribulation Period, chapters 4-18, and (b) The Kingdom Period, chapters 19-22.

It is the purpose of this work to delve into the views of Amillenialists and Premillennialists. Differences between the two result in a variety of interpretations. One such issue that divides the interpreters of Revelation is the question of the rapture of the Church. Amillennialists do not accept the view of a literal rapture of the Church while Premillennialists do. Some Premillennialists believe the Church will be raptured or taken to be with Christ in

Heaven before the Tribulation. Other Premillennialists believe it will occur midway through the Tribulation, and still others believe that it will come after the Tribulation. Here again is an area of disagreement. Just as Amillennialists do not believe in a literal rapture, it follows that they do not expect there to be a Tribulation period of seven years prior to the Second Coming of Jesus Christ.

An equally significant difference concerns itself with the interpretation of the Scriptures in general. Amillennialists tend toward a symbolic approach to the Revelation where as Premillennialists usually keep to standard rules of literary interpretation. That is to say, if the literature is poetry (e.g., Psalms), it should be interpreted in the light of ancient Semitic poetic forms. If a passage is history (e.g., Genesis 1, 2), it should be interpreted as history, not poetry.

Two questions arise in the interpretation of the Revelation. When was John attempting to convey truth by figurative language, and when was he making a plain statement of fact? Some passages are easy to identify as figurative, e.g., the seven stars and the seven lampstands in Revelation 1.

Other passages are rather difficult to interpret. The chain, for instance, in Revelation 20:1 is understood by some as a symbol of the power of God that constrains the forces of evil. Yet others think the chain will be a literal chain made by a spiritual being, God, for a spiritual being, Satan. Consequently, they say the chain should be understood as a literal chain designed to bind a spiritual person; however, they do not mean that the literal chain will be a material one. This type of interpretative problem arises throughout the Book of Revelation.

One further point that divides interpreters is related to the subject of Israel and the Church. Some make a sharp distinction between God's dealings with Israel and His dealings with the Church. Others look at Revelation as a message to God's people of all times; viewed in a spiritual sense rather than indicative of literal happenings. Also, there is some disagreement as to whether the revelations have taken place already or are still to come.

Being a mature believer is not a matter of ascribing to one particular interpretation of the Revelation. Instead, the mature believer is a person who is deeply rooted in Christ and growing in his understanding of and obedience to the Scriptures. This fact, however, does not mean that a mature Christian is apathetic about eschatological problems. On the contrary, maturity in Christ suggests a concern for understanding all of the Scriptures. Still, the mature believer recognizes that he is not always correct in his understanding of the Scriptures. He knows that every facet of the Word of God is important, but he thinks it is idealistic to expect every believer to come to the same interpretation of each passage. At the same time, he diligently seeks to interpret the Scriptures in the way God wants all believers to understand His Word.

Many people like to read a book that answers all of their questions. If you are looking for such in this study, you will be somewhat disappointed; for the purpose of this book is to show the distinctives of the Amillennial and Premillennial views of the Book of Revelation. Actually, no one can give a completely definitive interpretation of John's work. But there is a better reason than that for not attempting such a feat: If a Christian is going to mature in Christ, he needs to be stimulated to find answers for himself. Do not be disturbed, therefore, on occasions when you fail to find clear-cut answers to your questions. Instead, think through the viewpoints that are discussed. You should eventually accept the position that is best supported by the evidence.

Table of Contents

The Apocalypse

A Premillennial Perspective

by

Douglas J. Simpson

About Dr. Simpson

Author of ***The Apocalypse***

Dr. Douglas J. Simpson is uniquely qualified to write this Premillennial interpretation of the Book of Revelation. He earned the B.A. degree from Free Will Baptist Bible College, Nashville, Tennessee, in 1962; the M.A. and Ph.D. from Bob Jones University, Greenville, South Carolina in 1963, 1965; the M.Ed., from Middle Tennessee State University, Murfreesboro, Tennessee in 1967; and, another Ph.D. at the University of Oklahoma in 1970.

Dr. Simpson's graduate concentrations were about equally divided in the areas of the history and philosophy of education, religious studies, and psychology and counseling.

His travels have taken him to Canada, Mexico, and extensive travel in the United States. In Europe he has traveled in Ireland, Scotland, Wales, England, France, Luxemburg, Italy, Austria, Germany, Belgium, and Switzerland.

Dr. Simpson's professional experience includes:

1965-68	Free Will Baptist Bible College, Nashville, Tennessee
1970- 73	Memorial University of Newfoundland, St. John's, Newfoundland, Canada
1973- 76	Free Will Baptist Bible College, Nashville, Tennessee
1976- 88	Tennessee State University
1989-99	Texas Christian University
1999-	University of Louisville

Representative publications from his pen have appeared in *The Negro Educational Review, Psychology for Living, The British Journal of Educational Studies, Focus, Journal of Education, Journal of Thought, Contact,* and *Religious Education.*

Dr. Simpson is also the author of the analytical study of *The Book of Daniel* published by Randall House Publications.

1

An Introduction to The Revelation

Study Text: Revelation 1:1-20

Introduction

1. The Introduction to the Book (Revelation 1:1-8)
    a. The Superscription (verses 1-3)
    b. The Salutation (verses 4-8)
2. The Vision of Christ (Revelation 1:9-20)
    a. The Time of the Vision (verses 9-11)
    b. The Person in the Vision (verses 12-16)
    c. The Interpretation of the Vision (verses 17-20)

Introduction

Probably no book in the entire Scriptures stimulates the mixed responses that the Book of Revelation does. Some folks even seem fascinated with the very name of the book, Revelation. Immediately, horses, beasts, seals, trumpets, and bowls go dancing through their minds. They freely talk of a rapture, an Antichrist, a Tribulation, a millennium, and a new Heaven and a new earth. These people are thrilled with knowing what lies ahead in God's timetable and the implications of such for their personal lives.

Not all Christians experience this ecstasy when thinking of the Apocalypse. The very thought of the Apocalypse conjures up notions of lavender locusts, crazy-looking horses, and other strange characters that seem straight off the pen of someone who had never had a course in "How to Say What You Mean"!

Hopefully, this study of the Apocalypse will help the latter of these two groups to come to a better understanding of what Jesus Christ revealed to the Apostle John. This is not to say, however, that the latter group will automatically become members of the first group. The purpose of this work is much more modest than that.

Instead, the design of the book is to whet one's appetite for the Revelation of the Lord Jesus Christ.

Before we move any further in our study of the Apocalypse, it will be worth your time to read the "preface" if you have not already done so. From it, you will obtain a general introduction to the Apocalypse and get an idea of how John's book is approached in this volume.

Exposition

In order to properly focus the Book of Revelation, it is appropriate to stress that the Apostle John wrote the book while in exile on the Isle of Patmos around A. D. 90. The revelation he recorded for all believers may be roughly divided into four divisions:

(1) The Revelator, chapter 1; (2) The Recipients, chapters 2, 3; (3) The Revelation, chapters 4-21; and (4) The Reminders, chapter 22. John's presentation of the revelation centers on a series of sevens: (1) the seven churches, chapters 2, 3; (2) the seven seals, chapters 5-7; (3) the seven trumpets, chapters 8-11; and (4) the seven bowls of wrath, chapters 15, 16. These series of sevens are preceded by an introduction (chapter 1) and followed by a discussion of Babylon, the triumph of God's kingdom, and the New Jerusalem and the new Heaven (chapters 17-22). Occasionally, the series of sevens are supplemented by parenthetical accounts of special events that are probably close-ups of activities during particular seals, trumpets, or bowls. The interludes come in the following order: (1) the two multitudes, chapter 7; (2) the angel, the book, and the two witnesses, chapters 10, 11; (3) the dragon, the woman, and the offspring, chapter 12; (4) the two beasts and the Lamb, chapters 13, 14; and (5) the harlot, chapters 17, 18. Let us now look at John's introduction to the Revelation of Jesus Christ.

I. The Introduction to the Book (Revelation 1:1-8)

When the elderly apostle was sentenced to live on Patmos by the Roman emperor Domitian, he may well have thought that he would be ending his life as a witness to a group of banished criminals. That may have been what John thought; however, God had a different plan for His servant who was exiled to his prison in the Aegean Sea. God wanted John to receive and to record a revelation that no other believer had ever known, a revelation that is a detailed picture of the last days of life on earth before Christ returns to set up His kingdom.

The Superscription (verses 1-3). The opening words of John indicate the nature of that which he is about to explain. The book concentrates on disclosing or unveiling (which is what *revelation* or *apocalypse* means) truths about the Lord Jesus Christ through some unidentified angelic being. The angel's method of disclosing this revelation is implied in the word *signified,* which suggests communication that is figurative or symbolic but may also include straightforward statements.

John the Apostle further clarified the nature of the disclosure or revelation by the words, "things which must *shortly* come to pass." Some commentators argue that the word shortly implies that the entire Book of Revelation had to be fulfilled a few years after John completed the writing of his book. The Book of Revelation, they insist, must be understood as referring to events that occurred during the first and second centuries.

This interpretation is certainly a plausible one. But some Premillennial expositors argue that upon closer examination, the word is better understood as suggesting that the Revelation of Jesus Christ, once it is started, will be completed quickly or suddenly. The same notion is found in John's statement about Christ's future return (Revelation 22:7). When Christ returns, He will suddenly appear even though He may have spent a couple thousand years away before returning. So, too, the prophecies mentioned in the Apocalypse will swiftly take place once they begin.

One additional interpretation of the term *shortly* needs to be mentioned. This interpretation, which also seems preferable to the first one, suggests that the emphasis be upon something that is *soon to take place.* Those who interpret the word in this way stress that prophecy in the Scriptures is seldom concerned with the sequence of events; the emphasis is on the fact of the event. As a result, the fact takes on the appearance of imminence or immediacy. Therefore, the prophecies of the Apocalypse are viewed as imminent while in actuality they were, from John's perspective, distant events.

The second verse further amplifies the nature of the revelation: It is the Word of God, not John's speculations. John himself was only a witness to the revelation as was Jesus Christ Himself. The witness that Christ gave is not exactly clear, but perhaps John's words refer to the witness mentioned in Revelation 1:11 as well as in Revelation 22:16.

At this point in his book, John pauses to mention a threefold blessing having to do with reading, hearing, and obeying the prophecies found in the Book of Revelation. The reference to reading is to the *public* reading of the Apocalypse since only a few copies of the manuscript were available; therefore, a number of Christians would have gathered to listen to the reader. But the particular blessing John speaks of seems to be for those who practice the truths recorded in the Apocalypse. Two significant thoughts stem from the latter part of this statement. First, John makes it clear that a person will be blessed if he continually lives in the light of God's truth. Second, it is obvious that there are practical applications of the Book of Revelation even though much of its content has to do with future events.

The Salutation (verses 4-8). As soon as John finished his description of the Book of Revelation, he turned his attention to greeting the people who would first read his book. The immediate recipients of his book were seven churches scattered in the western part of Asia Minor. They were historical churches in the area just like other congregations mentioned in the Scriptures in the same general area (Acts 20:5; Colossians 1:2). John was probably led to select these seven churches because he was familiar with them, and they were representative of different churches throughout the world in his time as well as in later periods of church history. Perhaps John was a special apostle to the churches throughout Asia Minor.

The customary way of greeting Christians in John's day was to express a desire for the grace and peace of God to fill a person's life. The desire for grace and peace was an abbreviated way of saying that one believer wanted another believer to experience daily God's normal provisions for Christians.

The sources of these riches of the Christian faith are identified as: (1) "him which is . . . was, and . . . is to come," (2) "the seven Spirits," and (3) "Jesus Christ." The first source denotes God the Father and probably alludes to Exodus 3:14 which refers to the eternity of God.

The seven spirits is a rather difficult phrase to understand. A number of people believe John spoke of seven special angels who minister to God the Father. Most interpreters, however, believe that John was conveying the thought of the fullness of the Holy Spirit. This view seems to be more consistent with the context than does the first, because it would be more consistent to connect the wish for peace and grace with the Father, Spirit, and Son than it would to connect it with the Father, seven angels, and the Son.

The last four verses all speak of the Lord Jesus Christ and clarify why believers can experience the grace and peace of God. One of the reasons Christians enjoy the favor and peace of God is because of who Jesus Christ is: (1) the faithful Witness (1:5), (2) the exalted Firstborn Son (1:5), (3) the Ruler of all human rulers (1:5), (4) the future Deliverer of Believers (1:7), (5) the Judge of unbelievers (1:7), and (6) the Alpha and Omega (1:8).

A second reason we Christians enjoy the rich privileges we do is because Christ "loved us, and washed us from our sins in his own blood" (1:5). The consequences of freedom in Christ are at least twofold: (1) believers constitute a New Kingdom, and (2) believers are priests before God. These consequences seem to suggest continuity and change from Old Testament times to New Testament times. In Old Testament times, only the nation of Israel was peculiarly God's kingdom, but now peoples of all nations who are true believers are pictured as making up God's present kingdom. Then a special class of people were priests, but now each believer may go directly to God. No wonder the apostle wrote, "Grace be unto you, and peace."

2. The Vision of Christ (Revelation 1:9-20)

John's brief introduction to the Book of Revelation is followed by an equally brief introduction to the Lord Jesus Christ. This section of the first chapter is divided into three portions: (1) The Time of the Vision (1:9-11), (2) The Person in the Vision (1:12-16), and (3) The Interpretation of the Vision (1:17-20).

The Time of the Vision (verses 9-11). These verses are essentially concerned with the circumstances that surrounded John's life when he received the revelation of Jesus Christ. John, like his readers, experienced tribulation for his faith in Christ. During every period of history, believers have experienced various kinds of persecutions. But these periods of tribulation are not to overwhelm the Christian; for, as John wrote in another book, Christ stated, "In the world ye shall have tribulation: but be of good cheer; I have overcome the world" (John 16:33). The believer in any age, like John when he was on Patmos, should be happy because Christ is not only the King of His kingdom of believers, but He is also ruler of all kingdoms of the world.

The most probable interpretation of "in the Spirit on the Lord's day" is that John was worshiping on the first day of the week. Over a period of time, first century believers came to see Sunday as a special time of worship, fellowship, and study. A second but less likely interpretation of the expression is that John was transported forward to the eschatological day of the Lord; that is, he was permitted to see a vision of how God will judge and rule over the world.

While worshiping the Lord, John entered some type of trance and heard the voice of Christ. He was commanded to write what he would see and then to send what he wrote to seven churches. The term *churches* here, as in a number of other places in the New Testament, probably does not refer to one particular church in each of the seven cities. Instead, there may have been several different groups of believers meeting in various places throughout each of the cities. Thus, the church at Ephesus probably included all of the believers who lived in Ephesus, not just one specific group of Christians who met in a certain building for worship. The same may be true of the churches in the other six cities.

The Person in the Vision (verses 12-16). The Person in John's vision is clearly the Lord Jesus Christ, who is in one sense the Author of the Apocalypse. The overall import of the vision seems to stress two characteristics of the risen Lord.

The first feature about Christ is His glory. One of the first allusions to the glorious position and character of Christ is in the phrase "the Son of man" (1:13). The expression was used by Daniel to designate the Person who came to God the Father (Daniel 7:13). Daniel recorded that there was given to "him dominion, and glory, and a kingdom, that all people, nations, and languages, should serve him: his dominion is an everlasting dominion, which shall not pass away, and his kingdom that which shall not be destroyed" (Daniel 7:14). Other indicators of the glorious nature of the coming Messiah are His priestly robes (1:13), purity (1:14), omniscience (1:14), strength (1:15), authoritative speech (1:15, 16), and brilliant countenance (1:16).

A second notion that throws light on the character of the Lord Jesus Christ is His concern for the Church. He is pictured as standing in the midst of the seven candlesticks (1:13) and holding in His right hand the seven stars (1:16). To those believers who were in the seven churches in Asia Minor and those who served these churches, it must have been very comforting to know that the risen, glorified Christ was in the midst of them and was sustaining them with His strength. Christ had not forsaken them in their time of tribulation, nor had He withdrawn His power from His faithful messengers. In essence, then, the seven churches were assured that the glorified

Christ was still keenly interested in them and was continually seeking to meet their needs.

The Interpretation of the Vision (verses 17-20). A likely consequence of receiving a vision from God is that a person is overwhelmed by the experience. Many illustrations in the Scriptures, especially the Old Testament, reveal that believers were overcome after receiving a vision from God. A significant cause of this response seems to be fear. Notice Christ immediately said to John, "Fear not" (1:17). When a believer encountered the eternal God, he was undoubtedly impressed with his own inadequacies as well as the divine glory of one of the members of the Trinity. Such an experience would seem to cause almost anyone to say, "Woe is me! for I am undone; because I am a man of unclean lips, and I dwell in the midst of a people of unclean lips: for mine eyes have seen the King, the LORD of hosts" (Isaiah 6:5). Sometimes people today claim they receive visions from God but seldom, if ever, do they mention that they were overpowered by the experience. The casual relationships they claim to have had with God seem almost foreign to the experiences of those Bible characters who encountered God.

After reassuring John, Christ explains who He is: the eternal, living Savior of mankind. But this is not all Christ said; He points out that He has the "keys of hell and of death" (1:18). The word *hell* in this case refers to the intermediate state of the dead much as the Old Testament term *sheol* does. The reference is not to the lake of fire or to the eternal abode of unbelievers (Revelation 20:15). Note, too, that Christ said He has authority over *death* as well as life after death. The message He gave to John, then, is that He has sovereign power over both physical death and life after death.

Christians in Asia Minor who received this message–and John was commanded to send it to them (1:19)–were no doubt excited when they received these truths. Christ, they were reminded, is the everlasting risen Savior of mankind; He controls the deaths and destinies of believers. No believer, John told his first century suffering brothers, will die because Christ is indifferent to his persecution. Similarly, he informed them that any believer who dies will do so only because Christ is in control; and even as he is dying; Christ will care for him.

Not only was John instructed to record these encouraging words of Christ, but he was told to "Write the things which thou hast seen, and the things which are, and the things which shall be hereafter"

(1:19). Three distinct aspects of time are covered in this directive to John. As a starter, he was instructed to write about his vision of Christ, i.e., "the things which thou hast seen." Second, he was told to describe the state of the seven churches, i.e., "the things which are." Finally, John was told to explain the rest of the Revelation of Jesus Christ that is related to the future conclusion to human history and to the eternal kingdom of God, i.e., "the things which shall be hereafter."

In the final verse of this chapter, Christ clarified a couple of points about the vision John had just seen. Three truths are mentioned. The first point is related to identifying the person "like unto the Son of man" (1:13). This person was indirectly identified by Christ when He said "in my right hand" (1:20).

A second aspect of the interpretation is related to the seven stars who are "the angels of the seven churches." The term *angel* has caused a number of explanations to be offered by expositors. Some of them suggest that John was actually told to write to seven angelic beings. These seven angels are, from this point of view, thought to be somewhat like ministering angels to individual believers. But this viewpoint is a rather odd one. Why, for instance, would Christ want John to write seven letters to non-human beings when the messages themselves seem clearly to be for the human beings in the churches? Certainly angels have ministries to believers and to groups of believers, but it would be a strange situation if they had to find out what happens on earth through some transcendental mailbox.

The best interpretation may be that John wrote to one key Christian worker or messenger in each city. Paul was inspired to write that God "gave some, apostles; and some, prophets; and some, evangelists; and some, pastors and teachers; For the perfecting of the saints, for the work of the ministry, for the edifying of the body of Christ" (Ephesians 4:11, 12). These four groups of people (pastors and teachers constitute one group, i.e., teaching pastors) were given by God to the early Church to prepare believers for ministering and edifying each other. Thus, these men usually worked with more than one local congregation of Christians. It is possible that John, an apostle, wrote to a member of one of the other three groups; that is, he wrote to someone he knew who was a prophet, an evangelist, or a teaching pastor. There were probably other Christian workers in each of the cities, but John wrote to a particular Christian leader who had contact with all of the believers in the city where he was located.

2

The Letters to Ephesus, Smyrna, Pergamos, and Thyatira

Study Text: Revelation 2:1-29

Introduction
1. The Letter to Ephesus (Revelation 2:1-7)
   a. Praise for the Church (verses 1-3)
   b. Condemnation of the Church (verse 4)
   c. Exhortation for the Church (verses 5-7)
2. The Letter to Smyrna (Revelation 2:8-11)
   a. Praise for the Church (verses 8, 9)
   b. Exhortation for the Church (verses 10, 11)
3. The Letter to Pergamos (Revelation 2:12-17)
   a. Praise for the Church (verses 12, 13)
   b. Condemnation of the Church (verses 14, 15)
   c. Exhortation for the Church (verses 16, 17)
4. The Letter to Thyatira (Revelation 2:18-29)
   a. Praise for the Church (verses 18, 19)
   b. Condemnation of the Church (verses 20-23)
   c. Exhortation for the Church (verses 24-29)

Introduction

The second chapter of the Apocalypse is the first chapter in the next division of the book. As may be noted by examining the outline at the back of this volume, this major division is entitled "The Church Age" and includes only the second and third chapters of the Book of Revelation.

There are two basic interpretations as to how these two chapters of the Apocalypse relate to the Church age or the era of history that stretches from the time of the apostles to the time of the Tribulation. The first viewpoint is that the seven churches are typical of seven distinct eras of church history beginning with the apostolic age and going through the last days. Although there are variations of this interpretation, the following designations are somewhat typical of the general position: (1) Ephesus: The Apostolic Church, A.D. 33-100; (2) Smyrna: The Caesarean Church, A.D. 100-312; (3) Pergamos: The Constantinian Church, A.D. 312-606; (4) Thyatira: The Medieval Church, A.D. 606-1517; (5) Sardis: The Reformation Church, A.D. 1517-1750; (6) Philadelphia: The Missionary Church, A.D. 1750-1900; (7) Laodicea: The Contemporary Church, A.D. 1900-Tribulation.

A popular variation of this viewpoint is that both the church of Philadelphia and the church of Laodicea started around 1750 and are still in existence today. Another variation is that Philadelphia represents the final stage of the Church age and that Laodicea represents the Church during the Tribulation.

While some variety of this general position is held by many Christians, others object to the position on a number of grounds. Although they are not necessarily given by the same critics, two frequently given reasons for rejecting this point of view are the artificiality of the view and the implications for the return of Christ.

Some feel this interpretation is artificial in two senses. First, there is no statement in the Scriptures which implies that this is the way the seven churches should be explained. Instead, it is argued that this is an interpretative scheme based upon speculation, not exegesis of the second and third chapters of Revelation.

The second sense in which this position is said to be artificial is that the descriptions of the seven churches do not naturally describe the periods of history usually given. For example, it is argued that the dead church of Sardis is hardly an adequate description of the movement started by the Protestant reformers. If anything, the Protestant Church was very much alive when compared with the Medieval Church.

Those Christians who reject this interpretation because of the doctrine of the return of Christ usually say the view is inconsistent with the belief that Christ could have returned at any moment after His ascension. For if this view is correct, it would have been impossible for Christ to have returned before the eighteenth century, or, according to some explanations, before the twentieth century.

A second basic way of understanding the seven churches of Asia Minor is that God selected them as recipients of John's letters for a couple of reasons. To begin with, the local churches during John's time were in need of particular spiritual advice; therefore, John wrote to each according to its needs. More than this was involved, however. Other churches, not in the seven written by John, had spiritual needs, too. These churches could find exhortation in the similarities found between them and one or more of the seven churches that received a letter. Finally, this interpretation suggests that the weaknesses and strengths of the seven churches are somewhat representative of many of the problems of churches in all periods of history. As a result, Christians today can profit by a study of what God considered to be weaknesses and strengths of these original churches of Asia Minor.

In order to help you visualize where John and the churches to whom he wrote were, FIGURE 1: A Map of the Apocalyptic Setting, is presented. Many of the islands in the Aegean Sea are not included on the map. You will also notice that geographic exactness has not been achieved. The only purpose of the map is to give the reader a general picture of the apocalyptic setting.

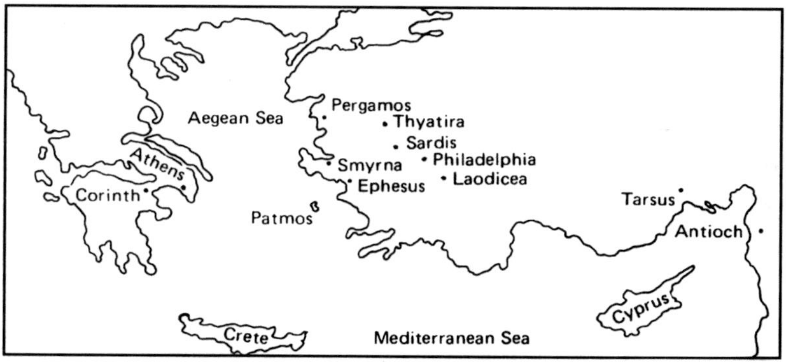

FIGURE 1: A Map of the Apocalyptic Setting

Exposition

In this chapter as well as the next, the procedure which John used in writing to the individual churches is quite similar. He usually identified the church itself, mentioned something about the person of Christ, praised the church if appropriate, rebuked when necessary, and then exhorted the church to live as Christ desired so that it could receive Christ's promises.

1. The Letter to Ephesus (Revelation 2:1-7)

The people in Ephesus who had God's particular message read to them lived in one of the most influential cities in the province of Asia. Ephesus was especially noted for its interest in the occult. The Ephesian church was probably founded as a result of the work of Aquila, Priscilla (Acts 18), and the Apostle Paul (Acts 19). Tradition says that the Apostle John also had a profound influence upon the believers in this Asiatic City.

Praise for the Church (verses 1-3). John begins his letter to believers in Ephesus by assuring them that the Christ who holds the stars and walks among the candlesticks is alert and constantly concerned for their welfare (2:1). Then he commends them for their overall behavior or works.

The behavior for which John particularly praised the Ephesian Christians was their perseverance in Christ, their testing and excommunication of false teachers, and their continued zeal for the glory of the Lord Jesus Christ. In modern-day language, we would say that the Ephesian Christians were maturing in Christ in a number of respects. That is to say, they were good Christians when it came to having the right motive for service ("my name's sake"), being consistently true to Christ ("patience" and "not fainted"), identifying teachers who denied essential Christian truths ("liars"), and forbidding false teachers from continuing as leaders and members of the church ("canst not bear them"). Thus, these Christians were remarkably perceptive, courageous, stable, and active. What more could God want from a group of believers? Our answer is partially seen in the next verse.

Condemnation of the Church (verse 4). The Ephesian Christians were staunch believers, but they were not perfect or completely mature Christians. They actively served God. They withstood the trials that came into their lives. They carefully identified heresies and disciplined heretics. Indeed, it appears they were much better Christians than many, perhaps most, contemporary Christians. But being better than even most Christians in any age is not the standard God uses for measuring spiritual depth.

The specific standard or truth that the believers in Ephesus ignored was love. They had forsaken their first love. Some folks say forsaking one's first love refers to not properly loving Christ. This opinion, nevertheless, may be partly negated by the fact that the Ephesians labored for Christ's sake (2:3). Another interpretation that may be more plausible than the first is that the continual battle with heretics had caused Christians in Ephesus to ignore their responsibility to cultivate love and fellowship with each other. As new believers, they had been thrilled with their "new family" (1 John 3:14). But their continual conflict with "false brethren" had caused them to ignore true believers.

Exhortation for the Church (verses 5-7). John's message to the Ephesian believers is essentially this: "Purity, loyalty, and service are admirable. Indeed, they are essential aspects of a well-balanced Christian life. Yet, you must repent of your lack of concern for fellow believers, or Christ will remove or eliminate you as a church that testifies of the true gospel. As a matter of fact, Christ's removal of you will simply be a natural consequence of your becoming increasingly unbalanced in your Christian life. A decision to remain unbalanced as a church is also a decision to become more unbalanced and will eventually turn your original virtues into vices."

For a moment John pauses to soften his criticism of the church in Ephesus by saying, "But this thou hast, that thou hatest the deeds of the Nicolaitans, which I also hate" (2:6). Little is known about the Nicolaitans, but three ideas are sometimes associated with them. Many interpreters believe the group was started by Nicolas, one of the original table-servers (Acts 6:5). Second, almost all expositors agree that the word *Nicolaitans* comes from two words meaning "lord of the people" and, therefore, may refer to the practice of some pastors having established dictatorial rules over the churches. If this is the case, John would be praising the Ephesians for having a proper understanding of the role of pastors and believers in general. A third notion sometimes thought to be a part of the Nicolaitans' teachings is that the sect advocated immoral practices as a part of their worship of God or taught that it was acceptable for Christians to engage in emperor worship. Each of these interpretations, of course, is somewhat speculative. But if either of the latter two is correct, the implication is either that God hates dictatorial pastors or that He detests compromise with a pagan culture. If the first is true, then the exhortation to believers is, at least in part, that a man, Nicolas in the case before us, who at one time had been wise, filled with the Spirit, and dedicated to the work of God can later start a movement that is hated by God. And whichever of these thoughts John had in mind, he said, "He that hath an ear, let him hear."

2. The Letter to Smyrna (Revelation 2:8-11)

Smyrna, like Ephesus, was a seaport town and was located about thirty-five miles north of Ephesus. The city was also like Ephesus in that it was a prosperous commercial town.

Praise for the Church (verses 8, 9). In the opening words to this church, Christ is alluded to as being the eternal One who died for man's sins and, then, arose from the grave. Christ's message to the believers at Smyrna began with an indirect praise for their being faithful to Him during their persecution by the Smyrnean unbelievers, especially by unbelieving Jews in the city. One of the consequences of their being persecuted was that they were suffering financially. In fact, they are described as being in poverty. They were, on the other hand, wealthy when it came to spiritual matters.

Exhortation for the Church (verses 10, 11). The exhortation given to the Smyrneans is that their problems are going to become more severe. The indication is that some of them might even die for their faith since they are encouraged to be "faithful unto death."

Commentators have been puzzled by the reference to ten days (2:10). Most interpreters suggest that the words are used symbolically to signify a brief period of time. Some suggest that this interpretation is supported by similar statements in Acts 25:6 and Daniel 1:12. A few expositors prefer an interpretation that sees the days as exactly ten days, e.g., some of the believers would be put in prison for ten days.

John, then, says to the Smyrnean Christians: "You are to be praised for your faithfulness during persecution, but be sure to continue to serve Christ in the future when your trials may be intensified." Those who respond positively to John's exhortation are told that they will be rewarded with eternal life and will not be in danger of "the lake of fire" (20:14).

3. The Letter to Pergamos (Revelation 2:12-17)

The city of Pergamos was the farthest north of any of the seven churches that John wrote, and it, like the remaining four, was an inland city. The people of this city were noted in Asia Minor not only because of their economic stability but also because of their cultural, educational, and religious interests.

Praise for the Church (verses 12, 13). The specific reference to Christ in these verses is found in the phrase: "he which hath the sharp sword with two edges." The allusion is to the word of Christ as it may bring judgment upon the believers in Pergamos if they do not repent of their compromise with unchristian teachings (2:16).

The key item of praise concerning the believers in Pergamos is that they had firmly stood for the Lord during their recent tribulation. Even though one of their fellow believers, Antipas, had died as a result of either mob violence or judicial processes, they had still resisted the pressure of the pagan society to surrender to the worship of the Roman emperor.

The words *Satan's seat* have been variously understood by expositors. Everyone seems to agree that the thought implied is that in some sense Pergamos was particularly influenced by Satanic power. But the exact meaning is debated. John's words may refer to the interest that the people of Pergamos had in pagan cults. Or, perhaps, the reference is to the worship of Esculapius, the serpent god. Then again the overall power of Satan may be epitomized in the strength of emperor worship in the city. Still another view is that the person who supervised emperor worship in the region lived in Pergamos. At any rate, Satan was in firm control of the minds and actions of the people of Pergamos.

Condemnation of the Church (verses 14, 15). Somewhat surprisingly, the believers in Pergamos had been influenced by two false doctrines: the doctrines of Balaam and of the Nicolaitans. The actions of Balaam that are condemned in this passage are his compromise with pagan idolatry and the immorality that are mentioned in Numbers, chapters 22-25, 31. In particular, the doctrine may refer to intermarriage between the Jews and heathen people. Observe, too, that the believers in Pergamos were rebuked for ascribing to that which the church in Ephesus was so ably resisting, the doctrines of the Nicolaitans.

Exhortation for the Church (verses 16, 17). The Christians who tolerated or even embraced the doctrines of Balaam and of the Nicolaitans are warned that if they do not repent of their lax attitude toward these views they will be judged by Christ. The implied judgment was undoubtedly due to the fact that no church that has departed from sound thought and practice can continue to be blessed by Christ. As Paul wrote, "A little leaven leaveneth the whole lump" (Galatians 5:9).

The promise made to those who would turn away from their lax attitude toward or acceptance of the specified doctrines is that, "To him that overcometh will I give to eat of the hidden manna, and will give him a white stone." The precise meaning of this promise is debated by commentators, but they usually agree that the manna includes fellowship with, and sustenance by, Christ either in the present life or during the marriage feast of the Lamb (Revelation 19). The white stone is probably a symbol of favor as it was used in courts to signify acquittal. Consequently, Christ's promise to the believers of Pergamos is that if they repent of their sins, favor, fellowship, and strength will be theirs.

4. The Letter to Thyatira (Revelation 2:18-29)

The fourth church addressed by Christ was the one in Thyatira, a town that was primarily noted as a trade center. It was probably the least important city of the seven to which John wrote. In some ways, it seems rather remarkable that a church in a relatively unimportant city would receive a message directly from Christ. Christ's interest in people, however, is not measured by the importance of the place they reside.

Praise for the Church (verses 18, 19). The basic difference between the description given of Christ in Revelation 1 and the one given here is that there He was spoken of as the Son of Man and here as the Son of God. This description, then, calls attention to Christ's deity and the fiery wrath and judgment that are promised to those who disobey Him.

This glorious Judge, John says to the believers in Thyatira, knows and praises you for your love, service, faith, and perseverance. As a matter of fact, John says recently ("the last") you have been manifesting these qualities more than you were when I first knew you ("the first"). These words of John are not to be taken lightly, for none of the previous three churches were praised for their growth in love, service, faith, and perseverance.

Strangely, however, growth in these areas had not made the believers in Thyatira mature, well-balanced Christians. More was necessary if they were to be satisfactory examples of what Christ wanted in His followers.

Condemnation of the Church (verses 20-23). The sins of some members of the church at Thyatira were associated with a person called Jezebel. The language is so picturesque that it is worth quoting in full: "Notwithstanding I have a few things against thee, because thou sufferest that woman Jezebel, which calleth herself a prophetess, to teach and to seduce my servants to commit fornication, and to eat things sacrificed unto idols."

As surprising as it may seem, this church was steadily maturing in its love, faith, service, and perseverance but was at the same time tolerant of what the members knew to be error. They were mature enough to recognize false teachings, like the Ephesians were; but, unlike the believers in Ephesus, did not deal with the false teacher and her followers.

The woman who led others into acceptance of her own heresies is called Jezebel. Her real name probably was not Jezebel, but she is called such since Jezebel was the prototype of her sins: leading people to support idolatrous practices and other heathen customs.

The Jezebel of Thyatira had already been given time to repent of her sins, but she had openly resisted the pressure of the Holy Spirit. As a consequence, she was to be thrown into a bed of physical affliction which would be in stark contrast to the bed of physical adultery she had enjoyed. Similarly, her followers ("them that commit adultery") who had compromised Christian truth with their pagan culture would experience great tribulation, perhaps implying severe physical suffering.

In addition, those people who ("her children") were totally committed to the teachings of the prophetess would experience death. Notice the progressive judgment that John recorded: a bed of affliction, great tribulation, and death. A word of caution may be in order at this point. Sometimes Christians wonder what sin another Christian has committed when he has an illness. This kind of suspicion is contrary to Christian love (1 Corinthians 13). One may properly say that God has chastised–and probably still does–people for their sins by bringing about certain illnesses, but this does not mean physical illnesses are necessarily signs of God's chastening hand.

Exhortation for the Church (verses 24-29). The believers who had not accepted the teachings of the first century Jezebel were instructed to cling to the truths that they already possessed (2:25). This thought seems to suggest that the believers who had not followed the doctrines of the prophetess would have to start resisting her views and "to exhort and to convince the gainsayers" (Titus 1:9).

Before proceeding to the promises made to those who were challenged to respond to Christ's command, let us briefly examine an ironical remark recorded by John. The irony is found in Revelation 2:24: "the depths of Satan." Evidently, the woman who had been leading astray the church at Thyatira promised them a deeper, richer experience with God. Christ Himself, however, said to the believers that she was actually introducing them to the depths of Satan! Similar ironies are found in the letters to Smyrna and Pergamos. In those letters the synagogue of the Jews was described as being of Satan (2:9), not God; and Pergamos was the place where Satan was on the throne (2:13), not Caesar. Satan, it seems, is able to so deceive people that they will believe that the exact opposite of the truth is the truth.

Two promises are made to the overcoming Christians of Thyatira. First, they will be given power to rule or lead in the millennial kingdom of Christ (2:26, 27). Second, they will be given the "morning star" (2:28). The first concept is rather easily understood, but the second is another matter. Perhaps the remark alludes to some type of glory that is promised to all faithful believers (Daniel 12:3). Then, again, it may be a reference to having intimate fellowship with Christ Himself who is "the bright and morning star" (22:16).

3

The Letters to Sardis, Philadelphia, and Laodicea

Study Text: Revelation 3:1-22

Introduction
1. The Letter to Sardis (Revelation 3:1-6)
   a. Condemnation of the Church (verses 1, 2)
   b. Exhortation for the Church (verses 3-6)
2. The Letter to Philadelphia (Revelation 3:7-13)
   a. Praise for the Church (verses 7-9)
   b. Exhortation for the Church (verses 10-13)
3. The Letter to Laodicea (Revelation 3:14-22)
   a. Condemnation of the Church (verses 14-17)
   b. Exhortation for the Church (verses 18-22)

Introduction

The third chapter of the Apocalypse contains addresses to three churches, i.e., Sardis, Philadelphia, and Laodicea. The letters to these three churches, of course, are really an integral part of the first major division of the Apostle John's book after his introduction. If you will glance at the general study outline at the end of this work, you will find chapter three is the second and final topic under the heading, "The Church Age." The words *The Church Age* may be understood in one of two ways. If a person ascribes to the view that the seven churches represent seven different periods of church history, he may use the heading to refer to the entire church age in a chronological sense.

On the other hand, if a person thinks the seven churches are not prophetic of all periods of church history but descriptive of seven churches in John's time, the words simply suggest that chapters two and three refer to part of the Church age and contain truths that are applicable to churches through all of church history. From this way of viewing Revelation 2, 3, the heading "The Church Age" merely means that this portion of the Book of Revelation is to be sharply distinguished from later portions of the book which deal with the Tribulation and Kingdom Periods. This way of understanding the heading seems preferable to the chronological explanation.

Exposition

This chapter divides neatly into three major divisions. The first section, the letter to Christians in Sardis, is found in Revelation 3:1-6. The second part of the chapter, Revelation 3:7-13, is addressed to believers in the church at Philadelphia. The church in Laodicea is spoken to in Revelation 3:14-22.

1. The Letter to Sardis (Revelation 3:1-6)

The believers who lived in Sardis were members of a community that was notorious for its wickedness and immorality. Perhaps a partial explanation for the character of the city is that a number of important Roman highways merged there, and travelers have a way of being less inhibited than people who are in their regular settings.

Economically speaking, the people of Sardis were dependent upon manufacturing woolen and dyed goods. The main religious attraction of Sardis was the Temple of Artemis, which was built several hundred years before the birth of Christ.

Condemnation of the Church (verses 1, 2). One of the noteworthy characteristics of this letter to the Christians in Sardis is that there is almost no mention of anything being praiseworthy. When there is a reference to a strength of the believers in Sardis (3:4), it is a rather casual and nearly unnoticeable compliment.

On the other end of the spectrum, the weaknesses of the church are both alluded to and specifically identified. One allusion to spiritual problems in Sardis may be the statement, "These things saith he that hath the seven Spirits of God." How, one may wonder, do these words imply anything about the spiritual condition of the people of Sardis? Perhaps the answer is that the words may imply that the believers in Sardis lacked the fullness of the Holy Spirit in their lives and that, in turn, was because they were not obedient to Christ and to His messengers who are alluded to in the words "the seven stars."

The candid condemnation of the church in Sardis is found in the words: "I know thy works, that thou hast a name that thou livest, and art dead." The omniscience of Christ enabled Him to know that the reputation of the church in Sardis was far from the true situation. No doubt believers in nearby cities thought that the Christians in Sardis were actively and eagerly engaged in serving the Lord Jesus Christ as a result of their deep love and devotion for the Lord Himself. Actually, the people themselves may have thought that they were alive to God and dead to the world.

Christ, however, did not see the Christians in Sardis as they saw themselves, or as others saw them. Christ did not detect any false doctrines in the church at Sardis, but He did recognize that the believers were spiritually dead, living a false profession. The empty profession and activities of these Christians were meaningless as far as Christ was concerned. The Christians in Sardis were not motivated to action by a compassion for Christ, for each other, or for the unbelieving world around them.

A related condemnation of the believers of Sardis is found in the ensuing words, "I have not found thy works perfect before God" (3:2). Their activities–which were obviously of the right variety–were incomplete; that is, they lacked something. The fundamental reason their works were imperfect has already been mentioned: The motives of the people were inadequate. Perhaps they worked out of a desire to satisfy their leaders, to impress other churches with their zeal, to maintain the customs of previous believers in Sardis, or to keep from being considered indifferent Christians by each other. Regardless of what their motive or motives may have been, Christ knew they were not spiritually interested in what they were doing.

The church in Sardis was not hopeless, however. If the believers would recognize their needs and would seek to restore that which was about to die, they could survive the crisis they were now experiencing. If they failed to so respond, no doubt the bit of life that still remained in them would soon disappear.

Exhortation for the Church (verses 3-6). An analysis of the exhortation given to the church in Sardis leads to several conclusions. To begin with, there was a residue of life that needed to be revived. Also, the believers were to recall the truths they had been taught, act upon those ideas and repent of their sins as the Spirit of God specified them. Third, the church was warned that failure to follow Christ's instructions would lead to the judgment of God. Every Christian who knew what he ought to change and refused to respond appropriately had reason to believe Christ would bring judgment upon him. Finally, the Christians were told that if they really listened to what Christ said, they would be given a white robe, i.e., they would be acceptable to the Father because of their righteousness in Christ.

In conclusion, we may ask, "What exactly did the Christians in Sardis need to do?" Obviously many of them did not need to do any more in the area of Christian service. Their weakness, instead, was that they lacked a quality of life that gave them the proper motivation for service. It seems, therefore, that they were in desperate need of being edified by each other, of having true fellowship–not merely socializing–with one another, and of truly worshiping Christ.

2. The Letter to Philadelphia (Revelation 3:7-13)

This letter to the Christians in Philadelphia follows the pattern set in the previous correspondence addressed to the churches in Ephesus, Smyrna, Pergamos, Thyatira, and Sardis. The Christians are first praised for their strong points and then exhorted by Christ.

Praise for the Church (verses 7-9). These verses indicate that Jewish opposition, rather than pagan pressure, was the major problem Christians in Philadelphia experienced. Notice, too, that no strong words of criticism are leveled against the church; only praise for the believers is mentioned. An allusion to a fault, however, may be found in the words, "Thou hast a little strength" (3:8).

In the opening words of His address to this church, Christ makes three observations about Himself. He is, first of all, holy and, therefore, thoroughly committed to the righteous standards of God the Father. Second, He speaks of Himself as being true. In this context, Christ may have been referring to Himself in contrast with false teachings, or He may have been referring to Himself as a Person who is faithful to the promises He makes to believers.

The third statement by Christ is variously interpreted. When Christ says He has the key of David, He is probably referring to His power to open doors of service to the Christians in Philadelphia. The words that follow this remark indicate such a notion. Some commentators, nevertheless, believe that more than this is implied. For example, it is possible that the key of David is an allusion to the throne of David. If this is so, perhaps Christ is indirectly saying that the Jews in Philadelphia who claim to be heirs of David and the true people of God do not really have Davidic rights. No, the rights only belong to those that Christ says may have them; that is, true believers of all racial backgrounds.

The fundamental item of praise that is found in Christ's words to Christians in Philadelphia is that they have stayed true to the teachings of Christ and have not succumbed to pressure to publicly deny Him. This seems to have been a very encouraging compliment from Christ when one considers that the church in Philadelphia was probably very small and that the opposition of the Jews was unusually strong.

The reference to Jews worshiping before the feet of the believers of Philadelphia is somewhat difficult to understand. Perhaps the statement is to be understood, as some suggest, as a promise that the Jews in Philadelphia were to be inwardly convinced by the testimony of the Christians that God loves and cares for those who personally accept His Son. This inner conviction was not to be necessarily followed by conversion but at least respect for the Christians may be implied.

At least one other interpretation should be considered. Christ's words may be framed in the light of Old Testament promises to the Jews. God promised the nation of Israel a day when other nations would respect it (Isaiah 60:14; Ezekiel 37:28). The Jews expected to be the recipients of those promises. Christ, however, may have been saying, "The promises apply to the true people of God, not to people who are God's in name only."

Exhortation for the Church (verses 10-13). The faithfulness of the Christians in Philadelphia, Christ says, will be rewarded by their being kept from a period of persecution. Commentators who believe that both the churches of Philadelphia and Laodicea represent the present church age (1750 to the rapture) say the deliverance spoken of is that of the rapture of the Church before the beginning of the Tribulation. Others suggest that John's comment describe a historical deliverance of the first century believers in Philadelphia but also includes the rapture of believers in the last days. Still other expositors, even though they believe (on the basis of other passages) in a literal Tribulation and a literal millennium, believe the words are best understood as referring to the first century Christians only. Or to put the thought in slightly different words, when persecution of Christians did spread throughout the Roman Empire, the tiny group of believers in Philadelphia was spared by God. This interpretation seems to be the best of the three.

In conclusion, Christ challenged the believers to maintain their interest in maturing in Him and not to lose that which they had earned by being faithful to Him. Then, in metaphorical language, He promised them honor in the Temple of God and identification with Himself ("my new name"). The reference to honor stems from the words "make a pillar in the temple." In some ancient cities, it was customary to honor an outstanding person by placing a pillar with his name on it in a pagan temple. Christ's idea, therefore, seemed to flow from this tradition that was probably practiced in Philadelphia.

3. The Letter to Laodicea (Revelation 3:14-22)

The final message to the seven churches of Asia Minor is addressed to the messenger of the church of Laodicea. The city was founded by Antiochus II during the third century B. C. and was located approximately forty-five miles southeast of Philadelphia and ninety miles east of Ephesus. The people of Laodicea had made their city famous for its wealth, and the medical school they had established had also attracted the attention of outsiders.

Condemnation of the Church (verses 14-17). Immediately before pointing out the inadequacies of the church in Laodicea, Christ identifies Himself as "the Amen, the faithful and true witness, the beginning of the creation of God." By saying this, Christ was referring to Himself as a reliable and trustworthy person and as a faithful communicator of the truth. The final phrase, "the beginning of the creation of God," should be understood in one of the two following ways: (1) Christ is the first of all that was originally created by God, or (2) Christ is the source of the creation of all that exists.

The first idea is clearly inconsistent with Revelation 1:17, 2:8, and other passages penned by the Apostle John (John 1:1-3). This being the case, the second explanation is the correct one. Christ was speaking of Himself as the source of all that we say God created. Indeed, as God, Christ was the originator of the entire universe.

The problem that plagued the people of Laodicea appears to have been threefold. First of all, the people seem to have been guilty of spiritual complacency. A second quality of the believers in Laodicea that troubled Christ was that the people were spiritually proud. Finally, the church was evidently unaware of its true spiritual condition and was, therefore, living in spiritual ignorance.

Let us examine further these three characteristics of the church in Laodicea. Spiritual complacency seems to be suggested by the fact that the people were "neither cold nor hot" but lukewarm. The three different spiritual conditions mentioned in this connection seem to be suggestive of the ensuing ideas: (1) Some people are totally indifferent or even hostile to the claims of Christ. (2) Others are complacent about the teachings of the Scriptures, and it is difficult to know whether these people are true believers. (3) A few Christians are zealous for the doctrines and moral teachings of Christ.

The Laodicean church was described by Christ as being in the second category: Observers could not easily tell if the church members were people who had really accepted the Lord Jesus Christ as their personal Savior. People probably wondered about their ultimate commitments in life. These folks were very different from the church members in Sardis who had a reputation–even though a false one–for being devoted to Christ. The complacency of the Laodicean Christians may have extended to part or all of their lives. For the purpose of illustration, they may have been only casually interested in doctrine, morality, evangelism, edification, fellowship, and worship. Or they might have been somewhat concerned in a few of these areas but were generally characterized by complacency. Either way, Christ detested their lack of full identification with Him and warned in metaphorical language that He would eventually reject the church if it persisted in its present sins.

The second sin, that of spiritual self-sufficiency, is identified in the statement, "I am rich, and increased with goods, and have need of nothing." The Laodicean church members probably never spoke those words. As a matter of conjecture, it is unlikely that the people even thought this way. The case that existed, however, was that they acted as though they needed no assistance from anyone, including the Sustainer of the universe.

The final sin mentioned by John is, at least in part, the reason for the other two sins. Evidently, the church members were ignorant of their true spiritual state in the sight of God and did not know that they were "wretched, and miserable, and poor, and blind, and naked." The spiritual ignorance was even worse than it appeared on the surface; the church no doubt could have known or, perhaps, even inwardly knew but deceived themselves so much that, for all practical purposes, they did not know themselves. Spiritual ignorance, then, can and often does lead to spiritual pride and spiritual complacency.

Exhortation for the Church (verses 18-22). The manner in which Christ exhorted the Laodicean church seems to be tinted with a bit of irony as well as with love, compassion, and sternness. He summons the professing believers to buy from Him gold that would make them spiritually rich, white garments that would cover their spiritual nakedness, and eye-salve that would cure their spiritual blindness. He, in other words, is capable of curing all of their spiritual problems, but they were not.

Second, Christ calls upon the Laodiceans to repent. It is significant that His call for repentance is prefaced by the words, "As many as I love, I rebuke and chasten." The Savior who is so insistent that the Laodiceans repent does so as a result of His love for the Laodiceans.

In concluding His appeal to the church, Christ clarifies His feelings further by announcing His intent to have intimate fellowship with them. Furthermore, He promises that those who are victorious in this life will reign with Him. Perhaps the reign alluded to both the millennial kingdom (2:26) and the eternal kingdom (22:5).

4

The Throne and the Book

Study Text: Revelation 4:1—5:14

Introduction
1. The Scene in Heaven (Revelation 4:1-11)
    a. The Throne of God (verses 1-5)
    b. The Living Creatures (verses 6-8)
    c. The Worship of God (verses 9-11)
2. The Sealed Book (Revelation 5:1-14)
    a. The Search for a Worthy Person (verses 1-4)
    b. The Lamb of God (verses 5-7)
    c. The New Song (verses 8-10)
    d. The Singing of All Creation (verses 11-14)

Introduction

By looking at the general study outline in the back of this volume, you will observe that this chapter is the first topic under the second major division of the Book of Revelation which is entitled, "The Tribulation Period." This heading is in keeping with many, perhaps most, Premillennial interpretations of Revelation 4-18. In actuality, however, Premillennialists have traditionally had a variety of interpretations as to when the events described in chapters 4 to 18 would take place. These differences will be further delineated in the next chapter. For the moment, the important idea to remember is that Premillennialists believe at least the majority of the events described in Revelation 4-18 refer to a future period of tribulation that will be realized near the end of human civilization on this planet. In particular, they say chapters 4 and 5 are introductory chapters, chapters that set the stage for understanding the prophetical drama described in Revelation 6-18.

One very important question needs to be raised before proceeding to the Biblical text itself. The question is as follows: Why do Premillennialists believe Revelation 4-18 refers to the future and especially to the Tribulation? Sometimes the answer given to this question is that the angel who spoke to John implied such when he said, "I will shew thee things which must be hereafter" (4:1). This answer, when carefully analyzed, is far from convincing, for the term *hereafter* is indefinite and could apply to any period of time after John received the vision recorded by him in the first century.

A better answer, even though it is not without its problems, is that if one examines the events in the Apocalypse in reverse order beginning with Revelation 22 and proceeding to Revelation 21 and so on there are good reasons for saying the majority of the events described in the Apocalypse are still future and related to what Premillennialists call the Tribulation.

For just a moment, let us indulge in examining the Book of Revelation in reverse order. Many of the events in Revelation 21, 22 are concerned with a new Heaven, new earth, and New Jerusalem. These verses clearly refer to a future realm of life for people who have accepted the Lord Jesus Christ as their personal Savior. Revelation 20 describes, among other events, the casting of unbelievers and Satan into the lake of fire. These events, too, do not seem to have been fulfilled as of now. And so the process of reasoning goes on to chapters 19, 18, 17, and so forth. Using this approach, the Premillennialist normally concludes that the events described in Revelation 6-22 will be fulfilled sometime in the future and are particularly related to events that will transpire during the Tribulation, millennium, and the eternal state of believers. Revelation 4, 5 provide a background for the rest of the picturesque drama that is unfolded to John in three acts: the seven seals, the seven trumpets, and the seven bowls.

Exposition

Even though there are other topics of importance in Revelation 4 and 5, the main concerns of these chapters are the throne of God, the Lamb of God, and the sealed book. The throne of God is of central importance in Revelation 4, but as chapter 5 is approached the Lamb and the sealed book are introduced.

1. The Scene in Heaven (Revelation 4:1-11)

The scene that John saw in Heaven introduced him to three different types of persons. The first was a member of the Trinity, God the Father. The second group of people are called "elders," and the third, "beasts."

The Throne of God (verses 1-5). Shortly after the apostle had received the first vision of Christ's concern for the believers in the seven churches of Asia Minor, he was given an additional revelation about future activities. The invitation to "come up" was an offer to show him what would happen at the end of the Church age. He was immediately in an ecstatic state ("in the spirit") as he had been in the earlier vision (1:10). Being in the Spirit brought him into the presence of God, although he was actually still on the Isle of Patmos.

Many Premillennialists like to stress at this juncture that John's entrance into Heaven is typical of the rapture of the Church before the Tribulation ever begins. These Premillennialists are known as pretribulationists since they believe Christ will return for His saints before the Tribulation starts. While the position taken by pretribulationists may be correct, it is important to remember that the idea of John's ecstatic state being typical of the Church's rapture is not explicitly supported by an exegesis of this passage.

John saw God seated on His throne, but we do not know precisely what he saw. We do know, however, that John did not describe God in anthropomorphic terms. Instead, he was impressed with the brilliance of God. The jasper is a clear, transparent stone while the sardine or Sardius that is mentioned is a bright red stone. The emerald green rainbow may have been in the form of an arc behind the throne, or it could have been a complete circle over the throne.

The significance of these stones and colors is disputed. Some interpreters insist the colors are symbols of God's purity, redemption, and mercy. The stones themselves are said to be symbols of the Jewish people since the jasper represented the firstborn of Jacob and Reuben, and the sardine the youngest of Jacob's sons, Benjamin (Exodus 28). An easier view to accept is that the overall emphasis is simply on the majesty and beauty of God and that John found God's appearance inexpressible.

Next, John says he saw twenty-four elders sitting on thrones next to God's throne. The identity of these elders is far from clear, but one interpretation that may be based upon too much imagination is that the elders represent the twelve apostles and the twelve patriarchs and, thereby, represent Old and New Testament believers. Little if any evidence from the text itself seems to support this conjecture.

A second interpretation is that the elders are representative of the raptured Church. One problem with this interpretation is that one has to first prove that the Church will be raptured before the events described here take place. Even if a person thinks he can accumulate evidence which strongly supports the rapture of the Church before this scene in Heaven takes place, this still does not prove the elders are raptured believers nor that they symbolize them. It has been suggested by some scholars that since the elders have on white robes and gold crowns they must be redeemed people since only believers will wear these in eternity.

A third position held by many expositors is that the twenty-four elders are some type of heavenly or angelic beings. The proponents of this viewpoint maintain that there is no conclusive evidence concerning the matter of whether only believers will have white robes and crowns in Heaven. What evidence, they ask, is there to support the notion that angels will not be robed in white?

Furthermore, some expositors argue, one of the elders seems to raise questions much like angelic beings are pictured as doing in other Biblical passages (7:13, 14). Likewise, the elders offer the prayers of saints to God just as an angel does later in John's revelation (8:3).

Finally, this view seems to be supported by the best translations of Revelation 5:9, 10. The King James Version suggests the elders were redeemed by God; however, most Greek authorities suggest that the key words would be better translated: "You were slain, and purchased for God with your blood, people from every tribe, tongue, people, and nation, and have made them a kingdom and priests to our God, and they shall reign on earth." In this song, the elders seem to be speaking of the redeemed as *another* group, i.e., *them.* Consequently, the elders may very well be a group of angelic beings who follow God's directives and pass them on to other angels who minister on the earth itself.

The final verse in this passage speaks of the presence of the Holy Spirit and of "lightnings and thunderings and voices." Similar manifestations occurred in the Old Testament when the power and glory of God were to be indicated (Job 37:2-5; Ezekiel 1:13). Perhaps here the intent is to add to the overall majesty of God as well as to draw attention to God Himself before His judgments are announced.

The Living Creatures (verses 6-8). In front of God's throne, John saw a sea that looked like glass but was not actually glass. The sea was probably only an aesthetic element in the overall vision of God, but some interpreters have spent a great deal of time arguing for some sort of symbolic meaning, such as the following: (a) The crystal sea represents a separation between God and man that can only be crossed by acceptance of the Lamb, or (b) the sea symbolizes God's ability to see all the activities on the earth beneath Him. While a person can agree with the truth contained in both of these viewpoints, one need not think the sea itself symbolizes either of these truths.

The four beasts, as the King James Version has it, are better understood as four living creatures. Probably the reason the King James Version has beasts instead of living creatures is that the creatures mentioned are said to be similar to a lion, an ox, a man, and an eagle. But the descriptions of the cherubim in Ezekiel 10 and the seraphim in Isaiah 6 are somewhat similar to the one given of the living creatures by John. Once again, then, it seems these characters may very well be another type of angelic being who serves God in some specialized capacity.

Another interpretation that seems somewhat less feasible is that the creatures represent some attributes of God or, perhaps, symbolize His majestic nature. This explanation is unusually awkward, because it suggests that some of God's attributes cry, "Holy, holy, holy, Lord God Almighty."

An additional point of view that is difficult to accept is that the four creatures are symbols of the four gospels. The creature that is similar to a man is supposed to represent Matthew; the one like an eagle, Mark; the one like an ox, Luke; and the one like a lion, John. This explanation of the creatures is not as awkward as the one previously discussed, but it does seem a little unnatural to think of the four gospels praising God.

The Worship of God (verses 9-11). In these final verses of the chapter, both groups of angelic beings worship God. The passage itself may imply some kind of relationship between the worship of the two groups; that is, when the group of four worships God, the group of elders joins in with them. In the case before us, the smaller group praised God for His eternal nature, and the larger group praised Him for His created works.

2. The Sealed Book (Revelation 5:1-14)

This chapter of the Apocalypse continues the apostle's account of his heavenly vision. God is still seated on His throne, but John's attention is drawn away from the splendor of God, the sea, and the angelic beings to a book in God's hand.

The Search for a Worthy Person (verses 1-4). The book that is mentioned by John is ordinarily thought to be a scroll made of either leather or papyrus. These pieces of material were pasted together to make a long strip. Most of the time the scroll was only written on one side, the inside. The scroll seen in God's hand, however, had writing on both sides. Seven seals were along the edge of the scroll in such a manner that all seven would have to be broken before a person could read the contents.

As John was looking at the scroll, he heard an angel raise the question, "Who is worthy to open the book, and to loose the seals?" John was terribly upset when he realized that no one in the entire universe was worthy enough to open the scroll. The reason John wept is not explicitly mentioned, but perhaps he did so because he was so deeply engrossed in the vision and realized that all of God's creatures were limited in their ability to break the seals on the scroll.

The Lamb of God (verses 5-7). The apostle's grief was short-lived, however. He soon learned that the Lion of the tribe of Judah, the Root of David, was able to break the seven seals. The words *the Lion of Judah* may be an allusion to Genesis 49:9, 10, and *the Root of David* a reference to Isaiah 11:1. Both passages appear to suggest a ruler will come who will be king during an age of universal deliverance from societal problems.

Suddenly the scene is changed, and John is described as seeing a Lamb who had been slain. In this way, the vision connects the Lion of Judah with the Lamb of God; the Lion who can open the book that brings judgment upon the world is one and the same with the Lamb who died that people might escape the very wrath of God that is to come.

The Lamb had an unusual number of horns, seven. Similarly, he had seven eyes, which are explained as being the Holy Spirit. The horns are left unexplained but may represent the complete power which Christ has.

The Lamb is depicted as taking the sealed book from God's right hand as He walks to the throne of God. The sealed book itself has been explained in several ways by expositors. One unlikely interpretation is that the scroll is the book of life that is mentioned several places in the Apocalypse. The events that transpire after Christ receives the sealed book seem to imply that the book mentioned here is not the same as the book of life.

A more popular interpretation of the sealed book is that it represents the last will and testament of God. Or the book is an allusion to the Old Testament practice of having a deed, which entitled a kinsman to buy back property that had been sold by one's family. If this explanation is accepted, the thought suggested is that Christ takes the deed to the earth, which has been under the control of Satan. While this position has much to recommend it, it is handicapped by the fact that the symbolism might suggest that God has to purchase the earth back from Satan.

The interpretation that seems most acceptable is that the scroll contained a revelation from God concerning the last days–the Tribulation, the millennium, and the eternal state of believers. A second way of stating this idea is that the book contained most of the Book of Revelation. The scroll may include the ideas presented in Revelation 8:1–22:21 or, perhaps, Revelation 7:1–22:21. Evidence for this viewpoint will be presented in the next chapter.

The New Song (verses 8-10). Praise for the Lamb of God is said to have broken forth as soon as He took the book from God. Both the living creatures and the elders first worshiped before Christ; they evidently assisted in some way with presenting prayers to Christ that had come from believers. Observe, too, the reference to harps. The text is silent on the matter, but the two groups may well have played the harps as they sang of the Lamb's act of redemption and how He had brought people to God by His blood from "every kindred, and tongue, and people, and nation."

The song that was sung makes it clear that the true Church is composed of people from all sections of the world. While many believers recognize this fact, very few seem to really live in the light of the truth. The maturing Christian ought to be concerned with the whole body of Christ, not simply the small portion of it that he sees weekly.

The universal Church is further described as a company of priests who constitute a kingdom. Presently, the universal Church may be described as a kingdom, but after the judgment of nations, the Church shall reign on the earth with Christ during the millennium (20:6). Both now and during the millennium, believers, as priests, may go directly into the presence of God.

The Singing of All Creation (verses 11-14). In vivid language, the apostle describes for us the number who sang praises to the Lamb. First, we are told an unnumbered host of heavenly beings–angels, living creatures, and elders–sang, "Worthy is the Lamb that was slain." Then John describes, much as he had done in Revelation 5:9, how everyone joins in to sing, "Blessing, and honour . . . be unto him that sitteth upon the throne, and unto the Lamb." In the former song, only the Lamb was praised. The latter song included praise for both the Father on the throne and the Lamb.

The worship service in John's vision closed with the four living creatures crying "Amen!" and the twenty-four elders falling down before the throne of God. Obviously, in Heaven people do not stymie their emotions; they freely worship the Lord of the universe. Even though living believers are not in Heaven, we may be well advised to examine our own worship of God to see if it is prompted by a self-effacing, spontaneous adoration of God.

5

The Seals and the Multitudes

Study Text: Revelation 6:1—7:17

Introduction
1. The Opening of the Book (Revelation 6:1-17)
   a. The First Seal: The White Horse (verses 1, 2)
   b. The Second Seal: The Red Horse (verses 3, 4)
   c. The Third Seal: The Black Horse (verses 5, 6)
   d. The Fourth Seal: The Ashen Horse (verses 7, 8)
   e. The Fifth Seal: The Martyred Souls (verses 9-11)
   f. The Sixth Seal: The Day of Wrath (verses 12-17)
2. The Two Multitudes (Revelation 7:1-17)
   a. The Angelic Beings (verses 1-3)
   b. The Sealed Tribes (verses 4-8)
   c. The Mixed Multitude (verses 9-17)

Introduction

A moment of recapitulation should help us get a clearer understanding of the context of these two chapters. The first chapter of the Apocalypse is concerned with a revelation about the Lord Jesus Christ, the Revelator of the Apocalypse. The second and third chapters are personal letters from Christ to seven historical churches of Asia Minor. The next two chapters, Revelation 4, 5, provide a background for understanding the sealed book that constitutes the fundamental revelations that were given to the Apostle John. As we have already learned, these revelations will be fulfilled at the end of or shortly after what is usually called the Church age. The major events discussed include the Tribulation, the millennium, and the eternal state of believers. Revelation 6, 7 are John's description of what will happen in the earliest stages of the "end times." His attention has been drawn away from God, Christ, and the angelic beings in this portion of the revelation and is directed toward the seven seals on the book Christ received.

Although there is some uniformity of interpretation among Premillennialists concerning the seals, there is also a tremendous amount of disagreement. A few of their major disagreements will be briefly noted before proceeding to an analysis of the text itself.

When looking at the seven seals, it is important to keep in mind that practically all Premillennialists think they are at least in part associated with the Tribulation. The Tribulation, however is understood in a variety of ways by Premillennialists. Some theologians argue that the Tribulation is a period of three and a half years as is specifically mentioned by Daniel (Daniel 12) and by John (Revelation 11). Others think the Tribulation is a general description of the troublesome times at the close of the Church age, not a description of any minutely calculated period of time. The majority of Premillennial thinkers ascribe to a seven-year period of Tribulation. The seventieth week mentioned in Daniel 9 is understood by this group to refer to the Tribulation. Many of this group, nevertheless, agree that John's concern is basically with the last half of the seven-year Tribulation, or with what is often called the Great Tribulation.

Now let us return to the seven seals. In some way, all three groups of Premillennialists just mentioned associate the seals with the Tribulation. For the sake of simplifying our discussion, we will illustrate the several interpretations of the seven seals with the way the majority of Premillennialists interpret the Tribulation, as a seven-year period of time. As a general rule, we will stick to this plan of explaining the Book of Revelation. On rare occasions, one of the other positions will be drawn into the discussion. This neglect of the minority views just mentioned does not mean that either or both of them are necessarily incorrect. This approach is taken for the sole purpose of convenience.

A commonly held point of view concerning the seals is that the first five seals refer to the first half or three and a half years of the Tribulation. The first seal or white horse will begin the Tribulation, and the sixth seal or the great earthquake will begin the second half of the Tribulation.

A second, but less popular, interpretation of the seals is that the first seal, the white horse, refers to the first half of the Tribulation. The second through the seventh seals describe events that will come to pass during the Great Tribulation.

The final interpretation we will mention is that some Premillennialists think the first six seals refer to a period of time shortly before the Tribulation, and beginning with the seventh seal or the seven trumpets the Tribulation itself starts. This position is held by some interpreters who ascribe to a three and a half-year Tribulation as well as some that hold to the seven-year interpretation.

We will not have time to debate the pros and cons of these interpretations, but you should consider these positions as you gradually develop your understanding of the Apocalypse. For the moment, we need to concentrate on obtaining a general grasp of the book.

Exposition

The exposition of both Revelation 6, 7 are rather difficult since there are a number of different interpretations that need to be noted. If we keep in mind the ideas discussed under the introductory section, it will make our job an easier one.

1. The Opening of the Book (Revelation 6:1-17)

One of the obvious points to keep in mind about the seven seals–at least the first five or six–is that the events associated with the seals seem to happen before the events which are contained in the sealed book *per se.* Looking at it from another perspective it appears that the seven seals (6:1-17; 8:1) describe events that will occur before the seven trumpets (8:2-9:21; 11:14-19), and both the seals and the trumpets appear to happen before the seven bowls (16:1-21).

Since this seems to be the case, two tentative conclusions may be drawn. One of these conclusions is that the first five or six seals are preliminary events that transpire before the great judgments of the trumpets and before the bowls are released upon the peoples of the earth. This idea may be interpreted so that it is consistent with either the view which says these seals describe events that will happen shortly before the Tribulation or with the position which teaches that these seals refer to activities which will take place before the Great Tribulation.

A second conclusion that seems plausible is that there is a close chronological relationship between the seals, the trumpets, and the bowls. This relationship is visualized in Figure 2. A glance at the diagram will reveal that the seventh seal actually includes the seven trumpets and seven bowls. In a similar way, the seventh trumpet includes the seven bowls or vials.

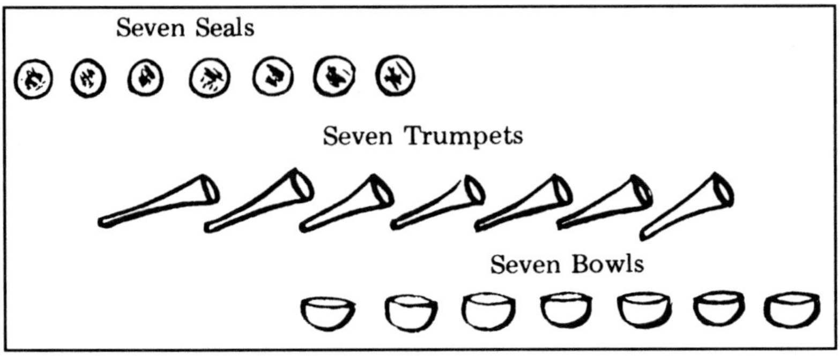

FIGURE 2: The Chronological Relationship of the Seals, the Trumpets, and the Bowls

The First Seal: The White Horse (verses 1, 2). The most widely disputed horse in the Scriptures is probably the one that John simply calls "white." A trend among some expositors is to identify the horse and its rider with Christ. If this view is taken, one usually argues that the white horse symbolizes the fact that Christ, sometime in the future, will begin conquering the earth at the beginning of the Tribulation so that He may establish His kingdom. Some interpreters believe this conquering will be in the form of a revival while others see it as a result of the judgments that are later described by the Apostle John.

Oddly enough, a second popular interpretation suggests the opposite of the first explanation: The horse represents activities associated with the Antichrist, not Christ. In this case, theologians say that the horse represents the peace which the forces of the Antichrist will bring to the world just before the wrath of God is emptied upon mankind. This peace is a pseudo-peace that is built by men as they desperately attempt to live apart from God, and it is directly spoken of by the Apostle Paul when he says: "For yourselves know perfectly that the day of the Lord so cometh as a thief in the night. For when they shall say, Peace and safety; then sudden destruction cometh upon them" (1 Thessalonians 5:2, 3).

Both of these interpretations seem to be consistent with understanding the white horse as referring to either a time before the Tribulation itself begins or as symbolizing the start of the Tribulation proper. Perhaps the view that the white horse represents the building of a pseudo-peace in the world sometime before the start of the Tribulation is the easier view to defend.

The Second Seal: The Red Horse (verses 3, 4). The idea that the white horse represents some kind of peace appears to be partially supported by a clear comprehension of the second seal, the red horse. The white horse may have temporarily conquered the world and established peace, but of the rider of the red horse it is stated:

"Power was given to him that sat thereon to take peace from the earth." Whatever peace the Antichrist, or the Willful King of Daniel 11, is able to build will be destroyed by the red horse that stands for various kinds of societal hostilities, including war. The evil desires of nations will be constrained for only a short time by the government of the Antichrist before human depravity will cause national and international problems. Once again this seal may be consistent with the thought that it will be fulfilled either before the Tribulation begins or during the early part of the Tribulation.

The Third Seal: The Black Horse (verses 5, 6). Following on the heels of war and, to some degree probably, occurring simultaneously with various facets of international unrest, the world will experience a famine. The troubles spoken of in the symbol of the red horse may be partly responsible for the food shortage. Or, the continually growing world population may be a significant factor. Then, again, God may alter weather conditions or influence the production of food in some other way.

Whatever brings about the famine, John has recorded for us the sobering idea that there is coming a time when the average worker in the world will have to pay his full day's salary (a penny or denarius) for a meal made from wheat or for three meals made from barley. An obvious implication is that except for those who are affluent, people will have to spend the overwhelming majority of what they earn for food. Food will be available, but it will be extremely expensive. The notion that the necessities will be available also seems to be suggested by the words, "See thou hurt not the oil and the wine." These commodities were staples in New Testament times, not luxuries as many expositors have supposed.

The Fourth Seal: The Ashen Horse (verses 7, 8). The ashen, green, or pale horse is generally recognized to stand for death that will overrun the earth during the latter days. The shortage of food contributes to the wholesale death of mankind. More than a food shortage is implied. Hunger is only one of the four causes identified in Revelation 6:8. The other three factors are the sword, pestilence ("death"), and animals. The basic idea, therefore, is that either one-fourth of the earth's geographical area or one-fourth of the world's population will die as a result of famine, epidemic diseases, killings of various sorts, and animals that are either wild or infected with diseases. This thought, just like the preceding ones, is not very comforting. If this seal refers to a fourth of the world's population, and if it is broken during the twenty-first century, billions of people will die.

The Fifth Seal: The Martyred Souls (verses 9-11). The passage dealing with the fifth seal appears to imply several thought provoking truths. Manifestly, one of these is that a number of people will die in the future as a result of persevering in their loyalty to Christ. Another point communicated in this passage is that those who martyr these Christians will not be judged until after "a little season."

While these two thoughts are clearly expressed in the verses before us, it is not so clear as to when these Christians will die. Nor is it obvious what is meant by the words *a little season.*

Many Premillennialists think that the believers who will be martyred will die during the Tribulation and after the Church has been raptured. This position is held by pretribulationists. Others, midtribulationists, think that the martyred Christians will die during the Tribulation but before the Great Tribulation starts, at which time the Church will be raptured. Posttribulationists see these people dying during the Tribulation; their view of the rapture taking place after the Tribulation is not a significant factor in understanding the problem at hand. Still others, including tribulationists of all persuasions, think the believers mentioned will be martyred before the Tribulation or "little season" even begins. Unfortunately, the seal itself does not clarify which of these interpretations are to be preferred.

The Sixth Seal: The Day of Wrath (verses 12-17). The "great day of wrath" spoken of in this passage is probably an allusion to at least part of the Tribulation as well as, perhaps, to the seventy-five days after the Tribulation that are mentioned by Daniel (Daniel 12:11, 12). Interpreters are divided, of course, as to the exact time that is meant. Some, for example, think this day of wrath refers to the entire seven years of the Tribulation, believing that the first five seals will come to pass before the Tribulation. Only the Great Tribulation is being referred to according to other Premillennialists.

Some expositors, midtribulationists, see such a strong similarity between these verses written by John and those recorded by Matthew that they believe the sixth seal not only indicates the midpoint of the Tribulation, but that Matthew 24:29-31 indicates the Church is raptured at this point. But the issue is not so easily solved, for the passage in Matthew 24 is open to several interpretations.

Writers are also split over whether the language employed by John is to be understood as primarily symbolic of social and political catastrophes on earth or to be interpreted in a largely literal manner of physical disturbances. The latter part of this passage (6:15, 16) probably supports a more literal interpretation. Keep in mind, though, the similes used throughout the passage: (a) as sackcloth, (b) as blood, (c) as a fig tree, (d) as a scroll.

The last three verses of Revelation 6 may suggest that unbelievers will know when the Tribulation or the Great Tribulation begins. They will know God and Christ are responsible for what occurs (6:16). These thoughts run counter to the view that the world will be engaged in a search to find out the cause of a chaotic world after the rapture.

2. The Two Multitudes (Revelation 7:1-17)

This chapter contains the first interlude or parenthesis of several that appear in the Apocalypse. One of the most troublesome aspects of attempting to understand the Book of Revelation is deciding how this and other parentheses fit into the timetable of the overall vision. For the sake of an illustration, we may ask this: Does Revelation 7 fit into one or several of the previously mentioned seals, or does it belong to the trumpets that follow the seals? Both answers are commonly found in literature; the matter will have to be ultimately decided, if it can be, by looking at the passage itself.

The Angelic Beings (verses 1-3). The verses of this section inform us that John's focal point is that of five angels. Four of the five are depicted as having the power to unleash plagues upon the earth as they stand "holding the four winds of the earth." The fifth, however, instructs the first four to refrain from releasing judgments upon the earth until the foreheads of God's servants have been sealed. In answer to the previously stated inquiry in Revelation 6:17, the reply seems to be this: Those who are sealed by the angel of God will be able to do so in "the great day of his wrath."

This thought may throw some light on the problem of identifying the time during which the two multitudes will be of prophetic significance. The two groups may be closely associated with the sixth seal. In other words, John's description of the two multitudes is a close-up picture of two groups of people who are important beginning with the sixth seal. If the Great Tribulation begins with this seal, the two multitudes will be of significance during this period of three and a half years.

The Sealed Tribes (verses 4-8). Premillennialists, like interpreters who belong to other millennial schools, have had no easy task when it comes to identifying the 144,000 people mentioned in this passage. A few of them believe the 144,000 mentioned by John refers to the Church, the true Israel. While there is the possibility that some Biblical passages may be understood to suggest that the true Jew is the believer of any race (Romans 2:28, 29), it is somewhat difficult to see how the detailed explanation of the twelve tribes is an attempt to refer to the Church.

It is not inappropriate to ask this of those who propose this interpretation: If the description given in Revelation 7:4-8 refers to the Church, what kind of description could John have given to refer to real, physical Jews? The description is so detailed that it would seem well nigh impossible for John to give another description that would cause a person to think more readily of Jews.

Probably the most commonly accepted interpretation of the twelve tribes is some form of the ensuing explanation: The reference is to a group of converted Jews who will be selected as witnesses for Christ during the Tribulation. The 144,000 Jews will be selected out of a multitude of Jewish people who will be saved during the end times. These select Jews will become missionaries for Christ during the Great Tribulation and will be instrumental in winning others, both Jews and Gentiles, to Christ.

This position encounters a number of problems, but the general notion still appears to be preferable to interpreting the tribes as a symbol for the Church. Perhaps it is worth noting, too, that a person may explain the 144,000 as Jews without being either a strict dispensationalist or a pretribulationist.

The Mixed Multitude (verses 9-17). The victorious group of mixed people mentioned in this passage of Scripture is not as difficult to identify as the 144,000. The apparent explanation is that this group represents a mass of people saved from throughout the world. They are specifically set apart from the angels, the elders, and the living creatures (7:11).

While there is little difficulty in giving a general identification of the mixed multitude, there is at least one moot question concerning the group. The question that arises is as follows: Is this multitude a group of martyrs?

One's answer to this question may be based upon how the words *out of* are understood (7:14). These words are sometimes said to mean that the mixed multitude "escaped from" the Tribulation. Some members of two separate groups of Premillennialists prefer to explain the words in this manner. A number of pretribulationalists believe the mixed multitude refers to the Church that will be raptured before the Tribulation begins. Midtribulationists, at least a few of them, ascribe to a similar viewpoint. They say the group mentioned is the Church but add that the Church will be raptured in the middle of the Tribulation just before the Great Tribulation starts.

On the other hand, other Premillennial expositors of all three tribulational positions argue that the group discussed by John refers to martyrs, not to raptured believers. The mixed multitude will suffer death during the Great Tribulation because they will not yield to the pressure of the Antichrist's government. Perhaps many of this group will be won to the Lord by the 144,000 Jews.

6

The Seventh Seal and the Six Trumpets

Study Text: Revelation 8:1—9:21

Introduction
1. The Seventh Seal (Revelation 8:1-13)
   a. The Silence in Heaven (verses 1-6)
   b. The First Trumpet: The Hail and the Fire (verse 7)
   c. The Second Trumpet: The Great Mountain (verses 8, 9)
   d. The Third Trumpet: The Great Star (verses 10, 11)
   e. The Fourth Trumpet: The Luminaries (verses 12, 13)
2. The First and Second Woes (Revelation 9:1-21)
   a. The Fifth Trumpet: The Locusts (verses 1-12)
   b. The Sixth Trumpet: The Horsemen (verses 13-21)

Introduction

After John concludes describing the two multitudes that appear to be of significance during and after the sixth seal, he merely records that the seventh seal was opened by Christ. He does not mention that the seventh seal has any content of its own; therefore, it seems logical to assume that the content of the seventh seal is in actuality all of the seven trumpets and, likewise, the seventh trumpet include the seven bowls of wrath. Interpreting the Apocalypse in this manner, we may conclude that the seventh seal is the most important of all because it depicts the completion of God's wrath upon the world.

The diligent student of the Book of Revelation is increasingly faced with a hermeneutic problem as he goes through the book. He constantly has to decide whether he will interpret passages in a literal sense or in a symbolic manner. In these chapters dealing with the seventh seal and the first six trumpets, the problem becomes acute. You will notice that the more literal vein is expressed herein unless there is evidence in the immediate context or in related passages elsewhere which implies a symbolic explanation should be sought.

Exposition

An examination of Revelation 8, 9 reveals that the first four trumpets appear to be fundamentally concerned with picturing judgments upon nature: the earth, trees, grass, sea, rivers, sun, moon, and stars. Only indirectly is mankind mentioned as being afflicted or dying, such as when ships are destroyed (8:9) and people die from the poisoned waters (8:11). Nature itself, therefore, will be the primary focus of the first four trumpets.

The fifth and sixth trumpets, on the other hand, will be directly aimed at human beings. For five months, the locusts will be able to inflict pain on mankind. Following their activities, the horsemen will be able to destroy a third of mankind.

The first series of judgments, then, will be designed to disrupt nature, destroy man's environment, and deprive him of the blessings he has so casually taken for granted. The second series will extend beyond man's environment, taking both his health and his life in some cases. While these judgments may seem severe, they are designed to bring men to repentance. Strange as it may seem, these judgments will not turn all men to Christ. Much of mankind will be so stubbornly engrossed in sin that it will prefer to curse the Creator of the universe rather than repent.

1. The Seventh Seal (Revelation 8:1-13)

In the light of the breaking of past seals, one might expect some cataclysmic or at least ominous event to be described as soon as the seventh seal is broken. Contrary to expectations, however, at first there is only silence. Later the expected, awesome holocaust is vividly depicted.

The Silence in Heaven (verses 1-6). The period of silence mentioned by John has no straightforward explanation, but perhaps it is reasonable to conclude that the silence symbolizes some sort of suspenseful lull between the breaking of the seal and the announcement of what it constitutes.

During the time of anticipation, John saw an angel offering incense with the prayers of believers upon an altar, perhaps the altar he saw was like the altar of incense used with the Tabernacle. In some manner, it seems that the actions of the angel are to convey the notion that the prayers of saints are connected with the judgments that are hereinafter discussed. The judgments do not come as a result of prayers of vengeance, but instead are partially a consequence of prayers of vindication (Luke 18:1-9).

John also notes that there were seven particular angels that caught his attention. The angels later reveal the contents of the seventh seal which opened the book or scroll itself. Rather strangely, the scroll is not mentioned again by John (unless he does so in Revelation 11), but this seems more reasonable when one recognizes that the contents of the scroll, i.e., the trumpets and the bowls, are the center of attention, not the scroll itself. Thus, the seventh seal which leads to the first trumpet appears to be the first glance we receive of the contents of the scroll itself.

The First Trumpet: The Hail and the Fire (verse 7). Probably few commentators would have any problem with a literal interpretation of this verse were it not for the term *blood.* A smaller but similar judgment without the blood was brought upon Egypt during the time of Moses (Exodus 9). But since the word *blood* is present in John's statement, many Premillennialists say the whole verse should be understood in a symbolic sense; that is, the scene describes God's chastening of the ungodly disorders of mankind.

This type of interpretation, nevertheless, does not seem to adequately deal with "the third part of trees . . . and all green grass." The suggestion that the trees represent people of high political and social positions and that the green grass symbolizes the ordinary, working man does not help matters either.

One of several interpretative possibilities seems to be left. A person may say the blood is mingled with the hail and fire after the latter two are thrown to the earth; some human beings and animals will be killed and their blood will be mixed with the hail and fire. Even though this is a possible explanation, many expositors argue that the more natural explanation is that all three will be cast upon the earth.

Another option for the student of the Apocalypse to consider is to say something like blood will be mixed with the hail and fire before being thrown to the earth. In this case, however, one does not have any more reason for saying something like blood will be thrown than he does to say something like hail and fire will be thrown.

A final consideration is that God will actually mingle blood with the hail and fire. The idea is unquestionably a strange one but not at all impossible. By the way, before we move on to the second trumpet, it is interesting to know that many interpreters think the fire that is spoken of may be a reference to an intense electrical storm.

The Second Trumpet: The Great Mountain (verses 8, 9). Expositors have the same problem with the second trumpet that they have with the first trumpet, the word *blood.* So, partly as a result of the term, many expositors suggest that the verses symbolize the fact that a great empire will be visited by God and thrown into internal chaos and violence. Other expositors are inclined toward a more literal interpretation and believe the waters will be turned blood red as a result of some chemical change that occurs. A bit of evidence might be found in the text for this interpretation. The words *as it were* before "a great mountain" are better translated *something similar to.* Thus, the notion is that something like a great mountain, perhaps a large meteoric object, will be thrown into the sea.

At least one difficulty arises, however, if one says that the apocalyptic language used by John may also indicate that we should conceive of the words *something similar to* before the word *blood.* That problem, briefly stated, is that one has no logical stopping place in this passage once he begins to apply the concept to anything other than the mountain itself. As a result, one could argue that *something like* creatures, a sea, and ships are involved. But then, the resulting meaning is rather ridiculous; for, what would be meant by something like a ship?

After considering the alternatives, it seems best to conclude that the second trumpet signals the time when a large meteoric mass will fall into some body of water on the earth and that a third of the ships of the world and the life of the sea will be destroyed. And, as far as we can tell, that body of water will be turned to blood or will be red as a result of the blood that comes from the death of a great deal of sea life.

The Third Trumpet: The Great Star (verses 10, 11). One major interpretation offered by symbolists of this trumpet is that God announced through an angel that some outstanding religious leader will fall into apostasy during the Great Tribulation and, consequently, the sources of spiritual and national life will be poisoned.

A more natural explanation is that an astronomical body will enter the atmosphere of the earth and will contaminate many of the rivers and waters of the earth. Literalists generally accept this interpretation.

The Fourth Trumpet: The Luminaries (verses 12, 13). Symbolic interpretations of these verses tend to describe the events here as referring to some kind of disruption of society or as an allusion to the withdrawal of spiritual light during the Great Tribulation. If the latter of these two views is accepted, the expositor usually says it will be much more difficult to find Christ as one's personal Savior during the Great Tribulation.

Those who ascribe to a more literal viewpoint are not in total agreement either. Some argue that the best interpretation of the passage is that the sun, moon, and stars will lose a third of their brilliance or that these luminaries are diminished by a third of their usual force. Many other literalists suggest God will in some way alter the natural properties of these luminaries so that they fail to be seen anywhere on earth a third of the time. The easier of these two general positions–symbolist and literalist–to accept is the literalist position. Yet it is not easily decided which of the two literalist views is the better.

2. The First and Second Woes (Revelation 9:1-21)

In Revelation 9 we are introduced to the fifth and sixth trumpets which are also referred to as the first and second woes. In all, there are three woes; the third woe is also the seventh trumpet, which is discussed by John in Revelation 11:14-19. These three trumpets are designated as woes because they are specifically aimed at human beings, not the natural environment. The implication of the term *woe* seems to be that the final three trumpets are more devastating, torturous, and frightening than the first four trumpets.

The Fifth Trumpet: the Locusts (verses 1-12). Although Premillennialists are not in perfect agreement as to the identity of the angel mentioned in verse 1, many of them think the angel is Lucifer or Satan. If the angel is Lucifer and not some other angelic being, then the fall mentioned here might be an allusion to the spiritual battle that is vividly portrayed in Revelation 12:7-9.

To the person who is referred to as a fallen star, John records that a key is given. The key enables the individual to open the bottomless pit or the place where demons are detained. The same pit is mentioned later in the Apocalypse. In the light of the reference in Revelation 20:1-3, many say it may be best to interpret the angel in this verse as someone other than Satan. Satan probably will not be given the power to release one of God's judgments upon the earth. Instead, God will probably send one of His own ministering angels to release this judgment; although the fifth trumpet and the eviction of Satan from Heaven may happen during approximately the same time period.

After the pit is opened, John says smoke rises to darken the sky. Out of the dense smoke, locusts appear. That these locusts are not to be understood as normal locusts is implied by the fact that they have an angelic king, perhaps Satan himself (9:11). Satan is ruler of the demonic world, and it appears that the "abnormal locusts" described by the apostle are demons; although, some commentators think, among other things, the locusts are atypical locusts that are demon possessed.

The demons, whether acting as themselves or through atypical locusts as some suppose, will be restrained from harming anything or anyone except people who do not have "the seal of God in their foreheads" (9:4). They are not to damage any of nature and cannot kill human beings who are believers. Their only function is to torture unbelievers for a period of five months, the normal season for literal locusts to be active in Palestine.

The excruciating pain that will be experienced by mankind during this part of the Great Tribulation is compared with that of the sting of a scorpion. So horrible will be the experience that people will wish to die so they can escape from their agonies. They will not be so fortunate, however; they will be afflicted throughout the story of the demonic forces.

The demons themselves are vividly described in Revelation 9:7-10. The main truth John wishes to get across is that the demons will bring both terror and fear to the hearts of mankind during their activities. Perhaps the demons will in some way be visible to people, e.g., inhabit atypical locusts. Whether they are or not, they will be fierce ("teeth of lions"), indestructible ("breastplates of iron"), intelligent ("faces of men"), and victorious in their mission ("crowns like gold").

In looking at this total passage, at least two problems surface for the average student. One of these is manifested in the following question: Do the forces described by the apostle torture any Christians during the Tribulation? Most people give a negative answer to this inquiry. It appears that the fundamental purpose of this trumpet is to turn unbelievers to God (9:21). If Christians suffer the same excruciating pain, there would seem to be no particular outward appeal to becoming a believer.

This question, nevertheless, becomes a little more difficult to answer when the words "but only those men which have not the seal of God in their foreheads" (9:4) are taken into consideration. The problem that develops is whether the 144,000 mentioned in Revelation 7:4 are the only Christians spared while other believers are tortured by the locusts. A possible answer that is given by a number of Premillennialists is that the 144,000 mentioned by the Apostle John should not be understood in a literal manner; that is, the number refers to the total number of believers who will be protected by God during the Great Tribulation.

Another suggestion that is put forth by many expositors is that the reference to those who are sealed by God is meant to include all Christians during this period of time. The sealed group is particularly mentioned because the group will be somewhat representative of all Christians during the time of God's wrath upon the unbelieving and unrepenting world.

An additional difficulty that arises in connection with this passage is related to the nature of the work of the demonic forces that are mentioned. Some folks think it strange that Satan will be working against himself during this portion of the Great Tribulation. Satan will be seeking to destroy believers on the earth, but this passage suggests his forces torture unbelievers as well. This problem partially disappears if one does not interpret the angel (9:1) as Satan and remembers that even if the angel is Satan he has never been a friend of unbelievers. Besides it seems that God will divide the forces of Satan in more than one way during the days immediately before the millennium (17:16).

The Sixth Trumpet: The Horsemen (verses 13-21). The blowing of the sixth trumpet will result in the release of four angels, perhaps fallen ones, who in turn release 200,000,000 horsemen. Unlike the locusts, the horsemen will be given the responsibility of bringing death to a third of the population of the world. If the fourth seal (6:7, 8) is understood to refer to the death of a fourth of the people of the world, then the combined destruction of the sixth trumpet and the fourth seal will account for the death of half of the people of the world during the last days. Such a massive loss of human life will undoubtedly seriously alter the total way of living on the entire globe.

When examining the army that will be so devastating, one faces a couple of moot questions. For instance, should the 200,000,000 horsemen be understood in a literal manner? Premillennialists are divided on the question, but there seems to be no significant reason for answering in the negative, especially in the light of the present population of the world.

A more perplexing question is how we should understand the very notion of horsemen. Some expositors believe the word is John's way of describing what will be a modern army. They stress such statements as "out of their mouths issued fire and smoke and brimstone" and "their power is in their mouth, and . . . tails" (9:17, 19). Many who follow this line of thinking believe the horsemen symbolize a gigantic Asiatic army that will gather during the Great Tribulation to fight the forces of the Antichrist in Palestine. They believe that this army may depict the early stages of what is later mentioned again in the sixth bowl (16:12-21). Other Premillennial expositors believe basically the same as this first group except they think the language is symbolic of an army that will be unusually destructive.

A number of more recent students of the Apocalypse think that the 200,000,000 persons mentioned in these verses are not human beings. They are demons. These demons will lead in some type of invasion on earth that will be directed by the four demons released earlier. The destruction they bring on the earth will primarily result from the three plagues of "fire, and by the smoke, and by the brimstone" (9:18). A somewhat similar view suggests that the demonic and human forces will be so mingled that they will be indistinguishable, much like the blending of the locusts and demons in the fifth trumpet.

7

The Angel, the Witnesses, and the Seventh Trumpet

Study Text: Revelation 10:1—11:19

Introduction
1. The Mighty Angel (Revelation 10:1-11)
   a. The Seven Peals of Thunder (verses 1-4)
   b. The Mystery of God (verses 5-7)
   c. The Eating of the Book (verses 8-11)
2. The Two Witnesses (Revelation 11:1-13)
   a. The Measuring Rod (verses 1, 2)
   b. The Ministry of the Witnesses (verses 3-6)
   c. The Death of the Witnesses (verses 7-10)
   d. The Restoration of the Witnesses (verses 11-13)
3. The Seventh Trumpet (Revelation 11:14-19)
   a. The Third Woe (verses 14, 15)
   b. The Announcement of the Elders (verses 16-19)

Introduction

The writer of the Apocalypse, after having sketched the components of the first six trumpets, turns to discuss a number of topics in detail. Earlier, in Revelation 7 when he discussed the two multitudes, he took a similar break from the basic outline of his book. During that break, he gave a close-up of events that will come to pass during the Great Tribulation. This interlude, however, is rather long when compared with the first one; for, it extends from Revelation 10:1 through Revelation 11:13 before returning briefly to discuss the seventh trumpet or third woe (Revelation 11:14-19).

The same question that confronted the interpreter of Revelation 7 once again challenges him at this time: When will the events described in the interlude occur? Will they fall during one of the first six trumpets? Will they overlap with several trumpets? Will they come to pass during the seventh trumpet? Some suggestions for answering these questions will be mentioned as the Biblical text itself is studied.

Exposition

When analyzing the present parenthesis, it is helpful to extract what seems to be the major truths that John wished to convey. As far as we can tell, he had a few major purposes in writing this section. A reason that is almost explicitly stated by him is that the information he presents will help prepare the way for a more mature grasp of the seventh trumpet. John's own words are as follows:

"But in the days of the voice of the seventh angel, when he shall begin to sound, the mystery of God should be finished, as he hath declared to his servants the prophets" (10:7).

The mighty angel's words to the Apostle John imply a second reason for the parenthesis: "Thou must prophesy again before many peoples, and nations, and tongues, and kings" (10:11). The angelic being, in a special way, wanted to encourage John to continue his ministry as a prophet and to assure him that his prophecies would be communicated, not to just a few people, but to "many peoples, and nations, and tongues, and kings."

Two other purposes are involved in this break in thought between the sixth and seventh trumpets. In this stage of the vision, John became an actor or participator in the revelation of the last days as he was commanded to "measure the temple of God." Finally, God wished to give a blowup or an enlargement of two particular prophets who will be key witnesses for Christ during the Great Tribulation. After accomplishing all of these purposes, John's vision turned to the seventh trumpet.

1. The Mighty Angel (Revelation 10:1-11)

In the division of the Apocalypse, the narrative centers on a person who is described by John as a mighty angel. The mighty angel is first of all described in his relation to the seven peals of thunder; then to the mystery of God; and, finally, to a little book.

The Seven Peals of Thunder (verses 1-4). As you have probably already observed, angels play an important role in the revelation that was given to the apostle. In the instance before us, the angelic being is described as mighty. Perhaps the word denotes an angel who had authority over other angels in addition to being powerful within himself.

John's introduction to the angel describes him as being "clothed with a cloud: and a rainbow was upon his head, and his face was as it were the sun, and his feet as pillars of fire" (10:1). This picturesque description may have been designed merely to draw attention to the glorious appearance of the angel. After introducing the angel, John turns his attention to the little book or scroll in the angelic being's hand. The contents of this small scroll are not mentioned by John; therefore, a number of speculations have emerged as to what it contained.

Some folks believe the scroll is a symbol of the Word of God. From this perspective, the contents of the scroll are the past revelations of God through His servants. If this thought is accepted, the reason the angel had the scroll is that it suggests he had God's authority to fulfill his particular mission at that time. One problem with this interpretation is why this angel would need such a symbol any more than the other angels who spoke to John.

Another way of attempting to understand the little scroll is to see it as representing a small portion of God's revelation. As a matter of fact, some Bible teachers argue that the little book contained the final eleven chapters of the Apocalypse. Yet, this viewpoint is not totally satisfactory either. Why, for example, is it considered a fragment of God's revelation if it is at least as large as the earlier portion of His revelation, Revelation 1-11? If the proponent of this position argues that the small scroll contained only a part of the rest of the Book of Revelation, this difficulty becomes less significant. However, the person then has the problem of saying which section of the Apocalypse is meant, and he also has the difficulty of justifying his answer.

Other expositors reason that the little scroll is a symbolic way of verifying the prophetic ministry of the writer of the Apocalypse, the Apostle John. While this point of view is not wholly without difficulties, it may be supported by the fact that John later eats the small scroll (10:9, 10).

A final interpretation that might have more merit than the others is that the small scroll is the same as the scroll with seven seals. The fact that John ate the book may figuratively convey the notion that believers during the Great Tribulation will experience both the bitter and the sweet aspects of life during that time.

Contrary to what might be expected, John was soon told not to record one of the segments of this specific vision. The reason for not being able to pass on to other believers what he himself saw in the seven peals of thunder is not clear. One can only be certain that God did not intend for believers to know about some of the events that will occur during the Great Tribulation.

The Mystery of God (verses 5-7). After the apostle was told not to record that which was revealed to him in the seven peals of thunder, the strong angel swore by God the Father. This oath suggests that the angel was not Christ as some exegetes have argued. The oath itself calls attention to the eternity of God, His creative acts, and His sovereignty. His sovereign rule is implied in the frequently misunderstood words "that there should be time no longer" (10:6). This common misunderstanding is reflected in a hymn that speaks of time ending at the return of the Lord Jesus Christ.

The words in verse 6 are better translated, "that there should no longer be any delay." The notion, therefore, is that the mighty angel announced that God would use His sovereign rule to bring to a quick end His planned judgments upon the earth. To rephrase the thought a little, the angel simply declared that when the seventh angel blew his trumpet, the mystery of God would be quickly finished.

Perhaps a word on the nature of time is important since the way verse 6 is translated in the King James Version has helped perpetuate a false understanding about it. Christians have frequently assumed that time refers to events that belong to the present world in distinction from events in eternity. Thinking of time in this way, Christians naturally come to the conclusion that time will one day come to an end. But time is better understood as the potentiality of relational activities or as the possibility of successive events. From this orientation there was time before the creation, and there will be time after the new universe is created because one event has always followed and always will follow another event. Eternity is properly understood as unending time, not as some existence without any time.

The mystery of God spoken of by John in verse 7 is not totally clear, but the essence of the thought in this case may center on God's judgment of people who reject His Son. In a broader sense, the mystery may also include other truths related to God's purposes for mankind. This point is supported by the reference to what God revealed to prophets during Old and New Testament eras.

The Eating of the Book (verses 8-11). The significance of John's eating the small scroll is far from being clear to the average expositor of the Book of Revelation even though he is inclined to express his opinion on the subject. The most commonly stated opinion is some variation of the thought that eating the scroll indicates how either the Word of God or the will of God is both sweet and bitter. In John's case, the prophetic messages he had to record and deliver to others is both pleasant and disturbing to him. The pleasure is derived from knowing the plan of God and how one fits into it. The bitter aspects of his assimilation of the book are associated with a natural grief that comes as a result of seeing the awful judgments that await unrepentant mankind as well as seeing the trials that come to faithful followers of Christ.

2. The Two Witnesses (Revelation 11:1-13)

This chapter of the Apocalypse is, like many other chapters, not too difficult to explain in a general way; but when it comes to specific questions, problems do arise. The basic problems are related to the nature of the Temple and the identity of the two witnesses that are discussed by the Apostle John.

The Measuring Rod (verses 1, 2). John's rather inactive role in the visions he saw came to an end for a short period of time when he was instructed, "Rise, and measure the temple of God, and the altar, and them that worship therein." But John's role as an actor is only implied, for the text does not elaborate on any of his actions. Instead, two witnesses are discussed at length.

The meaning of measuring the Temple is somewhat clarified by studying similar examples in the Old Testament. As a rule, the Old Testament examples suggest that someone or something is being set aside for destruction, discipline, or preservation. Since John was told not to measure the Temple court because it would be trodden "under foot forty and two months," it may be that the measuring of the Temple suggests it will not be harmed by the Gentiles during the same period of time.

Few Premillennialists ever think about what seems to be a contradiction that arises at this point if they understand the forty-two months to refer to the last half of the Tribulation. The problem is that most Premillennialists think the Antichrist will defile the Temple in the last half of the Tribulation by setting himself up as God (2 Thessalonians 2:4). If this is so, how can the measuring of the Temple be an allusion to God's preservation of it?

Not very many alternatives are open to Premillennialists if they wish to be consistent in their thinking. They may say that the measuring of the Temple suggests that God will preserve it from destruction but not from pollution. Or they may argue that the preservation spoken of refers to the first half of the Tribulation, not to the last half, as many have traditionally believed. A third way of handling this difficulty is to say that the Temple is not to be understood as a literal Temple, but as a symbol of the body of Christ. This third view will be encountered again in a few moments.

This difficulty, however, does not arise for those who see the rod as an instrument of discipline. They understand the symbolism to imply that God will chasten the Jewish people during the Great Tribulation.

Among Premillennialists the issue is fairly well settled that the Temple referred to here is an allusion to a literal Temple that will be rebuilt and be in existence during the entire Tribulation. If one ascribes to this position, a problem may arise for the traditional Premillennial viewpoint. For if the Temple is in use at the beginning of the Tribulation, it seems rather logical to say that the Church cannot be raptured until after the Temple is rebuilt. For if the rapture occurs at the time the Tribulation begins and the Temple is in use throughout the Tribulation, then the Temple must be rebuilt before the Tribulation as well as before the rapture. Thus, the rapture of the Church might not happen at any moment as many Premillennialists teach.

This problem does not bother too many midtribulationists and posttribulationists. They are almost by the very nature of their views committed to the soon coming of Christ rather than His imminent coming. So proponents of these two positions sometimes freely admit that the Temple must be rebuilt before the rapture, and that when it is rebuilt believers can be assured that the Tribulation will then be at hand.

Pretribulationists may select one of three ways to solve this problem concerning the Temple, the rapture, and the Tribulation. For those who wish to maintain that the Church's rapture is imminent, they can argue that the Temple can be quickly reconstructed as soon as the Tribulation begins.

Some pretribulationists, however, doubt that the Jews will so hurriedly build anything as sacred as the Temple. They think, therefore, that the Temple can be built after the rapture but before the Tribulation begins. For those who are used to hearing that as soon as the Church is raptured the Tribulation begins, this doctrine is difficult to comprehend. Pretribulationists, however, who ascribe to this position say there is no passage which teaches that the rapture initiates the Tribulation. The Scriptures simply teach, they say, that the world will go through the Tribulation after the rapture. They reason that a period of years could elapse after the rapture and before the Tribulation and, thereby, permit enough time for the Temple to be rebuilt. The coming of Christ for His Church, therefore, can still be at any moment.

Those pretribulationists who do not wish to defend the imminent return of Christ have no more problem with the Temple than do mid and posttribulationists. They simply admit that the Temple has to be rebuilt before the rapture and that it is best to speak of the soon coming of the Lord.

A final interpretation of the Temple needs to be mentioned before moving on to the two witnesses. A few Premillennialists do not think the reference to the Temple is to be understood as literalists understand it. These folks are convinced that the reference to the Temple signifies God's protection of a faithful Jewish remnant or His care for the Church during the Great Tribulation. Adherents of this position attack a literal interpretation of the Temple by asking. "Why would God want to protect unbelieving Jews during the Tribulation as well as their center of worship?" God would not want to do such, they believe; so, the passage must be understood as God's intention to protect true believers, whether Jews or Gentiles, during the Great Tribulation.

Yet the issue is not so easily solved. Those who believe in a literal Temple may give one of two rebuttals. They may argue that God speaks of protecting the Temple so that everyone can know that even though the Jews will not have complete control of Palestine, He will protect them from annihilation. Or, they sometimes argue that the whole idea of measuring the Temple does not signify protection but symbolizes that the Jewish people who do not worship Christ will be disciplined by God. A Premillennialist who ascribes to a literal Temple being rebuilt may like to stress that the figurative interpretation of the Temple very oddly implies, if 2 Thessalonians

2:4 is interpreted to be consistent with Revelation 11:1, that God will protect true believers while the Antichrist sets himself up among them as God Himself (2 Thessalonians 2:4).

The Ministry of the Witnesses (verses 3-6). To understand the two witnesses, it is important to understand the time of their ministry. The vast majority of Premillennialists are convinced that since this interlude comes after the sixth trumpet and just before the seventh trumpet, the events described will happen during the last three and a half years of the Tribulation or during the Great Tribulation. The specific identity of the two witnesses, however, is another matter. Expositors offer a number of interpretations.

Some of these writers suggest that the two witnesses symbolize the nation of Israel and the Scriptures, the two main ways people will learn of Christ during the Tribulation. If this view is accepted, one has an enormous problem in explaining the death of the witnesses as well as the restoration of them.

Other students of the Book of Revelation believe Elijah and Moses will return to the earth to witness for Christ and die for Him. The similarities between the activities and the descriptions of Moses and Elijah and the two witnesses are far from being conclusive evidence for this interpretation, however. Probably the best explanation is that during the Great Tribulation two men, who have powers similar to those of Elijah and Moses, will be outstanding witnesses for Christ.

The Death of the Witnesses (verses 7-10). The beast who will be responsible for the death of the two witnesses is generally thought to be the same beast who is described as coming out of the sea in Revelation 13:1. Conversely, a few believe the beast mentioned here is Satan and that John has here alluded to Revelation 9:1, 2, 11. In Revelation 9, the word *pit* or *abyss* is used; but the word *beast* is not employed. In either case, Satan will be ultimately responsible for the death of the two witnesses. If the beast out of the sea is meant, the allusion is to the Roman dictator, the Antichrist.

The Restoration of the Witnesses (verses 11-13). After the two prophets have been dead for almost four days, God will raise them from their "public graves." The apostle's description of what will take place suggests that the people around them will be characterized by great fear–probably because they will fear the power of the prophets or the wrath of God Himself. Their fears will be justified; for soon after the two prophets are raptured, an earthquake will occur that will shatter a tenth of the city and cause the death of thousands of people. The rest of the people, perhaps a reference to Jews, will become even more fearful because they recognize that God is responsible for the restoration of the dead prophets and the earthquake. This time their fear will lead them to give "glory to the God of heaven" (11:13). This phrase may imply that they will repent of their unbelief and trust in Christ. Whether similar acts of glorification will occur outside of Jerusalem is not specifically mentioned.

3. The Seventh Trumpet (Revelation 11:14-19)

John's words suddenly take a new direction as he returns to the trumpets he previously mentioned. He points out that the second woe is past, and the third is soon to begin. Later, we are told of the elders' announcement of God's judgment upon the nations of the world.

The Third Woe (verses 14, 15). Revelation 11:14 should, but seldom does, cause Premillennial writers to seriously consider the time of the third woe, the seventh trumpet, and the seven bowls. The events of Revelation 11:1-13 are usually thought to happen during the Great Tribulation or the last three and a half years of the Tribulation. After the Great Tribulation is over, the two prophets will lie three and a half days on a street in the city of Jerusalem. Then after the rapture of the two prophets, the third woe, seventh trumpet, and seven bowls seem to come. If this is the proper interpretation of these events, then it appears that all of the events described in Revelation 15:1–19:21 occur after the entire Tribulation has ended. Consequently, the seven bowls may come to pass after the Tribulation but before the millennium. This would be during the two periods of time, one of thirty days and the other of forty-five days, spoken of by the prophet Daniel (Daniel 12:11, 12). This interpretation, it should be remembered, is exactly that, an interpretation. Another explanation is that there will be some overlap of time between the trumpets and the bowls. Even if there is some overlap, there still seems to be strong evidence to suggest that at least Revelation 16:12–19:21 will come to pass after the Great Tribulation has ended.

The Announcement of the Elders (verses 16-19). The announcement of the twenty-four elders follows immediately after the angel blows his trumpet and says, "The kingdoms of this world are become the kingdoms of our Lord." The joint announcements indicate that the inception of Christ's rule has arrived and that the destruction of human rule is clearly over. A conclusion that may logically follow is that the Tribulation will be over when the seventh trumpet is blown and that the intervals spoken of by Daniel are about to begin (Daniel 12:11, 12).

8

The Dragon, the Woman, and the Offspring

Study Text: Revelation 12:1-17

Introduction
1. The Signs in the Heaven (Revelation 12:1-6)
   a. The Pregnant Woman (verses 1, 2)
   b. The Red Dragon (verses 3, 4)
   c. The Male Child (verses 5, 6)
2. The Battle in Heaven (Revelation 12:7-12)
   a. The Defeat of Satan (verses 7-9)
   b. The Salvation of God (verses 10-12)
3. The Persecution of the Woman (Revelation 12:13-17)
   a. The Flight of the Woman (verses 13, 14)
   b. The Wrath of the Dragon (verses 15-17)

Introduction

Having heard the seventh trumpet sound, the apostle might well have expected immediately to see a new series of divine judgments fall upon the earth. Yet this is not what he saw. A third interlude in the overall vision came before him. This parenthetical section begins with Revelation 12:1 and extends through Revelation 14:20. After this parenthesis is concluded, John is given the content of the seventh trumpet. The seventh trumpet seems to include the seven bowls (15:1-16:21) and, possibly, the judgment of Babylon (17:1-18:24).

The interlude between the announcement of the seventh trumpet and the description of it is concerned with a variety of individuals and groups. The symbolism utilized by the Apostle John to refer to these people is as follows: (a) a red dragon, (b) a pregnant woman, (c) a male child, (d) the other children of the woman, (e) a beast out of the sea, (f) a beast out of the earth, and (g) the Lamb of God. The specific symbols we are concerned with in this chapter are the dragon, the woman, the child, and the other children of the woman.

Exposition

As on other occasions, an important consideration in understanding the overall significance of this chapter is related to identifying the exact time the events discussed in this chapter occur. Will they occur before, during, or after the Tribulation? Or do some events happen during all three of these periods? If they are going to occur during one of these periods, at what specific time will they happen? That is to say, when Michael engages in a battle with Satan, will it occur before or during the Tribulation?

In addition to seeing and seeking to answer the aforementioned questions, it is important, too, that we realize that proponents of all three Premillennial positions–the pre-, mid-, and posttribulationists–find evidence for their particular positions in Revelation 12. This fact is sometimes confusing to the person who is just beginning his study of the Apocalypse, but it need not be overwhelming. A person does not have to be absolutely sure of the meaning of Revelation 12 in order to appreciate the Book of Revelation. Nor need he remain in some sort of theological limbo as a result. Through a study of the Apocalypse over a period of years, one can become more firmly convinced of a point of view and at the same time allow other Christians the freedom to develop and express differing viewpoints.

1. The Signs in the Heaven (Revelation 12:1-6)

Two signs or wonders are discussed in these few verses. The word *sign* suggests something of importance or great magnitude. The symbols used to convey truths that are of immediate importance to us are the pregnant woman (12:1) and the red dragon (12:3).

The Pregnant Woman (verses 1, 2). The signs that appeared to John in the heavens or in the sky are later depicted as occurring on the earth. Apocalyptic language is so flexible that at times it may be conceptually confusing. The remainder of the account, nevertheless, makes it abundantly clear that the events will happen on the earth.

The first sign in this story is that of a pregnant woman. She is briefly described as being "clothed with the sun, and the moon under her feet, and upon her head a crown of twelve stars."

Some Christians understand the description given in verse 1 to be presenting significant, detailed truths about the woman. For example, a person might argue that the reference to the twelve stars is an allusion to the twelve tribes of Israel and that the mentioning of the sun and moon is to be understood in the light of Genesis 37:9. Both sets of symbols, then, would be a prophetic way of identifying the woman as the nation of Israel.

Other believers think the first symbols are to be understood as a simple reference to the glory of the woman. The twelve stars are sometimes explained in the same manner as the first explanation presented, e.g., as a reference to the twelve tribes of Israel. But some argue that the stars stand for the twelve apostles.

While a person can get a relatively clear picture of this chapter without being settled on the precise interpretation of the symbols surrounding the pregnant woman, it is somewhat essential to understand what or who is signified by the woman herself. The proliferation of interpretations about the woman would be almost amazing were it not for the realization that proponents of all three tribulational positions find important clues to support their views.

The major interpretations of the woman may be summarized as follows: (1) She signifies Israel; (2) she symbolizes the universal Church; (3) she stands for the true people of God. The specific interpretation a person ascribes to concerning the woman is important within itself, but it is also significant in that the interpretation of the woman is somewhat related to one's view of the child she has. This relationship will be delineated when the male child is discussed. At that time the strengths and weaknesses of the various interpretations of the woman will be briefly sketched.

The Red Dragon (verses 3, 4). Determining the identity of the dragon seems unbelievably easy when compared with the task of attempting to decide what is symbolized by the woman, the child, and the remnant of the woman's seed. This should hardly be construed as saying that there are no problems at all concerning the dragon, however.

Even though the Biblical text says that the dragon is "the Devil, and Satan, which deceiveth the whole world" (12:9), some commentators have insisted that the dragon represents not only Satan but also the Roman Empire as revived or transformed in the last days and during the Great Tribulation. The grounds for saying this is that the dragon has "seven heads and ten horns" (12:3) just as does the beast out of the sea (13:1). No doubt the similarity does exist; however, it seems wiser to conclude that the similarity implies, if anything, a relationship between the beast and the dragon, not that both symbolize the same Roman Empire.

The stars that are raked from the heavens by Satan probably stand for the angels who will fall with him. On the other hand, some people think the reference is to Satan's overcoming social and political opposition during the Great Tribulation. The context makes the latter of these two interpretations difficult to defend (12:9).

The Male Child (verses 5, 6). As has already been mentioned, the way a person interprets the pregnant woman may to some extent influence his opinion of what or who is suggested by her male child. Before looking at the connection between the two symbols, let us first state the basic interpretations of the male child. Some of the more noteworthy interpretations of the child are that he represents the 144,000 Jews mentioned in Revelation 7, Christ, or the Church.

Now, let us examine the relationship between the woman and her child. Doing this in the light of pre-, mid-, and posttribulational interpretations may be beneficial. First of all, let us begin with the interpretations that are often ascribed to by pretribulationists or people who believe the Church will be raptured before the entire Tribulation. The most widely accepted interpretation by members of this group is that the woman symbolizes Israel and the child represents Christ. The ascension of Christ is alluded to by the words "caught up" (12:5). Israel will be persecuted by Satan for the last three and a half years of the Tribulation or during the Great Tribulation.

Not all pretribulationists are satisfied with this explanation. Some, but not all, who disagree with this interpretation argue that the catching up of the male child is better understood as referring to an event that happens in the middle of the Tribulation. Since the Church has already been raptured before the Tribulation, then the male child must represent the 144,000 sealed Jews who are active for Christ in the first half of the Tribulation and are later seen on Mount Zion with Christ (14:1).

Midtribulationists, unlike the first group of pretribulationists mentioned, hardly ever explain the child as being Christ. They do agree with the second group of pretribulationists in that they say that the male child seems to be raptured in the middle of the Tribulation. But, they argue, the male child represents the Church, not the

144,000 Jews. The 144,000 Jews appear in the last half of the Tribulation, not the first half.

True, midtribulationists admit, Christ presently sits on a throne in Heaven and will rule with a rod of iron during the millennium, but so will the Church. Christ Himself promised, "To him that overcometh will I grant to sit with me in my throne" (3:21). Moreover, He has clearly stated: "And he that overcometh, and keepeth my works unto the end, to him will I give power over the nations: And he shall rule them with a rod of iron" (2:26, 27).

Midtribulationists may interpret the pregnant woman in one of a couple of ways. Some of them think she represents Israel as the predecessor of the Church. Others see the woman as a symbol of the true people of God for all ages. But if the latter explanation is taken, one has a very difficult time explaining how the true people of God are still on the earth after the Church has been raptured (12:13).

The interpretation of posttribulationists for this passage generally runs something like this: The woman represents the Church and the child signifies Christ. During the Tribulation Satan will turn his attention to the Church in an attempt to destroy it.

How does a person decide which of these three fundamental explanations is the correct one? If a fully satisfactory answer were available, two of the views discussed would have disappeared if people were willing to accept the clearly correct interpretation. Since all three positions are very much alive today, we must conclude that either Christians will not accept the clear truth or the truth is not all that clear. The latter of these two alternatives appears to be the case: We have no completely adequate answer to the question.

Yet, we are not left without any guidelines. This interlude comes after the seventh trumpet has sounded but before the contents of the bowls are revealed. Almost all Premillennialists agree that the three statements about "a thousand two hundred and threescore days" (12:6), "a time, and times, and half a time" (12:14), and "forty and two months" (13:5) are references to the last half of the Tribulation. The emphasis of the interlude, then, is on the second half of the Tribulation. This being the case, it seems preferable to think that the events described in Revelation 12 are to be understood as happening shortly before and during the Great Tribulation. If this is so, it is best to understand the male child as some group of believers who will be taken out of the world just before the Great Tribulation begins.

2. The Battle in Heaven (Revelation 12:7-12)

The story takes on a different emphasis in these verses and indicates what will happen to Satan during the Tribulation. Some expositors think the passage, especially verses 7-9, refers to some past fall of Satan, but the context seems to support the idea that the fall spoken of here is a future event. If it is a future event, Satan's fall may be either at the beginning of the Tribulation or in the middle of the Tribulation. Since this parenthesis is vitally concerned with the last half of the Tribulation, the implication may well be that Satan will be cast out of Heaven just before the Great Tribulation begins; that is, he will be evicted by Michael and his angels before the final three and a half years of the Tribulation.

The Defeat of Satan (verses 7-9). Satan's plan will be to destroy the male child; but when the male child is raptured in the middle of the Tribulation, several important changes take place. First, Michael and the angels that serve with him will engage in a battle with Satan and his demons. The battle is difficult for us to visualize, so some folks say it is not a literal one. On the other hand, it may well be a literal battle (Daniel 10:13, 20, 21). The result of Satan's defeat is that he will no longer be able to accuse believers before God as he has historically been able to do (Job 2).

A second change that will take place is that Satan will no longer have access to the male child; therefore, he redirects his attack. This time he concentrates on the woman (12:13).

Those pretribulationists who believe that the male child symbolizes the 144,000 Jewish missionaries think, naturally, that Satan's original plan will be to destroy this group as soon as it appears during the first half of the Tribulation. His plan, however, will not reach fruition because God will have sealed this group for three and a half years.

Midtribulationists who think the male child represents the Church believe that when the Church is raptured in the middle of the Tribulation, Satan will then be evicted from Heaven for his days of accusation will be over. He will no longer be able to try to crush the Church; therefore, Satan will direct his attention toward the nation of Israel. At this time the Antichrist will break his covenant with the Jews (Daniel 9:27), and the last great anti-Semitic activities of society will commence.

The Salvation of God (verses 10-12). Satan's ejection from Heaven, then, appears to be a sign that the last half of the Tribulation or the Great Tribulation has begun. While Satan is not omniscient, the Apostle John does record that when Michael is victorious over him he will recognize "that he hath but a short time" (12:12).

The announcement, "Now is come salvation, and strength, and the kingdom of our God, and the power of his Christ" (12:10) has disturbed some believers. They have wondered, "How can the millennium or rule of Christ begin in the middle of the Tribulation?"

The question is a good one, and there are a couple of feasible answers to it. The first of these is that the announcement refers to an initial step by God in taking away Satan's realm of dominion. A second way of looking at the problem is to view the announcement as a proleptic statement. A proleptic statement assigns an event to a period earlier than its actual date. Such a statement is normally made shortly before the actual event is to occur, as in the case of politicians who will shortly become kings, Prime ministers, or presidents. So in this case, the proleptic statement indicates that the millennial reign of Christ is in the immediate future. The salvation of God is at hand.

3. The Persecution of the Woman (Revelation 12:13-17)

The woman that will give birth to the male child will be on the earth during the last part of the Tribulation. Since this is so, it appears that the woman is the nation of Israel. Some folks argue that she stands for the visible, apostate church, but it is difficult to see why God would protect her if this is the case (12:16). Others, some who believe that the true Church will go through the Tribulation, have contended that she symbolizes the true body of Christ, the Church. This interpretation, nevertheless, has great difficulty in explaining "the remnant of her seed, which keep the commandments of God, and have the testimony of Jesus Christ" (12:17). The best interpretation of the woman, therefore, is that she represents the Jewish people.

The Flight of the Woman (verses 13, 14). The figure of speech in this passage, "two wings of a great eagle," probably implies some providential care for Israel "for a time, and times, and a half time." The reference to times is like that found in Daniel 7:25 and 12:7. The word *time* can refer to any period of time, but the duration in both

Daniel and the Apocalypse suggests a year. Thus, a time, times, and half a time refer to three and a half years. For the last half of the Tribulation, Satan will diligently seek to destroy the Jews through his servants, the Antichrist and the false prophet. Some Premillennialists are convinced that Zechariah spoke of the last portion of the Tribulation, the partial destruction of Israel, and God's protection of many Jews in the ensuing words: "And it shall come to pass, that in all the land, saith the LORD, two parts therein shall be cut off and die; but the third shall be left therein. And I will bring the third part through the fire, and will refine them as silver is refined, and will try them as gold is tried: they shall call on my name, and I will hear them: I will say, It is my people: and they shall say, The LORD is my God" (Zechariah 13:8, 9).

The Wrath of the Dragon (verses 15-17). The anti-Semitism of Satan as manifested through the Antichrist is mentioned in these verses and seems to be spoken of by Daniel the prophet (Daniel 9:27). The flood mentioned by John is variously explained by Premillennialists as either a literal flood, a symbol for the Antichrist's military actions against the Jews, or a way of speaking of Satan's total program of attack against the Jews. The last of these three explanations is inclusive enough to embrace the anti-Semitic actions of people other than those who follow the Antichrist. Similarly, the opening of the earth is understood to be either a literal opening (earthquake) or a symbol of God's providential interventions.

9

The Beasts and the Lamb

Study Text: Revelation 13:1—14:20

Introduction
1. The Beast From the Sea (Revelation 13:1-10)
   a. The Appearance of the Beast (verses 1, 2)
   b. The Authority of the Beast (verses 3-8)
   c. The Exhortation for Believers (verses 9, 10)
2. The Beast From the Earth (Revelation 13:11-18)
   a. The Power of the Beast (verses 11-15)
   b. The Mark of the Beast (verses 16-18)
3. The Lamb on the Mountain (Revelation 14:1-20)
   a. The Redeemed From the Earth (verses 1-5)
   b. The Eternal Gospel (verses 6, 7)
   c. The Fall of Babylon (verse 8)
   d. The Worshipers of the Beast (verses 9-11)
   e. The Dead in Christ (verses 12, 13)
   f. The Harvest on Earth (verses 14-20)

Introduction

The interlude that the apostle began in Revelation 10, which he briefly interrupted in Revelation 11:14-19 and returned to in Revelation 12, is continued in Revelation 13, 14. The difficulty of trying to find out when the events in these chapters will occur is eased somewhat by statements in the Scriptures themselves. The period of the Great Tribulation and the time shortly thereafter was of prime interest to the apostle when he wrote these chapters.

Evidence to support this interpretation may be gathered from several statements in Revelation 13, particularly verse 5. Revelation 14, on the other hand, is not as easily placed into a timetable as Revelation 13. For one thing, there is no direct statement like that found in Revelation 13:5. Then, too, Revelation 14 is composed of a series of short visions or of excerpts from a vision that have no explicit indication of their chronological relationship. The problem of interpreting Revelation 14 is not insurmountable, however, as we shall shortly see.

Our present analysis of the Book of Revelation concentrates on the three main characters of Revelation 13:1–14:20. Accordingly, there are three major divisions with which we are concerned: (1) the beast from the sea, (2) the beast from the earth, and (3) the Lamb on the mountain.

As you may recall from our study of Revelation 11, some Christians believe there are three beasts discussed by John in the Apocalypse: (1) the beast out of the pit (11:7-10), (2) the beast out of the sea (13:1-10), and (3) the beast out of the earth (13:11-18). While this interpretation may be correct, perhaps it is better to think of the beast out of the pit and the beast out of the sea as the same beast in the light of Revelation 17:7, 8. In the former case, the beast's source of power is possibly being alluded to–the power is from Satan. In the latter case, the sea stands for people (17:15).

Exposition

The passage before us is one of the most intriguing in the entire Bible because it presents a close-up of two men who will be uniquely important in Satan's plan to control the world during the last days. These men are, in a sense, the best that Satan has to offer against God and His Son, the Lord Jesus Christ. From another perspective, they are the worst that Satan has in store for an unbelieving world during the "short time" that he will have to play havoc with both unbelievers and the new believers who will be saved during the Great Tribulation.

1. The Beast From the Sea (Revelation 13:1-10)

Perhaps no individual in the whole of Biblical prophecy has aroused more interest than the person spoken of here by the apostle as the beast that came out of the sea. The same person was spoken of by the Apostle Paul in his epistle to the Thessalonians (2 Thessalonians 2:3-9) and by the prophet Daniel (11:36-45). The progressive nature of divine revelation clarifies the type of person the Antichrist will be in these verses penned by the elderly Apostle John.

The Appearance of the Beast (verses 1, 2). Although the verses in this chapter do not at first appear to be connected with

Revelation 12, they are probably meant to be seen as naturally flowing from the preceding chapter. The grounds for this statement are found by carefully looking at the last verse in chapter 12 and the first verse of chapter 13.

An analysis of Revelation 13:1 will reveal that it is preferable to translate the words "And I stood" as "and he stood." The difference in the pronouns is not significant from one angle, but from another it illuminates the connection between Revelation 12 and Revelation 13. A resulting conclusion is that the dragon or Satan is pictured as standing on the beach, not the aged apostle.

This chapter, therefore, opens with John's comment that he saw the dragon standing on the beach watching a beast come up out of the sea. The beast himself is far from being a normal animal; for, he is described as having seven heads, ten horns, ten crowns on his heads, blasphemous names written on his seven heads, a mouth like a lion's, feet like a bear's, and in other ways he is like a leopard.

A glance at Daniel 7 reveals that the beast from the sea will be a composite of the first three of the four animals mentioned by Daniel approximately six hundred years before John wrote the Apocalypse. In Daniel, the lion symbolizes the Babylonian Empire; the bear, the Persian Empire; and the leopard, the Grecian Empire. The fourth beast–the great, terrible beast–"was diverse from all the beasts that were before it." Perhaps the reason Daniel said the fourth beast, which represents the Roman Empire, was different from all the others is that it was the abnormal mixture described by John.

The Book of Daniel tells us that the ten horns of the beast "are ten kings" (7:24). The Apostle John, in a later chapter of Revelation, presented a comparable thought about the horns of the beast out of the sea. His exact words are: "And the ten horns which thou sawest are ten kings, which have received no kingdom as yet; but receive power as kings one hour with the beast" (17:12). In this same context, John identified the seven heads of the beast as seven mountains but seems to have amplified his thought by adding, "and these are seven kings" (17:9, 10).

Disagreement among Premillennialists may again be seen when one thoroughly studies their writings about the beast, its horns, and its heads. Yet, they are in general accord that the beast is a symbol of the future Antichrist, a political leader who will rule in the Western world.

Some Premillennialists are convinced that he will rule a revived Roman Empire; others think he will be the dictator of a transformed Roman Empire or a Western world government that will have its roots in the culture of Rome. Most agree, too, that the Roman Empire, whether revived or transformed, will also have its cultural roots in Babylonia, Persia, and Greece and that such is symbolized by the reference to the lion, the bear, and the leopard. In the final days of human rule, therefore, Satan will give his tremendous power to the Antichrist who will be connected in some way with a group of ten kings and another group of seven kingdoms. More on this subject is presented by John in a later chapter, Revelation 17.

The Authority of the Beast (verses 3-8). The last word in verse 2 is *authority.* The idea, of course, is related to Satan giving power and authority to the beast when he comes out of the sea. Revelation 13:3-8 indicates some of the ways the future Antichrist will employ his power and authority during the Great Tribulation.

The words of verse 3 have puzzled many commentators, especially the statement that "I saw one of his heads as it were wounded to death; and his deadly wound was healed." A number of exegetes think that the head, a person, actually dies and will be raised from the dead. Many times they say it is the Antichrist himself who will die and then be raised from the dead. Certainly, there is some evidence that the Antichrist is in some way identified with the death mentioned here; John added in verses 12 and 14 that "the first beast, whose deadly wound was healed" and "the beast, which had the wound by a sword, and did live." The second of these verses figuratively suggests the manner by which the death occurred, i.e., by the sword.

No doubt this is a possible interpretation of the passage and is, in part, supported by the words *deadly wound* (13:3, 12). But other expositors believe the emphasis ought to be placed on the words *as it were* or, after being given a fresh translation, *as if it.* From this frame of reference, the passage is saying that the Antichrist appears to die but does not actually die. This view, too, has possibilities.

A third solution, perhaps the best one, to the problem that arises in verse 3 is to understand that the head symbolizes both a king and his kingdom. A kingdom is destroyed "by the sword" and will be eventually restored by the Antichrist. The fact that he is able to restore the kingdom amazes people–but it should not, for Satan empowers him to do such.

After the Antichrist restores or revitalizes what is the Roman Empire or some facet of it, people will worship him and inquire, "Who is like unto the beast? who is able to make war with him?" The second question supports the idea that the Antichrist will use military strength to restore an empire. Part of these activities may refer to the white horse (6:2), but the next verse definitely refers to the final aspect of the Tribulation (13:5).

The Exhortation for Believers (verses 9, 10). The short exhortation in these verses appears to have a threefold purpose. First, believers are encouraged to take seriously the words of John: "let him hear." Second, the first part of verse 10 implies that those who are led into captivity by the Antichrist will still be under the providential care of God. Finally, the one who kills by the sword–the Antichrist–will be similarly judged by God.

2. The Beast From the Earth (Revelation 13:11-18)

Many historians argue that absolute dictatorships are most easily achieved when political ambitions and religious ideals are interwoven. Satan obviously feels the same way; for, he will not only bring forth an unusually talented political leader during the final days of human rule, but he will also provide this dictator with a partner who is called by John the false prophet (19:20).

The Power of the Beast (verses 11-15). The reference to the second beast having the appearance of a lamb may suggest that he will be a poor imitation of the Lamb of God. His real nature will be revealed by his words which, John has stated, are as dreadful as those of the dragon, perhaps an allusion to his ultimate connection with Satan.

The power of the beast from earth will be totally devoted to getting people to worship the first beast, the Antichrist. In doing this, he will perform miracles and, thereby, deceive people throughout the world. Reminiscent of King Nebuchadnezzar's image, the false prophet will have an image made to honor the Antichrist and the kingdom he rules.

Unlike Nebuchadnezzar's image, however, the Antichrist's image may be totally unique in that John wrote that the false prophet will "give life unto the image of the beast, that the image of the beast should both speak, and cause that as many as would not worship the image of the beast should be killed" (13:15). The language used by John so naturally suggests that the image comes to life that some commentators either wish to ignore the passage or say it defies human explanation. Others attempt to explain the image in terms of some robot that will speak by means of a mechanical device. Rare is the expositor that is willing to grant the false prophet the power to give life to an image. But, then, the passage might ascribe the uniqueness of the image to the power of the false prophet.

The Mark of the Beast (verses 16-18). Whatever the image's nature, he or it will become a part of Satan's scheme during the Great Tribulation. Political, religious, and economic life will be partially manipulated by the image. The majority of mankind will be induced to receive the mark or the name of the Antichrist. The number of the beast is 666.

In the light of all the speculation about the proper interpretation of the number 666, it is very humbling to read the apostle's introductory words: "Here is wisdom. Let him that hath understanding count the number of the beast." It is easy to wonder whether anyone has much understanding or wisdom after reading the many different interpretations that commentators give. Interpretations have ranged from Nero to Hitler and, more recently, to a couple of twentieth century Americans. Those expositors who stress the symbolic use of numbers think that 666 is to be understood as God's way of saying the Antichrist will be short of the perfection that is represented by the number seven. Or, as others like to say, the number implies the Antichrist will fall short of the deity of Christ. All interpretations seem to have their weaknesses and, perhaps, the meaning of the number will become clear only when the Antichrist begins his climb to world-wide power.

3. The Lamb on the Mountain (Revelation 14:1-20)

The title for this section is taken from the first part of the revelation that is recorded in chapter 14. The title is a little misleading, for the whole chapter contains a series of short visions that are sometimes thought to be disconnected. This may be partly true; however, as we will attempt to show shortly, the visions are not totally unrelated. Regardless of one's view of the overall relationship of these visions, just about everyone agrees that the entire series of visions are designed to give comfort to believers since the previous facets of this interlude (Revelation 12, 13) are not necessarily encouraging to believers.

The Redeemed From the Earth (verses 1-5). The 144,000 people mentioned in these verses are probably the same as those discussed by John in Revelation 7:4. They are Jews who will be set apart for service during the Great Tribulation. In verse 1, they are seen on Mount Zion with Christ. Expositors usually give three possible explanations of this scene. One opinion that is found in Premillennial literature is that this scene is descriptive of Christ's return to the earth after the entire Tribulation is over. The fact that Christ is seen with the 144,000 may be interpreted in one of two ways. First, it may symbolize that He will preserve the 144,000 through the Great Tribulation. Or, second, it might signify–as those who interpret the male child as being the 144,000 like to stress–that the 144,000 will be raptured in the middle of the Tribulation and that they will return with Him when He comes to judge the world.

A second major interpretation of the Mount Zion scene explains it as a reference to the millennium and, in particular, to the New Jerusalem. The third basic explanation is that Mount Zion figuratively stands for Heaven. Those who hold this view emphasize that verse 2 describes an event in Heaven and argue that *they* in the third verse refers to the 144,000. If this latter view is taken, it is possible that the group here will be martyred for Christ after the witnesses have finished their ministries just as the two prophets will be (Revelation 11). Both of the other views seem to demand that a second group of believers is in Heaven singing the new song. It is possible, however, that the apocalyptic language jumps first to Mount Zion and, then, to Heaven with the same 144,000. The people described in verses 4 and 5–probably the 144,000–are described as being spiritual virgins, obedient to the Lamb, guileless, and faultless. This description of the 144,000 explains why they were originally selected by God.

The Eternal Gospel (verses 6, 7). Much debate has centered on the nature of the gospel that will be preached by the angelic being mentioned by the Apostle John. A number of folks think it is the gospel of the kingdom of God or of the millennium. Another group explains it as the same gospel Christians know today. But there is no need for speculation; the angel's gospel is explained in verse 7: It is a message to encourage people to repent because the time of God's judgment has come. The judgment mentioned might be a reference to the judgment of the peoples of the world that will take place when Christ returns.

The Fall of Babylon (verse 8). While the angel who preaches the eternal gospel announces a judgment that is to come, the second angel makes a further statement on the subject. The judgment to come is specifically related to Babylon "because she made all nations drink of the wine of the wrath of her fornication." The judgment of Babylon is further delineated in Revelation 17 and 18, but here the emphasis seems to be on the reason for her judgment, i.e., she has led the peoples of the world to participate in her corrupt manner of living.

The Worshipers of the Beast (verses 9-11). This cursory vision may build on the previous ones. First, there is the announcement that those who do not fear God will be judged (14:7). Then, there is the implication that those who drink Babylon's wine will also experience the wrath that will come to her. At this juncture, a third angel elaborates on those who will experience the wrath of God: those who feared the wrath of the beast out of the sea or the Antichrist.

An extra dimension is added, too, in this announcement of God's just punishment of those who will worship the beast. This time there is the mentioning of "fire and brimstone" and "the smoke of their torment ascendeth up for ever and ever." The rebellious men who will curse God during the Great Tribulation will be punished by spending eternity in the lake of fire (20:14).

The Dead in Christ (verses 12, 13). God's justice is only one side of His nature. The apostle also described another aspect of the eternal being we call God. This characteristic caused Him to encourage those who are faithful to His Son, the Lord Jesus Christ. Especially does He seek to strengthen those who will die during the Great Tribulation for their loyalty to Christ. This special encouragement is found in the following words of John: "Blessed are the dead which die in the Lord from henceforth: Yea, saith the Spirit, that they may rest from their labours; and their works do follow them."

The Harvest on Earth (verses 14-20). After encouraging those who are faithful to Christ, John turned to describe more about the judgment of God upon mankind shortly after the end of the Tribulation. Two harvests may be hinted at in this passage. The first, if there are two, will be by Christ (14:14-16) and the second by an angel (14:17-20). Conversely, there may be only one harvest that is described from the perspective that both Christ and His angels will be involved in the judgment.

If there are two distinct harvests at the return of Christ, some surmise that the first by Christ will be concerned with His gathering the remaining believers who are still alive. Posttribulationists can find support for a rapture after the Tribulation if they find two harvests here. Both of the other Premillennial positions, however, can also interpret the passage as having two harvests.

Whether one or two harvests are meant, the final verses of Revelation 14 are usually understood to be a reference to the battle of Armageddon. The language of the text seems to suggest that the battle will center in Palestine (the space of a thousand and six hundred furlongs or approximately 200 miles) and in Jerusalem ("the city").

Furthermore, the text may imply that the wrath of God is in some way mingled with the activities of mankind, i.e., war. The battle will be so terrible that blood will come out "even unto the horse bridles." The meaning of the phrase is debatable, and it may be interpreted as follows: (1) a symbol of the great number of deaths that occur, (2) a literal statement of blood being several feet deep, or (3) a literal statement implying the blood is splattered to the bridles of horses. The first and third views, separately or combined in some form, are preferable to the second explanation.

10

The Seven Bowls of Wrath

Study Text: Revelation 15:1—16:21

Introduction
1. Introduction to the Seven Plagues (Revelation 15:1-8)
   a. The Songs of Moses and the Lamb (verses 1-4)
   b. The Temple of the Tabernacle (verses 5-8)
2. The Wrath of God (Revelation 16:1-21)
   a. The First Bowl: The Sores on Men (verses 1, 2)
   b. The Second Bowl: The Death of the Sea (verse 3)
   c. The Third Bowl: The Death of the Rivers (verses 4-7)
   d. The Fourth Bowl: The Scorching Sun (verses 8, 9)
   e. The Fifth Bowl: The Darkened Kingdom (verses 10, 11)
   f. The Sixth Bowl: The Drying of the Euphrates (verses 12-16)
   g. The Seventh Bowl: The Lightning, Thunder, and Quake (verses 17-21)

Introduction

With the extensive interludes concerning the dragon, the pregnant woman, the male child (Revelation 12), the two beasts (Revelation 13), and the short visions of comfort (Revelation 14) behind him, John goes on to explain what is revealed to him in the seven bowls of God's wrath. As was pointed out earlier, the exact time these seven bowls will be poured out upon the earth is a subject of debate for Premillennial commentators. If the seven bowls are emptied after the death of the two witnesses (Revelation 11), then it appears likely that the bowls are symbols of the judgment God will bring upon the earth between the Tribulation and the millennium. If this indeed is the case, the seven bowls are released upon the world during the seventy-five days spoken of by the prophet Daniel (Daniel 12:11, 12).

We have already seen that Revelation 11:14 may imply that the seven bowls of wrath will come to pass after the Tribulation has come to an end, but there is additional evidence to support the notion that at least some of the seven bowls will come after the Great Tribulation. The battle of Armageddon will apparently take place immediately before Satan is bound for the millennium (19:19-20:2). Both the sixth and seventh bowls are related to the battle of Armageddon (16:16) and the destruction of Babylon (16:19); therefore, it seems that at least these two bowls will come to pass after the Tribulation has ended, and it is plausible that the first five will as well.

Sometimes an overview of a subject is helpful in keeping all of the particulars within a proper context; therefore, let us attempt to get a general grasp of Revelation 15 and 16 before we study the specifics of these two chapters. First, notice that John continues with a previously discussed truth from Revelation 14 (there is victory for those who are faithful to Christ) as he combines it with a new element in Revelation 15 (there will be some final judgments of God upon an unrepentant mankind). These two thoughts are gracefully blended when John speaks both of the "seven last plagues" (15:1) or the "seven golden vials full of the wrath of God" (15:7) and those who achieved "victory over the beast" (15:2).

The second phase of John's description of God's concluding judgments upon the world is elaborated on in Revelation 16. The apostle's language, if it is to be understood in its ordinary sense, leads us to believe that those who worship the beast out of the sea will be afflicted with sores, see the life in the sea and rivers come to an end, experience abnormally hot weather, and go through several different kinds of cataclysmic events, including a ravaging earthquake. More than this will be a part of life during the final days of life before Christ sets up His millennial kingdom. The darkening of the kingdom of the beast out of the sea and the releasing of unclean spirits by the beast, the dragon, and the false prophet will be part of those last few days. All of these events will apparently occur in rapid succession, perhaps coming within a few days or weeks of each other.

Exposition

Revelation 15 may be subdivided into two sections. The first of these divisions centers on a group of victorious believers who sing "the song of Moses . . . and the song of the Lamb" (15:3). The other division is fundamentally concerned with activities that are related to "the temple of the tabernacle" (15:5). Both scenes seem to take place in Heaven.

1. Introduction to the Seven Plagues (Revelation 15:1-8)

As in the case of the judgments that were associated with the seven trumpets, the seven last plagues are announced to John by angelic beings. These plagues are called the last ones; and when the seventh angel pours out his bowl, a voice from the Temple cries, "It is done" (16:17). Between the initial announcement (15:1) and the statement indicating accomplishment (16:17) lie some truths that the apostle carefully recorded for all believers.

The Songs of Moses and the Lamb (verses 1-4). In leading up to the songs of Moses and the Lamb, John first explains that he saw "another sign." The words cause one to think back to the signs mentioned by John in Revelation 12:1, 3. The sign in this case is that of a tremendous judgment which will be brought upon mankind by God. In particular, John stated that in the last seven plagues, which implies that the previous seals and trumpets are also plagues, are "filled up the wrath of God." The words *filled up* suggest that God's wrath has been brought to its ultimate conclusion. These concluding manifestations of divine judgment, John writes, will soon be announced by seven angels.

During this aspect of the revelation, John becomes keenly interested, not in the seven angels themselves, but in a group of people and a sea. The sea or body of water is often identified by expositors with the one that John saw earlier (4:6). No conclusive evidence for this exists, however. One difference is that the first sea was described as being "like unto crystal" while this sea is said to appear as if "it were a sea of glass mingled with fire."

On the other hand, there really is not any convincing evidence for rejecting the idea that the sea in this chapter is the same as the sea in Revelation 4. The fact that fire is mentioned in this chapter does not prove the sea is a different sea. At any rate, the sea is only a contextual factor for the group of people John was observing. The fire he mentions may be an allusion to the divine judgment which he later describes, but it is difficult to say if the standing on the sea represents any specific truth. Maybe this is just a part of the overall apocalyptic vision which has no specific meaning.

The people spoken of by the Apostle John are carefully identified by him: They are the ones who have "gotten the victory over the beast, and over his image, and over his mark, and over the number of his name." Even though it would have been easier to simply say this group was victorious over the Antichrist or the beast out of the sea, John took the time to specify at least three distinct truths about these people. They will choose to serve Christ rather than the Antichrist; they will refuse to be deceived and coerced by the image made by the false prophet; and they will resist the economic pressure to be approved by the Antichrist's mark or number. As a result, these people can be none other than the believers who will be true to Christ during the Great Tribulation. The context may imply that these Christians will be martyred by some of the people who are faithful to the Antichrist.

The next two verses, 15:3, 4, give expositors a difficult time. The language, which includes a definite article before each song, appears to suggest that two songs were being sung, i.e., the song of Moses and the song of the Lamb. Yet, the words recorded by the apostle seem to indicate that only one song was being sung. Perhaps the solution to the problem lies in the possibility that the thoughts of both songs have been combined into the one song recorded by John. Or it may be that only the song of the Lamb is recorded here, and readers are expected to look elsewhere to discover the song of Moses. Several suggestions for locating the song of Moses include Deuteronomy 22, Exodus 15, and Psalm 22.

In the portion of the song that has been recorded by John, several truths are prominent. God is described as follows: (a) mighty, (b) just, (c) true, (d) holy, and (e) regal.

The Temple of the Tabernacle (verses 5-8). The words "after that I looked, and, behold" once again indicate a major shift in John's thoughts. His attention is suddenly drawn away from the martyrs of the Tribulation to another heavenly scene. This scene may be a blend of two historical sites, the tabernacle of the wilderness and the Temple of Jerusalem, into one picture to stress the presence of God. Expositors differ on the subject, though. Some argue that the temple specifies the Holy of Holies and that the tabernacle refers to the whole tabernacle structure. The reference to testimony, most interpreters agree, alludes to the tables of the Ten Commandments.

The seven angels are pictured as coming in splendor from the Temple or the very presence of God. The implication, therefore, is that they will be sent forth by God Himself when the time for these judgments comes. As the angels come out of the Temple, John notes that they are each given a bowl filled with "the wrath of God." One of the four living creatures (4:6-9) gives each angel a bowl. The term *bowl*, or vial, as it is translated in the King James Version, refers to a shallow bowl that was used for drinking purposes.

2. The Wrath of God (Revelation 16:1-21)

A comparison of the seven bowls of wrath with the plagues that came with the seven trumpets indicates a number of similarities between the two different judgments. But, then, there are unique features in each; the intensity and severity of the seven bowls seems to be much greater than that of the seven trumpets or at least the first six trumpets, for the seventh trumpet appears to include the seven bowls.

The First Bowl: The Sores on Men (verses 1, 2). The voice which the apostle says originates in the Temple undoubtedly is that of God Himself. His commandment is to the seven angels who have just received bowls filled with His wrath. God's wrath, it will be noted, is to be poured out upon the beast and his followers. The first of these seven angels will one day have the power to inflict men with sores. Whether this power will be to use some existing disease and cause an epidemic or to initiate something new is not specified.

The sores may be somewhat like the boils of Egypt (Exodus 9) or, as some argue, something like a malignant ulcer. In either case, the suffering that will result is basically left up to the imagination of the reader, for John himself does not depict the consequences of the disease.

Some Premillennialists strongly emphasize that these sores are not literal, physical ailments but are to be understood as some sort of moral affliction. This interpretation, however, does not significantly enlighten one's understanding of the first bowl; it seems to do little more than open the door for unbridled speculation.

The Second Bowl: The Death of the Sea (verse 3). Those who are inclined to interpret Revelation figuratively sometimes suggest that this verse speaks of the ultimate immoral condition of mankind during the Tribulation, but it is very difficult to defend this interpretation. A thorough study of this verse seems to lead to the conclusion that it is preferable to interpret it in one of three ways: (a) The sea will be turned to blood; (b) it appears to be turned to blood;

(c) the death of sea life causes it to be colored with blood. The natural interpretation of the language seems to favor either the first or third viewpoints.

One question that arises among some commentators is whether the sea spoken of here refers to the Mediterranean Sea or to all the large bodies of water throughout the world. No definitive answer is given in the text, but it does not seem incorrect to conclude that all major bodies of water are included. For more than likely, all the peoples of the world will be afflicted with sores during the first bowl, and it seems logical to conclude that this will be a worldwide judgment, too.

The Third Bowl: The Death of the Rivers (verses 4-7). This plague includes the turning of both "the rivers and fountains of waters" into blood (16:4). The rivers spoken of probably refer to all the rivers of the world because the judgment is later described as being upon those who have "shed the blood of saints and prophets" (16:6). Believers will be killed throughout the world during the rule of the Antichrist.

This universal judgment of rivers and fountains during the third bowl probably means that all water will be unfit for human consumption. Even the salt-water of the world will not be suitable for processing. God will vividly illustrate to the people who are living during the days immediately preceding the return of Christ that He has not forgotten His saints who were slaughtered by the Antichrist.

Some Premillennialists reject the aforementioned interpretation of the third bowl. As far as they are concerned, the third bowl of God's wrath simply signifies that the natural sources of human pleasure will be destroyed by God during the latter days. Undoubtedly, the waters of the world are natural sources of pleasure, but it is difficult to conceive of this interpretation being little more than a vague way of dealing with the judgment itself.

The Fourth Bowl: The Scorching Sun (verses 8, 9). The apostle's description of the events that occur after the initiation of the fourth plague should cause us to recognize just how depraved mankind is. Those who are on the earth during this plague will be unmoved by the sovereignty and omnipotence of the Creator of the universe. They appear to know that God has "power over the plagues" that have come upon them, but they still refuse to repent and, still worse, blaspheme Him. The hatred of unbelievers will be so blatant during this time that even those who describe man as "basically good" may be shocked.

The interpreter who is a symbolist may conclude that in this bowl the Apostle John is depicting the fact that the Antichrist's government will bring intense suffering to mankind. Literalists, nevertheless, think the language implies an actual intensification of heat during the last few days of man. This intensification of heat may be the result of an act wholly initiated by God, or it could be partially a consequence of man's unintentional disruption of atmospheric conditions that causes him to greatly multiply the heat from the sun.

If you will think back to the three previous plagues, you can see how this bowl of God's wrath may produce almost unbelievable suffering. If people still have sores on them, have no water to drink, and then an extremely hot season comes, this will inflict terrible suffering on them. The remarkable fact about this period of time is that people still will not repent of their sins.

The Fifth Bowl: The Darkened Kingdom (verses 10, 11). If the darkness spoken of here is to be understood as some symbolists would have us believe, the meaning John wished to convey to his readers is that people during the last days will suffer from an impregnable moral darkness. The language, however, once again seems to suggest a more literal meaning, i.e., the area that the Antichrist will be ruling will be darkened by some supernatural action.

A topic that divides even literalists is whether the darkness covers the entire earth or just a part of it. Some Premillennialists think that the Antichrist's kingdom will have already been fractured by the time of the fifth bowl. Therefore, they conclude that only the part of the world that he still controls will be darkened. Others think the whole world will be darkened.

John does not explicitly explain what will happen to increase the pain of the unbelieving world at this time. No doubt, though, part of the suffering is to be associated with the continuation of the first plague (16:11), but the apostle left the remainder unexplained. As is stated, when some of the other plagues are poured out upon the world, mankind will continue to blaspheme God and will not repent of its "deed."

The Sixth Bowl: The Drying of the Euphrates (verses 12-16). Attempting to interpret this passage may be the most difficult task of the entire chapter. Even a casual glance at the literature written on this section of Revelation 16 will support this thought; so, the observations made herein will be somewhat abbreviated and simplified.

Two major Premillennial interpretations arise out of this passage, both of which have a number of variations. The first major school of thought suggests that these verses, as well as much of Revelation 16:17–19:21, speak of the uniting of all armies of the world to fight Christ at His return to the earth. Evidence for this viewpoint is taken from Revelation 17:14 and the fact that the battle mentioned is called "the battle of that great day of God Almighty" (16:14). A problem with this interpretation is that this viewpoint seems to suggest that the Antichrist and his forces will know both when and where the Lord will return to the earth. While this problem is not totally insurmountable, it is significant enough to make many, probably most, Premillennialists reject the view.

The second major position, ascribed to in some form by most Premillennialists today, is that the Antichrist's empire will be fractured in its final stage. He will not be able to continue to provide the world the peace and prosperity it originally expected from him. The segments of his former worldwide empire may be alluded to by John and by the prophet Daniel in chapter 11 of that book. The Antichrist will continue to control much of the Western world; but the rest of the world may be divided along what is presently described as Oriental peoples, Arabian-African peoples, and Slavic peoples. All of these sections of the world may be struggling to control each other immediately before Christ returns.

The Antichrist's armies, so adherents of this position say, will be in control of Palestine, and other peoples of the world will be seeking to wrestle the area from them. A series of battles (Daniel 11:40-45) will lead up to a final battle called the battle of Armageddon (16:16). The sequence of battles will bring about much of the destruction that is mentioned in Revelation 16:12–19:21. During the final moments of the battle of Armageddon, Christ will return. His return will cause the armies–even enemies–to turn their attention to Christ. Christ will then speedily destroy the forces of the Antichrist and of his enemies who will have gathered to fight him in Palestine. The only enemies specified by the Apostle John are "the kings of the east" (16:12). Demonic spirits are able to entice "the kings of the earth and of the whole world" to come to the battle of Armageddon (16:13, 14).

The Seventh Bowl: The Lightning, Thunder, and Quake (verses 17-21). In the setting of this devastating war, the seventh bowl of God's wrath will be emptied upon mankind. The primary consequence noted by John is "a great earthquake, such as was not since men were upon the earth" (16:18).

The description given by John in these verses has caused many Premillennialists to think a symbolic meaning should be sought. Usually the conclusion of those who take this approach is that the quaking refers to a total destruction of world governments.

Those who lean toward accepting the natural implications of John's language may adopt one of two approaches. One group of interpreters believes that the entire world will be basically destroyed by a supernatural earthquake, hail stones that weigh a hundred pounds each, and accompanying events. A second group thinks John described not only the battle of Armageddon but also creation of the new heavens and earth in these verses. Some believe his blending in of the new earth is a proleptic description of what will happen after the millennium. Others think the new earth will be created after the battle of Armageddon but before the millennium.

Now that we have looked at the seals, trumpets, and bowls, it is time to make a few summary comments about them. If our analysis has been correct, the first five seals will be broken sometime before the Great Tribulation. Perhaps those five seals will occur during what is often called the first half or the first three and a half years of the Tribulation.

Moreover, we may conclude that beginning with the sixth seal and continuing through the sixth trumpet that the events described will take place during the Great Tribulation. When the sixth seal is broken, people will say, "The great day of his wrath is come" (6:17). After the three and a half years of the Great Tribulation are over, then the seventh trumpet will be blown (11:14-19).

Finally, it seems that the seventh trumpet, which includes the seven bowls, will begin the seventy-five-day interval spoken of by Daniel the prophet (Daniel 12:11, 12). So we have seals (1-5) that describe events that will occur before the Great Tribulation, seals (6, 7) and trumpets (1-6) that depict activities during the Great Tribulation, and a trumpet (7) and bowls (1-7) that refer to a short period after the Great Tribulation.

11

The Destruction of Babylon

Study Text: Revelation 17:1—18:24

Introduction
1. The Mystery Woman (Revelation 17:1-6)
   a. The Invitation to John (verses 1, 2)
   b. The Description of the Woman (verses 3-6)
2. The Interpretation of the Angel (Revelation 17:7-18)
   a. The Explanation of the Beast (verses 7-14)
   b. The Explanation of the Woman (verses 15-18)
3. The Fall of Babylon (Revelation 18:1-24)
   a. The Angel's Announcements (verses 1-8)
   b. The Sorrow of Mankind (verses 9-19)
   c. The Thankfulness of Believers (verses 20-24)

Introduction

The events of the Apocalypse were being disclosed at a breakneck speed when John was discussing the seven bowls of God's wrath, but then he was directed by the Holy Spirit to slow down in order to amplify a thought that he had mentioned in the seventh bowl. That casual reference in Revelation 16:19 is more thoroughly treated in Revelation 17, 18.

Notice if you will in the general study outline at the end of this volume, that this chapter, "The Destruction of Babylon," is the final subdivision under the second major division of the Apocalypse which is entitled "The Tribulation Period."

A critical review of this outline indicates that it may be misleading in several respects. The first possible way it may mislead the reader has already been mentioned on several occasions. If the seven bowls (15:1–16:21) come after the Great Tribulation has ended, then the outline is misleading. Second, the return of Christ and the supper of God (Revelation 19) should be understood as being closely associated with the seven bowls and the destruction of

Babylon, not necessarily with the kingdom of God during the millennium or during eternity.

So keep in mind that the general study outline was determined as much out of convenience as it was from the Biblical text. More will be said concerning the outline at a later time. For now it is sufficient to note that the Apocalypse may have more divisions than we have suggested in our outline. That is to say, rather than dividing the book as has been done in the general study outline, it might be better to use the ensuing broad divisions: (a) An Introduction to the Apocalypse, chapter 1, (b) The Churches of Asia Minor, chapters 2, 3, (c) The Tribulation Period, chapters 4-14, (d) The Interval between the Tribulation and the Millennium, chapters 15-19, and (e) The Kingdom Period, chapters 20-22. Even this outline will need to be revised as you continue to get a better grasp of the Apocalypse.

Exposition

The two chapters before us have caused an enormous amount of dispute in Premillennial circles. The disagreements that have arisen are not simply over the minutia of these chapters, either. Instead of being divided on a few minute details, interpreters are divided on such major points as the identification of the harlot and the beast upon which she is seated.

The harlot herself is the major point of disagreement. Historically, many Premillennialists have felt that the harlot, Babylon, symbolizes some type of unbiblical religious system. Some feel that the papacy will be the major controlling religious component depicted by the harlot. Others suggest the papacy will be one of many apostate religious parties. A similar viewpoint suggests the harlot represents the apostate religious system of all ages.

While the religious or ecclesiastical interpretation of the harlot still exists and actually flourishes among Premillennialists, many other Premillennialists offer somewhat different interpretations of the harlot. Sometimes expositors say Babylon, the harlot, represents not just the religious system of the world but the entire world system at the end of time, e.g., political, social, economic, and religious values that are contrary to the teachings of the Scriptures.

Another perspective of the harlot is that she represents a literal city, either a rebuilt Babylon on the Euphrates River or another city that stands for the same things that ancient Babylon did. The conjectures as to which city is meant have included such cities as Rome, London, New York, Berlin, and Paris.

A third non-ecclesiastical interpretation of the harlot combines the two positions just described. In this explanation, the harlot stands for both a literal city and the world system that has continually been opposed to the system of thought and life expressed in the Old and New Testaments.

Some grounds can be given for each of these positions; but they cannot, of course, all, as distinct views, be correct. A study of the chapters themselves should clarify which positions are better than other ones.

1. The Mystery Woman (Revelation 17:1-6)

The first six verses of Revelation 17 give a cursory introduction to the person who is said to be a mystery (17:5). Later in Revelation 18 a more detailed picture of the woman is presented.

The Invitation to John (verses 1, 2). John's invitation to see another revelation of God is this time extended by one of the angels he had seen with the seven bowls of God's wrath. The invitation itself was to see "the judgment of the great whore" (17:1).

The partial description that John was first given of the woman (17:1, 2) is later followed up with a somewhat extended description (17:3-6). The brief description implies several key characteristics or qualities about the woman. First, she is guilty of some type of prostitution, i.e., "the great whore." Second, she is over and, perhaps, supported by "many waters." Third, she has had a worldwide influence on both leaders and common folks, i.e., "kings . . . and the inhabitants of the earth."

The Description of the Woman (verses 3-6). The words "carried me away in the spirit" indicate that once again the apostle was in a state of prophetic ecstasy. The wilderness that is mentioned seems incidental to the overall scene as John concentrates on describing the woman. In his detailed description of the harlot, she is first depicted as sitting upon a scarlet colored beast. The beast, no doubt, is the one spoken of in Revelation 13:1-10.

A number of expositors, especially those who ascribe to the ecclesiastical interpretation mentioned earlier, argue that since the woman is seated upon the beast, it is clear that the woman and the beast represent two different aspects of the world system during the last days–the woman represents the religious world system that dominates the beast which stands for the political world system.

A person would be hard pressed to totally disagree with this interpretation. The woman and the beast do not appear to symbolize exactly the same thing. Yet, it is not clear that the woman symbolizes an ecclesiastical system during the last days and the beast a political system. Reasons for this statement will be presented when the angel's interpretation is analyzed.

But having said this, it does seem likely that there is an intimate relationship between the woman and the beast. The two complement each other; each adds to the overall wickedness of the other; each enhances the infamy of the other; both are somewhat dependent on each other; the greatness of the woman may be basically because of the support of the beast; the pleasure of the beast is largely due to the influence of the woman.

Differences given by John are few but important. The beast is noted for its blasphemy (17:3). But the woman is noted for her luxurious lifestyle (17:4), wicked living (17:4), initiating various kinds of ungodly practices (17:5), and promoting the death of those who faithfully serve Christ.

2. The Interpretation of the Angel (Revelation 17:7-18)

Some of the differences of interpretation that have divided Premillennialists could have been partly, though not totally, avoided had more attention been given to the interpretation that God Himself provided through the angel who was speaking to the Apostle John. The angel's method of explaining things seems almost strange at times, but there is probably a point of truth that is to be gained by noting the rather unique way he handles his subject.

The Explanation of the Beast (verses 7-14). The strangeness of the angel's explanation is partly manifested in that while he knew that John was puzzled by seeing the woman (17:6), he told John that he would interpret both the "mystery of the woman, and of the beast." John was troubled by the woman herself; the angel said he would explain the woman and the beast.

Another oddity of the situation is that the angel spent the overwhelming majority of his time talking about the beast and devoted very little attention to the woman who had caused John to be puzzled in the first place. The manner in which the angel answered the apostle's implied question may suggest that the woman and the beast cannot be ultimately separated; the two are different aspects of a world setting during the end times, and both will be destroyed by God.

The explanation itself is at times bewildering, but several truths still surface in an analysis of the angel's comments. Of particular importance is the notion that emerges from the words, "the beast that was, and is not, and yet is" (17:8). These words may well refer to the thought mentioned earlier by John when he records: "And I saw one of his heads as it were wounded to death; and his deadly wound was healed" (13:3). Thus, the angel may have been saying that the beast would exist for a while, then disappear, and later reappear. Premillennialists are generally agreed that this refers to different phases of the Roman Empire.

Significance can also be found in connection with the discussion about seven heads. They are first identified as seven mountains (17:9) and later spoken of as seven kings (17:10). In the light of this double identification, some argue that the angel intended to associate seven kingdoms or empires with the city of Rome which was originally built upon seven hills. Others believe the mountains are symbols of seven powers, and the powers are identified as seven kings or kingdoms.

The seven kings and the beast, or the eighth king, present an interpretative problem that may be impossible to settle, especially in a brief analysis. Suffice it to point out that a popular view among Premillennialists is that the fallen kingdoms refer to successive empires, perhaps to Assyria, Egypt, Babylonia, Persia, and Greece. The kingdom that is (17:10) refers to the Roman Empire of John's day and the "other" that is to come refers to a revived or transformed Roman Empire that is to exist during the last days. The eighth empire will arise out of the latter-day Roman Empire and is the World Empire of the beast or the Antichrist. Notice that the seventh kingdom will last for just a little while (17:10).

In addition to the truths about the resurrection of the beast (17:8) and the eight successive empires (17:10, 11), John also recorded that the beast's ten horns are ten future kings who will rule for a while with the beast or the Antichrist. The major function of the group of kings, after the beast comes to power, will be to support the Antichrist's ambitions. From Daniel 7:8, one may infer that the Antichrist himself may dispose of three of these kings for some reason. In the last verse of this passage, the angel seems to have jumped ahead of his story to say these are the kings who will oppose the Lamb (17:14; 19:19).

The Explanation of the Woman (verses 15-18). Turning his attention slightly away from the kings, the angelic being interprets the waters upon which the woman sits. The waters symbolize, so the apostle has stated, "peoples, and multitudes, and nations, and tongues" (17:15). Pause for a moment to look at the details of the harlot's positions. She is first seen seated upon many waters (17:1), then upon the scarlet beast (17:3), and finally upon the seven heads of the beast (17:9). All of these references may be designed to stress one particular truth: The woman is supported by and rules over successive generations of people right up to the time of the Antichrist.

In one sense it appears the woman and the beast are inseparable. Conversely, the two may be somewhat separated in the final stage of human civilization; the final stage of the beast–the Antichrist's kingdom–hates "the whore, and shall make her desolate and naked, and shall eat her flesh, and burn her with fire" (17:16).

Those who are proponents of the ecclesiastical interpretation of the woman say that during the Tribulation, probably before the Great Tribulation begins, the Antichrist will overthrow the ecumenical religious system because he will no longer need it. Other interpreters see the Antichrist destroying a city. A number of others understand the passage to mean the Antichrist will lead his followers to destroy not only a city but a worldwide influence of ungodliness, including economic, religious, and social phases. Regardless of the particular identification of the woman, it is strange to read that the Antichrist will destroy that which is totally against Christ. The strangeness disappears, nevertheless, when we read, "For God hath put in their hearts to fulfil his will" (17:17).

The last verse of Revelation 17 finally identifies the woman: She is the great city. Perhaps the city symbolizes something else as the mountains symbolizes kings (17:9, 10). This is only speculation, however, for the only comment of the angel is that "the woman . . . is that great city." On the basis of this evidence, then, the woman does not stand for an ecclesiastical system at the end of the age. She represents an unspecified city, but a city that will have a worldwide influence: "which reigneth over the kings of the earth" (17:18).

3. The Fall of Babylon (Revelation 18:1-24)

Revelation 17 is an amplification of one aspect of the seventh bowl, the fall of Babylon. This final bowl is so important to God that He inspired John to continue to expound on the same theme in Revelation 18.

The Angel's Announcements (verses 1-8). John soon learned that there was more to be said about the fall of Babylon. Its destruction will be so thorough that nothing of value will remain in the city (18:2), and other cities will crumble with it (16:19). The reason for her destruction is clear: her influence on the rest of the world (18:3). Perhaps it is noteworthy that in Revelation 16:19 the destruction of Babylon is depicted as coming at approximately the same time that "the cities of the nations" fall. The picture John has painted suggests that the seventh bowl brings a judgment by God along with the destruction of Babylon which is brought about by the Antichrist's supporters (17:16, 17). So devastating will be the destruction of Babylon that the angel's second announcement is to warn any believers in the city to flee rapidly. The final announcement of the angel is that Babylon's judgment will be a just judgment.

Let us pause for a few seconds to look at some evidence that supports the idea that Revelation 18 is talking about the woman of Revelation 17. Those who teach that the woman represents apostate religion believe that Revelation 18 describes the destruction of the beast or a political system. Yet the context, especially verse 7, seems to support the idea that the woman is being discussed in both chapters. Key words in Revelation 18:7 are "I sit a queen." The harlot has been pictured as sitting on several occasions; and only she, not the beast, can be appropriately called a queen. In like fashion, the words "that great city," which were originally used by John to identify the woman (17:18), are used in this chapter again (18:10, 21).

The Sorrow of Mankind (verses 9-19). The appalling destruction of Babylon by God through the forces of the Antichrist will horrify all mankind, especially two groups. The first of these groups to be shocked will be the political leaders of the world (18:9). The other group will be the economic leaders of the world (18:11, 15, 17). Both of these groups, from one angle, will have the most to lose by the destruction of Babylon because the city seems to be a vital link in the economic system of the world.

Some commentators feel this allusion to material goods provides a clue about Babylon. There are some expositors who think the leading industrial city of the world at the time of the Tribulation will be the Babylon spoken of by John. Others stress that part of that which God so greatly hates is implicit in this passage of Scripture: God hates the influence the city has had upon the world in making it a materialistic civilization. The city leads the world in the worship of the material aspects of life. Actually, it is possible that both of these views could be combined and be correct.

The weeping of mankind for the city symbolized by Babylon, perhaps the capital city of the Antichrist, may be a little misleading. The grief of the people is probably not so much for the city itself as it is for themselves. They have lost Babylon. Moreover, the picture may be somewhat unclear in that the events might seem to indicate that political and commercial leaders of the world are standing by as Babylon is destroyed. As a matter of fact, these leaders will be among the fallen, for Babylon represents them. Cities of all nations will fall along with the city represented by Babylon (16:19-21).

The Thankfulness of Believers (verses 20-24). The closing observation of John is that believers will rejoice over the destruction of a city and a civilization that has progressively become more hostile to God. The joy of believers will not issue from a desire for personal vengeance but from thankfulness that at last God's justice and righteousness are in ultimate control of the world, no longer under the dominion of Satan, the Antichrist, and the false prophet. Christians will know, too, that it will not be long before the rule of the Son of God will come to the earth.

12

The Return of Christ

Study Text: Revelation 19:1—20:15

Introduction
1. The Second Coming of Christ (Revelation 19:1-21)
   a. The Hallelujahs in Heaven (verses 1-5)
   b. The Marriage of the Lamb (verses 6-10)
   c. The Smiting of the Nations (verses 11-16)
   d. The Great Supper of God (verses 17-21)
2. The Millennial Reign of Christ (Revelation 20:1-15)
   a. The Binding of Satan (verses 1-3)
   b. The Resurrection of the Dead (verses 4-6)
   c. The Release of Satan (verses 7-9)
   d. The Lake of Fire (verses 10-15)

Introduction

Our time spent thus far in the Apocalypse has been taken up with three major aspects of the book. Those parts of the book are designated in the general study outline in the ensuing manner: (a) An Introduction to the Revelation, chapter 1; (b) The Church Age, chapters 2, 3; and (c) The Tribulation Period, chapters 4-18. The final chapters of the Book of Revelation are discussed under the general heading, "The Kingdom Period."

We have previously pointed out that these major divisions do not adequately describe the details presented by the Apostle John. Generally speaking, the outline is acceptable if one recognizes that it is a tentative and partial guide to interpreting the Apocalypse. These observations are especially pertinent at this time since the present chapter treats topics that might be classified in a number of ways. The second coming of Christ (Revelation 19), for example, is sometimes treated as the last event of the Tribulation, but not everyone so interprets His coming. Many expositors see His second coming as the first step in establishing the millennial kingdom and, therefore, the first event in the establishment of God's eternal kingdom on earth. The important thought is not whether everyone decides to get on one side of this issue or the other but that a person understands the slightly different slants that may be taken by exegetes.

Exposition

The two major subjects of this chapter are the second coming of Christ and His millennial reign. On the latter of these two topics, one finds that Premillennialists are in essential agreement, except for an occasional expositor. The former subject, the return of Christ, finds Premillennialists offering a number of different explanations. Many times these differences are not so much concerned with Christ's return *per se* as with other activities that are mentioned in Revelation 19. These variations in thought are particularly noticeable when one does an analysis of "The Marriage of the Lamb."

1. The Second Coming of Christ (Revelation 19:1-21)

After the Apostle John receives further explanation about the fall of Babylon, he hears the voices of a large number of people exclaiming their praise for God. During this portion of the overall revelation, he is granted a brief view of the marriage supper, the judgment of nations, and the great supper of God.

The Hallelujahs in Heaven (verses 1-5). The rejoicing that is announced in Revelation 18:20-24 is, in a sense, continued in these verses. The fundamental difference between the two accounts is that the earlier words concern rejoicing over the fall of Babylon, and in this chapter, the rejoicing is an expression of thanks to the person, God, who brought about the fall of Babylon.

The praise recorded in this passage is directly related to the salvation of God. This salvation is a reference not to a personal deliverance from sin through faith in the Lord Jesus Christ, but to God's providential care for believers when the Antichrist and his followers seek to coerce them into compliance with the culture of Babylon.

The judgment of God upon Babylon is referred to as both true and righteous. In this scene, God is praised for avenging the deaths of saints who were killed for not submitting to the Antichrist's Babylon. The second alleluia (19:3) precedes the words, "And her smoke rose up for ever and ever." One possible way of explaining this verse is that the reference to burning forever does not refer to the city as a conglomeration of buildings but speaks of the people of the city who will spend eternity in the lake of fire (20:15). Another suggestion for understanding the verse is that the praise is expressed in a semi-poetic manner and refers to the totally devastating destruction that will come upon the city, much like the idea expressed in Revelation 14:11.

The twenty-four elders and the four living creatures are next described as worshiping God. As John observed, he heard a voice from the throne of God say, "Praise our God." Some commentators have suggested that God Himself spoke these words, but such seems unlikely. It is awkward to think that God Himself said, "Praise our God." An easier interpretation to accept is that either an elder or a living creature made the remark.

The Marriage of the Lamb (verses 6-10). The marriage of the Lamb (19:7), or the wedding feast of the Lamb as some prefer to stress (19:9), is announced to John next, but the event itself is nowhere explained. If some details had been given, perhaps so many interpretations would not be around today. Let us hurriedly examine some reasons for the various interpretations of the marriage supper. One topic that divides interpreters is where the marriage supper will take place. Many expositors argue that the wedding and feast will take place in Heaven. But just as many, if not more, argue against this viewpoint and in favor of the marriage supper being on earth sometime in the future.

The question of where the feast occurs is very much related to the issue of when the supper will occur. Three answers are forthcoming to the question. First, some believe the feast will occur after the rapture. The rapture, spokesmen for this position say, will occur before the Tribulation. This position, then, has the marriage supper occurring in Heaven during the Tribulation.

A second interpretation agrees in part with the first position. This viewpoint, however, distinguishes between the marriage of the Lamb and the marriage supper of the Lamb. The former will occur in Heaven after the rapture during the Tribulation while the latter will occur after the Tribulation on the earth.

The third stance sometimes taught is that the text makes no essential difference between the marriage of the Lamb (19:7) and the marriage supper (19:9). The metaphor blends the two, and they will occur on earth after the Tribulation. As a matter of fact, exponents of this position argue that the marriage of the Lamb will occur when

Christ returns to be forever with all believers. The marriage, therefore, symbolizes that Christ will, from the point of His return on, dwell with His people. This position seems to be supported by the reference to the bride of Christ, the New Jerusalem, and those who dwell therein (Revelation 21:9-12, 22-27).

One final point needs to be touched upon before analyzing the next part of Revelation 19. Many expositors insist that there is a difference between the wife (19:7) and those who are called to the marriage supper (19:9). If metaphorical language were supposed to be pressed for interpretations of all the details, then this position might be correct. Yet metaphors, like parables, are not to be interpreted in all of their particulars. Instead, one basic truth is to be sought. So in the case before us, it seems that the wife and those invited to the marriage supper represent the same group: saints of all ages. A careful study of the parables Jesus used (Matthew 22, 24; Luke 14) about feasts in general, as well as about marriage feasts, supports the notion that the emphasis is on those who attend the feasts, not the bride. The passage before us appears to be best interpreted when we see the "blessed" and the "bride" as the same group.

The Smiting of the Nations (verses 11-16). The marriage of the Lamb, a figurative allusion to the close relationship of Christ and His people that will begin when He returns, cannot occur until Christ Himself returns to judge the forces of the Antichrist or those who live in agreement with the values of Babylon.

The picturesque language used by John to describe the return of Christ suggests a number of truths. Christ Himself, to begin with, will return as He has faithfully promised. The long wait for His return will one day be over. Also, when He returns, He will judge fairly and righteously. While many are prone to question the justice of God today, the omniscient King will not be accused of such at His return. The Antichrist will not hesitate to oppose Him, but it is hardly likely that he will call Him unjust.

Third, Christ will return as a glorified King, having the right to judge all since He is "KING OF KINGS, AND LORD OF LORDS." Whether all unsaved people will be destroyed at the return of the Lord as some believe, or whether many who are unsaved but who are not openly supporting the Antichrist will be spared and allowed to enter the millennium as others believe is not clear. The latter interpretation may be supported by the fact that Christ will have to rule with a rod of iron during the millennium.

The Great Supper of God (verses 17-21). The great supper of God, which is actually a feast of various kinds of vultures upon the masses of people who are killed at the return of Christ, is to be the last phase of God's judgment upon the empire built by the Antichrist. This great supper will undoubtedly follow the battle of Armageddon.

The precise sequence of events and details of the battle of Armageddon are not stated in the Scriptures. Yet a skeleton of events may be gathered from the Apocalypse. This skeletal viewpoint is as follows: The seventh bowl (16:17) will produce cataclysmic events that jar the entire world. At that time, God will recall the iniquity of Babylon and will pour out His wrath upon the city (16:19). In some way, He will use the allies of the Antichrist to destroy the city symbolized by Babylon (17:16-18). During this moment of worldwide judgment by God, the Antichrist and supporting nations will be experiencing trouble with nations that were formerly faithful to the Antichrist (Daniel 11:40-45). Seemingly, the Antichrist and his allies will gather to fight former allies, but instead they will "make war against him that sat on the horse" (19:19) because Christ will return at this climactic moment of history. At the battle between Christ and the forces that are gathered at Armageddon, the Antichrist and his false prophet will be taken directly to the "lake of fire" while his armies and allies, as well as his enemies, will be destroyed (19:20, 21). The precise manner of destruction is not mentioned by the apostle.

These events may begin during the last part of the Great Tribulation and continue over into the seventy-five days between the end of the Tribulation and the beginning of the millennium (Daniel 12:11, 12). Neither the exact time of the fall of Babylon nor the precise moment the battle of Armageddon occurs is specified by the apostle. Perhaps these events will occur in the last forty-five of the seventy-five days mentioned by the prophet Daniel. One point that does seem to be relatively clear is that shortly after the Antichrist is cast into the lake of fire Satan will be bound (19:20; 20:2). The battle of Armageddon may end just a matter of a few days before the millennial reign of Christ begins.

2. The Millennial Reign of Christ (Revelation 20:1-15)

The redirection of John's attention is obvious from a glance at the first few verses of Revelation 20. The Great Tribulation, as far as this particular revelation is concerned, is over; the interval between it and the millennium had also ended. Now John is introduced to the rule of Christ on earth. The end of the rule of Satan through the Antichrist and the false prophet has come, and many of the beautiful creations of man are in shambles.

The Binding of Satan (verses 1-3). The overwhelming majority of Premillennialists believe that sometime in the future Satan will be bound for a period of a thousand years or a millennium. Some believe he will be bound by a real, though not physical, chain. More believe the chain symbolizes the concept that Satan's freedom and power will be curtailed during the millennium.

In studying the millennial question, it is important to recognize that not all Premillennialists take the thousand years mentioned by John as exactly a thousand years. Some, but very few to be exact, think the words are to be understood as a real but not exact period of time. The period of time will be what God considers an ideal enchainment of Satan.

The Resurrection of the Dead (verses 4-6). At least two significant truths emerge from a study of these verses. A truth that is not entirely clear is that some believers, maybe all, will live and reign "with Christ a thousand years" (20:4). The text itself is not explicit about who will rule with Him, but it seems that the saints who died during the Great Tribulation are primarily in focus. Perhaps others are implied in the less specific words, "the souls of them that were beheaded." Regardless of one's interpretation of these words, other passages make it clear that other believers will reign with Christ (2:26, 27).

The other point of significance is that there are two resurrections or two kinds of resurrections. Posttribulationists like to stress that there will be two resurrections. The first will be for all true believers after the Tribulation. This being so, the Church will not be raptured before or during the Tribulation. If there were a resurrection before or during the Tribulation, then the resurrection mentioned by John would have to be the second resurrection, not the first.

Pretribulationists and midtribulationists prefer to speak of two kinds of resurrections. The first kind of resurrection refers to the resurrection of believers and includes those raised in Christ's time (Matthew 27), those before or in the middle of the Tribulation, and those after the Tribulation as mentioned here by the apostle. The second kind of resurrection refers to the unbelieving that will be raised at the end of the millennium (20:5). This interpretation of the first resurrection and second resurrection parallels the notion of the first death and the second death.

The Release of Satan (verses 7-9). The details of life during the millennium are left to the imagination of the reader of the Apocalypse, for John does not describe activities of that future period of life. He does, however, mention a rebellion that will come about after the millennium.

Satan, after being released, will quickly deceive much of mankind. The implication seems to be that many who will live under the rod of iron will not actually worship Christ; for, if they are so easily led astray by Satan, it seems they will also lack a fundamental commitment to Christ (20:8).

The justice of God in sending unbelievers to an eternal Hell probably would not be questioned by very many people if they realized the full import of this passage: Many people who live with Christ Himself during the millennium will prefer to serve Satan once he is released. The human desire for truth, justice, and love is not nearly as strong as many folks would have us believe.

The words *Gog* and *Magog* have been bothersome to expositors. As a result, a couple of major explanations for the terms are offered. An explanation that has a large number of followers is that the words are to be taken as representing the enemy of God. This interpretation results from Ezekiel's usage on another occasion (Ezekiel 38). A slightly different variation of this interpretation is that the words signify the futile efforts of mankind in trying to thwart the sovereignty of God.

A second major explanation found in Premillennial literature is that, as in Ezekiel, Gog refers to the leader of a nation and Magog to the people themselves. If this position is accepted, the thought may be that Satan will deceive many nations or peoples through one outstanding leader.

Satan's last attempt to be the god of the universe will be futile. When the people who follow Satan prepare to attack Jerusalem ("the beloved city"), God destroys them with fire (20:9). Observe that this verse implies that Christ will rule from Jerusalem during the millennium.

The Lake of Fire (verses 10-15). It is doubtful that anyone enjoys thinking about the eternal abode of unbelievers, the lake of fire. Yet the lake of fire is a necessity for those who refuse to accept

Christ as their personal Savior. If there were no such place, all eternity might be "little seasons" for Satan to deceive and lead rebellions against the God who created him.

Those who will spend eternity with Satan will be resurrected after Satan is defeated at Jerusalem. Satan will then be cast into the lake of fire, and all unbelievers will be judged at what is normally called the great white throne judgment. Many Christians think that this judgment will take place in a moment of time as "the earth and the heaven" flee away, are renovated, or are completely destroyed and the new heavens and the new earth appear.

In concluding this chapter, perhaps a diagram of the way the events of Revelation 19, 20 occur will be helpful. While hardly any diagram conveys all that a person may wish to say, the following one may at least convey some of the sequential relationships that have been discussed. The term *interval*, of course, refers to the seventy-five days spoken of by the prophet Daniel. The other terms are better known; therefore, they need no explanation.

The Interval	**The Millennium**	**The Little Season**	**The White Throne**
The Return of Christ	The Resurrection of Believers	The Loosing of Satan	The Resurrection of Unbelievers
The Marriage of the Lamb	The Binding of Satan	The Activities of Gog and Magog	The White Throne Judgment
The Battle of Armageddon	The Rule of Christ from Jerusalem	The Battle of Jerusalem	The New Creation of the New Universe
The Antichrist thrown into the Lake of Fire	The Rule of Believers with Christ	The Casting of Satan into the Lake of Fire	

FIGURE 3: The Sequence of Events From the Return of Christ to the Creation of the New Universe

13

The New Universse

Study Text: Revelation 21:1—22:21

Introduction
1. The Eternal State of Believers (Revelation 21:1-27)
   a. The New Creation (verses 1-8)
   b. The Wife of the Lamb (verses 9-11)
   c. The Shape of the City (verses 12-17)
   d. The Beauty of the City (verses 18-21)
   e. The People of the City (verses 22-27)
2. The Final Aspects of the Revelation (Revelation 22:1-21)
   a. The Throne of God (verses 1-5)
   b. The Angel of God (verses 6-13)
   c. The Destiny of Mankind (verses 14, 15)
   d. The Invitation to Mankind (verses 16, 17)
   e. The Warning and the Benediction (verses 18-21)

Introduction

The final two chapters of the Apocalypse are now before us. As we will see shortly, the last two chapters of the Book of Revelation are essentially concerned with a description of the New Jerusalem (21:1–22:5) and John's epilogue (22:6-21).

A treatment of these passages, however, will be delayed until we have an overview of the Apocalypse clearly in mind. The revelation John received from God is essentially concerned with the ensuing points. First, there is a description of the glorified Revelator, Jesus Christ (chapter 1). Then John described and attempted to correct some of the problems seven historical churches of Asia Minor were experiencing (chapters 2, 3). These churches, while probably not representative of seven periods of church history, are somewhat typical of the kinds of churches that appear in any era of time since Christ established His Church. They represent many of the ways in which a church may become unbalanced as a community of believers.

Third, John discussed the sealed book which contained revelations that are described in terms of seven seals, seven trumpets, and seven bowls (4:1-16:21). The events symbolized by the book probably occur shortly before, during, and after the Great Tribulation. Most of the material included by John in his parenthetical discussions (chapters 7, 10-13) seems to be related to events that will transpire shortly before and during the Great Tribulation, or the last half of the Tribulation. One parenthesis (14:1-20) appears to be basically concerned with the latter part of the Great Tribulation and shortly thereafter.

The fourth major division of the Apocalypse is concerned with Babylon and the return of Christ (17:1–20:15). Much or all of this material may constitute John's final parenthesis and probably falls in the interval between the Great Tribulation and the Millennium. Some events, especially in Revelation 20, will occur during the millennium and shortly thereafter.

Scanning back over the Apocalypse, then, the book may be divided into five particular revelations: (1) The Revelation of the Glorified Christ, chapter 1; (2) The Revelation of the Churches of Asia Minor, chapters 2, 3; (3) The Revelation of the Sealed Book, chapters 4-16; (4) The Revelation of Christ as King of Heaven and Earth, chapters 17-20; and (5) The Revelation of the Eternal State of Believers, chapters 21, 22.

Exposition

Even though the revelations John received from God are not as comprehensive and as detailed as a person might desire, man's desire to know about the future may not be exactly in keeping with God's purpose in revealing the future. God seems to want to convey the truths that He is sovereign, that He is concerned for His people, and that He will keep His promises to believers and unbelievers. In Revelation 21, 22, God reveals through John that the promise of eternal life with Him is a certainty, and He briefly describes something of what the eternal state of believers will be like. In conclusion, however, God clarified His invitation to unbelievers: "Come. And let him that heareth say, Come. And let him that is athirst come. And whosoever will, let him take the water of life freely" (22:17).

God wants believers to understand a little of what the eternal state will be like, but He wants unbelievers to understand that they can freely come to Him and participate throughout eternity in the affairs of the New Jerusalem on the new earth. As Peter clearly stated, God is "Not willing that any should perish, but that all should come to repentance" (2 Peter 3:9).

1. The Eternal State of Believers (Revelation 21:1-27)

Interpreting Revelation 21 may seem somewhat easy after having struggled with some of the earlier chapters. This feeling of ease may be only partially correct, however. Christians have had a difficult time deciding on whether the chapter refers to the eternal state of believers or to the millennium. A large number of expositors are convinced that Revelation 21:9–22:7 refers to Christ's millennial reign; whereas Revelation 21:1-8 speaks of the eternal state. Another large group of interpreters argues that the entire passage, Revelation 21:1–22:7, describes the eternal state of believers.

Some of the reasons for this disagreement will be noted as we progress through Revelation 21. For the present, it may be observed that in one sense the eternal state of believers will begin with the millennium. Therefore, it is permissible, if a bit confusing at first, to describe both the millennium and the state we often term Heaven as the eternal state of believers. Then, too, it may be worth thinking about the possibility that what we often call Heaven will not be drastically different from the millennium. Some differences, of course, are obvious, e.g., only believers will be in "heaven."

The New Creation (verses 1-8). Contrary to the popular concept of "heaven," John describes the eternal state of believers as on a new earth, perhaps new in the same sense that believers will have new bodies throughout eternity (1 Corinthians 15:51-54). One distinct difference between the old and new earth is that there will be "no more sea" (21:1).

The new earth, which will be encompassed by a new Heaven, will be the site of the New Jerusalem. The New Jerusalem, while probably a literal city, seems to signify the eternal presence of God with believers. Look at the words, "he will dwell with them" (21:3). No longer will we live merely by faith. Instead, God Himself will be with us.

During eternity, God will have so changed existence that there will no longer be any sorrow, crying, pain, and death. Some folks argue that because God wipes away all tears, He will judge Christians just before eternity begins, and we will be greatly grieved over our sins and, therefore, weep. As a result, God will wipe away our tears after a judgment of saints. The context itself, however, does not support this interpretation. The context suggests that not only will God wipe away tears at this time, but He will also eliminate death, sorrow, and pain. Death, sorrow, and pain are not caused by some judgment that will take place just before the eternal state begins, and neither should we think of the crying as being caused by some unmentioned judgment. And as a conclusive factor in this argument, John associated tears, death, pain, and sorrow with "the former things" (21:4). The former things spoken of here refer to the former way of life, or life before the eternal state. The point of emphasis, then, is that in the eternal state no one will have any kind of undesirable experience.

There is the implication in this passage that spiritual sustenance, blessings, and the abundant life are, as always but in a fresh new way, directly related to God Himself: "I will give unto him that is athirst of the fountain of the water of life freely" (21:6). John's words, "He that overcometh," must have had a special meaning to the Christians in the seven churches of Asia Minor for to each group of believers there was a promise to the overcomer.

The Wife of the Lamb (verses 9-11). After John hears the comments about those who will spend eternity in the lake of fire, an angel invites him to view the Lamb's wife, the New Jerusalem. Some commentators say the scene quickly changes from the eternal state to the New Jerusalem during the millennium. No thoroughly convincing reasons, however, have been given for this position; although, some reasons are often stated and will be mentioned later. The basic point to keep in mind now is that the apostle has presented another close-up in these verses: Further details on the New Jerusalem that was mentioned in verse 2 are being presented. This pattern of treating subjects is seen throughout the Apocalypse.

The fundamental truths found in the wife metaphor in these verses are that the traditional beauty of the bride applies to believers and the intimacy of the wife and husband will be shared by believers and Christ. Christ and His lovely bride will live in an intimate relationship throughout eternity.

The Shape of the City (verses 12-17). The description of the New Jerusalem presented by the apostle has concerned expositors for a long time. Time and again they have asked, "How much, if any, of the description is to be understood in a literal manner?" Answers, naturally, vary. For our purposes, a couple of observations will be sufficient. First, the reason a person–if he does–rejects some of the literal aspects of the city and accepts a somewhat symbolic interpretation of the New Jerusalem should not be because of some preconceived idea of what eternity will be like. Our ideas should be based upon the Scriptures, not upon a folkloristic theology.

Second, no line of reasoning or Biblical evidence appears solid enough to cause the believer to say John's description of the New Jerusalem is to be understood in a totally symbolic fashion. No doubt, some aspects of the city, which are real within themselves represent particular truths; certain other aspects of the city are metaphorical allusions to ancient truths. On the other hand, the new earth seems to be a literal earth and so, too, does the New Jerusalem appear to be a literal city.

We can find at least three important thoughts in Revelation 21:12-17. The first two of these concepts are found in the words *the twelve tribes of the children of Israel* and *the twelve apostles of the Lamb* (21:12, 14). The prominent roles of Israel and the apostles in the development of the Scriptures and the Church will be memorialized throughout eternity.

The third notion of importance in these verses is related to the shape of the city. Many Christians focus their attention on the size of the city, but perhaps the shape is more important. The city will be of equal length, breadth, and height: twelve thousand furlongs. A furlong is 582 feet; therefore, the measurement spoken of is comparable to approximately 1,350 miles. Some translators round off the number to 1,500 miles.

The shape of the city is usually thought to be that of a cube. A few expositors, nevertheless, think that its shape is that of a pyramid. While the pyramidal theory may be correct, it seems more likely that the city will be a cube to signify the presence of God with man. The shape of the city may be to remind us of the holy of holies, which was in the form of a cube.

The Beauty of the City (verses 18-21). A careful examination of these verses reveals that little is really said about the New Jerusalem itself. Most of the description is concerned with the wall of the city. The foundations of the wall, unlike most, are pictured as being above ground and their beauty is a reflection of God's concern for beauty both now and for eternity.

The beauty of the city is reflected in the fact that it will be "pure gold, like unto clear glass" (21:18) and have streets (street is to be understood collectively) of "pure gold, as . . . transparent glass" (21:21). Two interpretations of these words are found in Premillennial literature. One of these is that the city and its streets will be gold-colored glass. The other is that in some way God will make gold itself transparent. No doubt the magnificence and splendor of the New Jerusalem will surpass that ever seen in any human civilization. The King of kings will dwell in a city that is well suited for Him. And His children will have access to that city as well as the rest of His new creation.

The People of the City (verses 22-27). In these verses, we find two ideas that have caused a number of interpreters to think the New Jerusalem in Revelation 21:9–22:7 refers to the city during the millennium. The earth itself is depicted as being inhabited by nations and kings (21:24). The following words of John also cause a problem: "And there shall in no wise enter into it any thing that defileth, neither whatsoever worketh abomination, or maketh a lie" (21:27). In the light of these statements, some conclude the New Jerusalem will be suspended over the earth during the millennium, and only saved people will be allowed to enter it.

Several possible solutions may be given to the aforementioned problem. Perhaps John used the only language he knew, a terrestrial or earthly vocabulary, to describe a heavenly or eternal idea. Thus, he was simply saying that all redeemed people will have access to the New Jerusalem and to God (21:24) and that no one except believers will be with God throughout eternity (21:27).

One suggested solution to the problem caused by the word *nation* is to interpret it to mean Gentiles. From this perspective, the proper interpretation is that Gentiles, too, will be allowed into the New Jerusalem. A difficulty that arises with this standpoint is that the word *kings* still needs to be explained.

A final consideration rests in the suggestion that there will be nations and kings (rulers) under God throughout eternity. That no unsaved peoples will be present is clear from verse 27, but God's eternal order will include giving men responsibilities in the realm of leadership just as angelic beings have different levels of responsibility. This position seems too earthy or secular to many folks, but a counter argument that may be given is that our view of Heaven is "too heavenly"; we have been influenced more by a folkloristic interpretation of "heaven" than we have been by the Scriptures themselves.

The final position one takes on this issue has little to do with his view of who will be in the New Jerusalem. Folks agree that only believers will be in the New Jerusalem along with the Trinity and, probably, angelic beings.

2. The Final Aspects of the Revelation (Revelation 22:1-21)

The first few verses of Revelation 22 are structurally related to the previous chapter; therefore, the first five verses of this chapter are thematically related to Revelation 21. The latter portion of Revelation 22 may be divided into four sections. Each of these divisions will be treated after an analysis of the first five verses is completed.

The Throne of God (verses 1-5). The source of "a pure river of water of life" will be the throne of both God and the Lamb. The reference to the tree suggests that fullness of life in eternity will be inseparably related to God Himself and will be available to all. The tree of life will not be governed by the ordinary cycles of growth, which symbolize the complete victory God has over all death. Likewise, the fruit of the tree will be the source of strength and life for all who eat of it. The word translated *healing* is better understood to mean health providing. Thus, the spiritual health of people will continue to be directly related to God.

Two phrases, "no more curse" (22:3) and "they shall reign" (22:5), are worthy of our attention. The former may refer to the curse recorded by Moses (Genesis 3:17). If so, then the lifting of that curse will mean that the new earth will be similar to the Edenic splendor and innocency (Romans 8:19-22).

The latter phrase illustrates a paradoxical notion: Believers will be both servants (22:3) and rulers (22:5). The precise manner in which each takes place is not described. As is often the situation, God only gives a glimpse of the future.

The Angel of God (verses 6-13). Basically this passage is not difficult to understand; yet several problems do arise for the careful reader. To begin with, it is difficult to know who is speaking in Revelation 22:6, 7 as well as in Revelation 22:12, 13. Was Christ the speaker? Was the angel quoting Christ? Or did John just insert Christ's own words as he wrote? No absolutely certain answer is found in the text, but some think Revelation 22:16 implies Christ Himself injected comments.

A second problem for the careful student of the Apocalypse is this: Why would John worship an angel (22:8)? Especially is this curious since he had previously been rebuked for such (19:10). The answer may lie in that the apostle had seen a continual stream of revelations that filled him with awe; therefore, he succumbed to the inclination to express his awe, even to the wrong person.

A final difficulty is found in Revelation 22:11. To modern ears the words of this verse sound insensitive, even harsh. Why would the evildoer be encouraged to continue in his sins? Although it seems John was encouraging unbelievers to remain in unbelief, another interpretation must be sought; for this interpretation is inconsistent with the whole trend of New Testament thought and, in particular, with Revelation 22:18.

Some expositors think the answer to this problem is that John is simply saying, "If the revelations recorded by me do not cause you to repent, then nothing else can effect such a change. Likewise, those of you who are believers should be motivated to purify yourselves even more if you take seriously the prophecies I have recorded."

Other interpreters think the answer is to be found in a different line of thought. Proponents of this point of view believe John is thinking of the time of the end, the Great Tribulation; he sees the day when those who are totally committed to the Antichrist will be solidified in their wickedness just as believers will be so devoted to Christ that they will be martyrs for Him.

The Destiny of Mankind (verses 14, 15). Two alternatives are open to people in the light of John's words. A person may dwell eternally with God and have access to the New Jerusalem. Or for those who reject the sacrificial death of Christ, there will be an outside, i.e., a place where people will be outside the blessings of God.

The word *dogs* is the only term in Revelation 22:15 that needs to be explained. To the reader in John's day, the word carried the notion of a vicious or malicious person.

The Invitation to Mankind (verses 16, 17). The destiny of a person is determined by himself; John has clearly stated that both the Holy Spirit and true believers eagerly invite all who will to participate in the eternal life God offers. The person who rejects the invitation makes the most serious mistake of his life; he ultimately chooses to enjoy some aspects of this life rather than have the abundant life in this world and eternal life with Christ.

The Warning and the Benediction (verses 18-21). The urgency of John's warning to neither alter nor to add to the revelation he had received is seen in the judgments promised to those who ignore the warning. The warning is not to believers who unintentionally misinterpret the Apocalypse but to those who intentionally deny or distort portions or all of the Book of Revelation. Similarly, the warning is to those who claim that God has given other revelations not in the Christian Scriptures.

The profundity and complexity of the revelations of the Apocalypse are overshadowed in John's words, "I come quickly." Differences of interpretations will surely exist until Christ returns. At times we may have no satisfying interpretations at all, but everyone understands, "I come quickly." The believer who is maturing in his faith can wholeheartedly say with John, "Even so, come, Lord Jesus."

Study Outline

An Introduction to The Revelation 1:1-20

1. The Introduction to the Book, 1:1-8
   a. The Superscription, 1:1-3
   b. The Salutation, 1:4-8
2. The Vision of Christ, 1:9-20
   a. The Time of the Vision, 1:9-11
   b. The Person in the Vision, 1:12-16
   c. The Interpretation of the Vision, 1:17-20

Part I: The Church Age

A. The Letters to Ephesus, Smyrna, Pergamos, and Thyatira, 2:1-29
   1. The Letter to Ephesus, 2:1-7
      a. Praise for the Church, 2:1-3
      b. Condemnation of the Church, 2:4
      c. Exhortation for the Church, 2:5-7
   2. The Letter to Smyrna, 2:8-11
      a. Praise for the Church, 2:8, 9
      b. Exhortation for the Church, 2:10, 11
   3. The Letter to Pergamos, 2:12-17
      a. Praise for the Church, 2:12, 13
      b. Condemnation of the Church, 2:14, 15
      c. Exhortation for the Church, 2:16, 17
   4. The Letter to Thyatira, 2:18-29
      a. Praise for the Church, 2:18, 19
      b. Condemnation of the Church, 2:20-23
      c. Exhortation for the Church, 2:24-29

B. The Letters to Sardis, Philadelphia, and Laodicea, 3:1-22
   1. The Letter to Sardis, 3:1-6
      a. Condemnation of the Church, 3:1, 2
      b. Exhortation for the Church, 3:3-6

2. The Letter to Philadelphia, 3:7-13
   a. Praise for the Church, 3:7-9
   b. Exhortation for the Church, 3:10-13
3. The Letter to Laodicea, 3:14-22
   a. Condemnation of the Church, 3:14-17
   b. Exhortation for the Church, 3:18-22

Part II: The Tribulation Period

A. The Throne and the Book, 4:1—5:14
  1. The Scene in Heaven, 4:1-11
     a. The Throne of God, 4:1-5
     b. The Living Creatures, 4:6-8
     c. The Worship of God, 4:9-11
  2. The Sealed Book, 5:1-14
     a. The Search for a Worthy Person, 5:1-4
     b. The Lamb of God, 5:5-7
     c. The New Song, 5:8-10
     d. The Singing of All Creation, 5:11-14

B. The Seals and the Multitudes, 6:1—7:17
  1. The Opening of the Book, 6:1-17
     a. The First Seal: The White Horse, 6:1, 2
     b. The Second Seal: The Red Horse, 6:3,4
     c. The Third Seal: The Black Horse, 6:5, 6
     d. The Fourth Seal: The Ashen Horse, 6:7, 8
     e. The Fifth Seal: The Martyred Souls, 6:9-11
     f. The Sixth Seal: The Day of Wrath, 6:12-17
  2. The Two Multitudes, 7:1-17
     a. The Angelic Beings, 7:1-3
     b. The Sealed Tribes, 7:4-8
     c. The Mixed Multitude, 7:9-17

C. The Seventh Seal and the Six Trumpets, 8:1—9:21
  1. The Seventh Seal, 8:1-13
     a. The Silence in Heaven, 8:1-6
     b. The First Trumpet: The Hail and the Fire, 8:7
     c. The Second Trumpet: The Great Mountain, 8:8, 9
     d. The Third Trumpet: The Great Star, 8:10, 11

e. The Fourth Trumpet: The Luminaries, 8:12, 13
2. The First and Second Woes, 9:1-21
a. The Fifth Trumpet: The Locusts, 9:1-12
b. The Sixth Trumpet: The Horsemen, 9:13-21
D. The Angel, the Witnesses, and the Seventh Trumpet, 10:1—11:19
1. The Mighty Angel, 10:1-11
a. The Seven Peals of Thunder, 10:1-4
b. The Mystery of God, 10:5-7
c. The Eating of the Book, 10:8-11
2. The Two Witnesses, 11:1-13
a. The Measuring Rod, 11:1, 2
b. The Ministry of the Witnesses, 11:3-6
c. The Death of the Witnesses, 11:7-10
d. The Restoration of the Witnesses, 11:11-13
3. The Seventh Trumpet, 11:14-19
a. The Third Woe, 11:14, 15
b. The Announcement of the Elders, 11:16-19
E. The Dragon, the Woman, and the Offspring, 12:1-17
1. The Signs in the Heaven, 12:1-6
a. The Pregnant Woman, 12:1, 2
b. The Red Dragon, 12:3, 4
c. The Male Child, 12:5,6
2. The Battle in Heaven, 12:7-12
a. The Defeat of Satan, 12:7-9
b. The Salvation of God, 12:10-12
3. The Persecution of the Woman, 12:13-17
a. The Flight of the Woman, 12:13, 14
b. The Wrath of the Dragon, 12:15-17
F. The Beasts and the Lamb, 13:1—14:20
1. The Beast From the Sea, 13:1-10
a. The Appearance of the Beast, 13:1,2
b. The Authority of the Beast, 13:3-8
c. The Exhortation for Believers, 13:9, 10

2. The Beast From the Earth, 13:11-18
   a. The Power of the Beast, 13:11-15
   b. The Mark of the Beast, 13:16-18
3. The Lamb on the Mountain, 14:1-20
   a. The Redeemed From the Earth, 14:1-5
   b. The Eternal Gospel, 14:6, 7
   c. The Fall of Babylon, 14:8
   d. The Worshipers of the Beast, 14:9-11
   e. The Dead in Christ, 14:12, 13
   f. The Harvest on Earth, 14:14-20

G. The Seven Bowls of Wrath, 15:1—16:21
1. Introduction to the Seven Plagues, 15:1-8
   a. The Songs of Moses and the Lamb, 15:1-4
   b. The Temple of the Tabernacle, 15:5-8
2. The Wrath of God, 16:1-21
   a. The First Bowl: The Sores on Men, 16:1, 2
   b. The Second Bowl: The Death of the Sea, 16:3
   c. The Third Bowl: The Death of the Rivers, 16:4-7
   d. The Fourth Bowl: The Scorching Sun, 16:8, 9
   e. The Fifth Bowl: The Darkened Kingdom, 16:10, 11
   f. The Sixth Bowl: The Drying of the Euphrates, 16:12-16
   g. The Seventh Bowl: The Lightning, Thunder, and Quake, 16:17-21

H. The Destruction of Babylon, 17:1—18:24
1. The Mystery Woman, 17:1-6
   a. The Invitation to John, 17:1, 2
   b. The Description of the Woman, 17:3-6
2. The Interpretation of the Angel, 17:7-18
   a. The Explanation of the Beast, 17:7-14
   b. The Explanation of the Woman, 17:15-18
3. The Fall of Babylon, 18:1-24
   a. The Angel's Announcements, 18:1-8
   b. The Sorrow of Mankind, 18:9-19
   c. The Thankfulness of Believers, 18:20-24

Part III: The Kingdom Period

A. The Return of Christ, 19:1—20:15
  1. The Second Coming of Christ, 19:1-21
    a. The Hallelujahs in Heaven, 19:1-5
    b. The Marriage of the Lamb, 19:6-10
    c. The Smiting of the Nations, 19:11-16
    d. The Great Supper of God, 19:17-21
  2. The Millennial Reign of Christ, 20:1-15
    a. The Binding of Satan, 20:1-3
    b. The Resurrection of the Dead, 20:4-6
    c. The Release of Satan, 20:7-9
    d. The Lake of Fire, 20:10-15
B. The New Universe, 21:1—22:21
  1. The Eternal State of Believers, 21:1-27
    a. The New Creation, 21:1-8
    b. The Wife of the Lamb, 21:9-11
    c. The Shape of the City, 21:12-17
    d. The Beauty of the City, 21:18-21
    e. The People of the City, 21:22-27
  2. The Final Aspects of the Revelation, 22:1-21
    a. The Throne of God, 22:1-5
    b. The Angel of God, 22:6-13
    c. The Destiny of Mankind, 22:14, 15
    d. The Invitation to Mankind, 22:16, 17
    e. The Warning and the Benediction, 22:18-21

The Unsealed Book

An Amillennial Perspective

by

Wade T. Jernigan

About Dr. Jernigan

Author of *The Unsealed Book*

Dr. Wade Jernigan is well known as an Amillennialist. His beliefs and education have prepared his ability to write on the subject of his deep conviction.

He has attended Free Will Baptist College, Oklahoma Baptist University, Oklahoma University, Sacramento Baptist Bible College and Seminary, and Baptist Christian University, acquiring a Bachelor of Science, Bachelor of Arts, Master of Arts, and Ph.D. Besides his earned degrees, he has been honored by five other colleges.

During his fruitful lifetime, Dr. Jernigan has served as an evangelist, pastor, and has held many leadership roles on every level of his denomination. For 9 years he served as the president of California Christian College. He has authored 7 books and 27 songs, and his writing is well known in other denominational publications.

While in his early 70s, he is active as a pastor and is employed by Hillsdale Free Will Baptist College.

From the Author

This brief analytical study sets forth an Amillennial view of the Book of Revelation. No attempt has been made to exhaust Amillennialist tenets. This book should be read with that in mind.

Revelation is not a handbook on Amillennialism. It is primarily God's message through John to the persecuted first century Christians in Asia Minor. Every effort has been made by this writer to disclose the message as it arises naturally from the text and to avoid bringing a "system" to the book and imposing it upon John.

This study is presented as a positive, affirmative answer to the sweeping controversies surrounding Revelation. Revelation is the "unsealed book." The honest student can still expect to understand exactly what John the Apostle said and what the Lord Jesus meant.

–Wade T. Jernigan

1

An Introduction to the Book of Revelation

Introduction
1. Revelation Can Be Understood
2. Revelation Is Relevant
   a. Past
   b. Present
3. Revelation Was Written Under the Domitianic Period
4. Revelation Was Written in Apocalyptic Language
   a. Symbols
   b. Numbers

This writer would like to write with the same definiteness which possessed Dr. Luke when he wrote the introduction to his first book:

> Forasmuch as many have taken in hand to set forth in order a declaration of those things which are most surely believed among us, Even as they delivered them unto us, which from the beginning were eyewitnesses, and ministers of the word; It seemed good to me also, having had perfect understanding of all things from the very first, to write unto thee in order, most excellent Theophilus, That thou mightest know the certainty of those things, wherein thou hast been instructed.
>
> Luke 1:1-4

Of course, only those who wrote by inspiration could make such a claim. Many have taken in hand to set forth in order, as they see them, a declaration of those things which are most surely believed by them; it seemed good to this writer also, but of course no claim of perfect understanding will be made. Luke wrote by divine direction; I will not. He wrote under inspiration; I cannot. His was perfect order because he had perfect understanding; I do not. It is hoped, however, that the things written will be in such order that every Theophilus (lover of God) will know the certainty of those things.

Damon C. Dodd, author of *The Book of Revelation, A Study Guide,* though of a different interpretive persuasion, wrote the truth when he stated, "The Book of Revelation can be understood and with the understanding comes a surge of hope and joy for the people of God."[1] Dr. Ray Summers wrote, "Neglected, misunderstood, and grossly perverted, the Book of Revelation stands quite alone in the New Testament."[2] Many, possibly most, have contented themselves to pass it by with the flippant attitude, "No one understands Revelation anyway." Others have found in the book a particular kind of fascination. Curiosity has played a significant role as some have endeavored to study the Apocalypse. Multitudes have despaired of ever securing a comprehensive interpretation because there has been such a profusion of conflicting opinions about the true meaning of the book. Some groups have unscrupulously and extensively used it to prove almost anything by a manipulation of the symbols. Such careless handling of the Word follows an error related to a principle basic to interpretation: Scriptures obscure in meaning should be interpreted in the light of clear passages. Profitable interpretation can come forth only when such a policy is followed.

A close examination by a conscientious student of the voluminous books written on Revelation will reveal how sorely mistreated this book is in the hands of the uninformed. Revelation is not to be abandoned, shunned, or left unread. At one juncture in Martin Luther's life he refused to count the book as canonical, for in his opinion it was impossible to understand. Such an attitude cannot be taken if in fact the book is God-breathed. Believing that Revelation can be understood, the purpose of this volume is to present an approach by which every reader may come somewhat closer to the problem of the exegesis.

Two things in particular are to be determined in this study: the meaning of the book for the suffering saints of Asia Minor and the consequent meaning by application to the conditions, peoples, and the church now.

How cruel it would have been for John to have written to the persecuted saints of Asia Minor about things that would transpire millenniums to come. No amount of information about an apostate Roman church, a history of ages to come, or some by and by Utopia would have given them the courage to be faithful unto death. A key to the identity of the original recipients is given in verses 4 and 11 of chapter one, "John to the seven churches which are in Asia . . . unto Ephesus, and unto Smyma, and unto Pergamos, and unto Thyatira, and unto Sardis, and unto Philadelphia, and unto Laodicea." Though the letters were addressed to these particular churches, the number "7," which is symbolic of completeness, would suggest that the book was for all the churches in Asia Minor. There is reason to believe that these seven were representative of all the churches. Conditions dealt with in each letter spoke most definitely of the local congregation addressed; and yet, in each letter there are reflections of problems existing in each church. Those churches receiving the letters were to make the message known to all of the other churches. Each church written was on the great circular road. From their vantage point, communication was made much easier. That such was the practice of the early church can be seen in Paul's statement in Colossians 4:15, 16, "Salute the brethren which are in Laodicea . . . And when this epistle is read among you, cause that it be read also in the church of the Laodiceans; and that ye likewise read the epistle from Laodicea."

Generally speaking, John wrote the book to the saints of Asia Minor. The message was meant first for them, however, it did carry with it a universal note. For every Christian in every age the message of victory is clearly seen. Christ, the principal character of the book, vindicates His message made to His followers in Matthew 16:18, ". . . Upon this rock I will build my church; and the gates of hell shall not prevail against it." This is the message they needed for the time. Unnoticed for several decades by the Roman government, Christianity, when learned it was not a part of the Jewish religion, came under the frown of Rome. Judaism was a legal religion in Rome. However, because of the Jews' political ambitions, there were times when they were persecuted. Titus' move against the Jews at Jerusalem in A.D. 70 bears out this point. Christ had prophesied about this conflict in Matthew 24, Luke 17, and Luke 21.

Nero persecuted the Christians in Rome and made them the scapegoat when he set fire to Rome. His persecution was severe, but it was local rather than kingdom wide. At the time John was writing (Domitian's reign), persecution broke out far beyond Rome. It had reached into one church in particular (Antipas had died a martyr), and too, John had been banished to Patmos by Domitian because of his testimony for Jesus Christ. Several reasons can be cited for the antagonism brought against the believers. When these are studied, there should be no doubt left in the mind of the serious student about to whom the prophet wrote and why.

Probably the most outstanding reason for persecution was that the Christians would not worship the emperor. Emperor worship was the state religion. The Jews gave at least token worship, but the Christians most definitely refused. There was no recognition on their part of the monarch in their worship. If the believers had been satisfied to recognize the ruler as superior to Christ, they could have participated in the Christian religion unmolested. This they refused to do.

Second, the Christian populace was believed to be traitorous. Because of the practice of wearing certain idolatrous insignia and a portion of the soldiers' oath that bound the soldier to the service of the idol of the state, they refused induction. And too, they strongly held to the teaching, "He that killeth with the sword must be killed with the sword" (Revelation 13:10).

In the third place, Christianity was looked down upon because it appealed mostly to the poor and downtrodden. Those in the higher circles looked scornfully upon the adherents to this sect.

Their conflict of interest in regard to allegiance stood them in ill repute. For the most part, the Romans saw the empire as supreme, but the Christians held that the Kingdom of God was most important. Viewing the Kingdom as they did, they sought to make the religion of God's Kingdom universal.

Enthusiasm and exclusiveness put them in a bad light with the government and the philosophers of the day. Branded as fanatics in their enthusiasm, they shocked the sensitive philosophers. The Christians' refusal to mingle with the heathen in worship and social practice caused the Romans to look upon them as enemies of the accepted gods.

Their love for one another (their badge of identity, John 13:35) caused the authorities to be suspicious. Also, they held secret night meetings. Their affection for one another and the secrecy of the meetings caused the Romans to accuse them of meeting to gratify the lust of the flesh. Cannibalism was another accusation hurled against them. They were heard to speak of "eating flesh and drinking blood" in their meetings. Of course, they had reference to the

Lord's Supper. Misunderstanding and popular hatred brought much persecution to bear.

The Christians in their state of unrelentingness were accused of being worse than Jews. The Jews at least to some degree compromised, but not these Christians! Only contempt was held for them.

Many other reasons could be named, but space would not permit writing about them all. There is one other thought that should be mentioned. Christianity with its interest came into sharp conflict with the temporal interest of the overwhelming majority of the Roman priests, makers of idols, vendors of the sacrifices, etc.

The seer aligned himself as brother and companion with this persecuted kingdom in 1:9. Internal evidence that John wrote Revelation during the reign of Domitian is plenteous. According to his own testimony, the prophet was exiled on Patmos. Origen says John wrote while in exile on Patmos, and Victorious went further by stating that John wrote Revelation on Patmos where he was in exile by the order of Domitian. Hippolytus, Jerome, Clement, and Hegesippus also held the same view. Such evidence indicates the belief that the book was written during the Domitianic persecution. Situations described in the churches speak of a later period than that of Nero. Conditions call for a time of more intense persecution than that experienced under Nero. And too, the inner life of the churches had greatly changed since Paul. A deterioration had set in at several of the churches. It was true that some groups of the Nicolaitans grew rapidly, but to put the time under Nero would have allowed only four or five years from Paul, and such was just not the case. Heresies described in the book show clearly an acquaintance with Gnosticism which calls for a later period than A.D. 70. More time was needed for such heretical development. Persecutions reflected fit the Domitianic period. Several persecutions to some degree had been carried out under Caligula, Claudius, Nero, and Vespasian, but it was said that Domitian bathed the empire in the blood of the Christians. His persecution came as a result of enforcing emperor worship. Several Scriptures certainly point to the practice of emperor worship at the time of John's writing. Many forms of punishment were inflicted upon the Christians; they were put to death, they were tortured to the point of confessing that the emperor was divine, their property was taken, they were exiled, and some had all of these things happen to them. All of this is reflected in the Book of Revelation.

Another thing that speaks for the Domitianic period is the *Nero-Redivivus* myth. This myth took several years to develop. It held that Nero did not die but rather escaped to the East. Held also was the belief that he would return–leading the armies of the East into conflict against Rome. John alludes to this myth several times in his writing.

"Fundamental to the primary thesis of this book," said Jay Adams, "is the proposition that when the angel said, 'I will tell thee the mystery' (Revelation 17:7), he did just that."[3] When this phrase is understood in the terms of the book itself, it means "I will tell you the meaning of the mystery," or "I will interpret for you the symbols."[4] A good example is found in chapter one. John saw a vision of Christ standing in the midst of the seven candlesticks holding seven stars. The angel then interpreted the vision: "The seven stars are the angels [messengers] of the seven churches: and the seven candlesticks . . . are the seven churches" (Revelation 1:20). Adams further states that the interpretation is introduced with the words "As for the mystery (i.e., the meaning of the mystery) of the seven stars . . . and the seven candlesticks . . . ."[5] Therefore, in Revelation, the first chapter, the "mystery" is the meaning or interpretation of the vision. So when "the mystery" of other visions is told by the Angel (example: Revelation 17:7), one may expect an interpretation.

One writer has even proposed, "Its symbolism belongs to the first century, not to our age."[6] The book is full of strange symbolism. However, since the angel has interpreted the major symbols, there is good reason to believe the book can be understood. For many modern men, Revelation remains a closed book; it should not be so for in reality the book was never closed, but has forever remained open (Revelation 22:10).

No study of Revelation should be attempted without a careful look at the symbolism of numbers. The Oriental mind was also fascinated by the significance of numbers. Summers has this to say about numbers and the Oriental mind, "In that early day, when language was primitive and the vocabulary meager, one Hebrew word sometimes was compelled to do duty for a score of diverse meanings."[7] When the conditions prevailed, men came to use numbers in like manner as modern man uses words. Numbers came to express certain concepts. Because of the association of numbers repeatedly with certain ideas, objects, and things, some numbers became symbols. To endeavor to interpret them with an exact literal meaning as one would employ when dealing with a math formula is to miss the true thought being conveyed.

Not all numbers used in that fashion will be listed and dealt with, but key numbers used in the writing of Revelation will be touched upon.

"One" does not appear used in symbolic form in the book, but in dealing with the significance of numbers used symbolically, to interpret "1" is to give a better understanding of the other numbers. When the Orientals saw a single object they came to associate the number "1" with uniqueness, aloneness, unity, and independency.

"Two" suggests strength. It only stood to reason that two men could stand together against a common enemy better than one. Two could also pursue a common interest better than one. Even in the writing of the Law two could make a stronger witness than one. Strength, courage, companionship, and energy came to be symbolized by the use of the number "2." One cannot help but see this type thinking even when observing the sending policy of Jesus–He sent them two by two. Such made for a more effective, confirming witness. God's truth is confirmed in the Book of Revelation by two witnesses. A strong witness is thus symbolized by the number "2."

Most students have little trouble with the number "3." Ask anyone who has spiritual sense and scriptural knowledge what the number "3" brings to their mind, and they will respond, "the Triune God." It has been long held that in his primitive environment, early man saw in his home something very divine–love of father, mother, and brother. Through the expression of their affection toward one another in the home, man came to associate the number "3" with divine things. "Three" symbolized the Divine. In early Hebrew writings, the Divine is expressed by the use of "3." A good case in point is the visit of the three men with Abraham on the Plains of Mamre in Genesis 18. Note that the three are spoken of as Lord several times. Hardly anyone would argue to the contrary on the symbolism of this figure.

Man's observation of the universe naturally brought to mind the figure "4." His knowledge of the world was far from that known by the modern mind. Even until more recent times men held that the earth's surface was flat. To them the earth being flat had of necessity four corners. Such thinking caused them to associate the world with "4." It became the number of the world. Two examples of how "4" is used in the Apocalypse is the four living creatures which symbolized the four divisions of animal life of this world and the four horsemen who symbolized the destructive powers of the world. A study of the four angels standing on the four corners holding the four winds will make the meaning even clearer.

In a study about himself, man could not help but notice that he had, unless he was injured, maimed, or deformed, five toes on each foot and five fingers on each hand. Man saw completeness in this. A perfect man had all of his fingers (10) and all of his toes (10). Five doubled to ten came to represent completeness. Man's complete duty to his God lay in ten commandments. Ten comes into play many times in Revelation, either as a single unit or a multiple. Revelation reveals in its symbolism that complete world power lay in a beast with ten horns. Both the "first" beast and the "scarlet" beast have ten horns. In reference to the last beast, the Book of Revelation itself gives us the meaning of the ten horns–ten kings–which symbolizes the complete world power as it lay with Rome and her provincial system. A multiple of ten can be seen in larger numbers used in Revelation. Needless to say, seventy is a very sacred number, and one thousand is a multiple of ten which shows ultimate completeness. To give to these numbers an exact true numerical value is to miss the message conveyed in the symbol.

"Six" is a sinister number in the thinking of the Hebrews. Jews seem to have observed "6" as many today look at "13"–an evil number. If for one moment a student thinks this to be absurd, call the local hotel and request a room on the 13th floor. They will offer rooms on 12, 12A, 14, etc., but not on the 13th. When it comes to superstition, even people who appear otherwise do not care to sleep on the 13th floor! Seven is the sacred number. Six comes close to seven but falls short. When the number of the beast (666) must be dealt with, keep in mind the Jews' thinking about the number "6." The number "666" is a multiple of "6," thus standing for or symbolizing immense evil.

"Seven" seems to have been one of the most sacred numbers in the thinking and writing of the Hebrews. John uses "7" more than any other number, and for good reason. This number took on its particular symbolic meaning because man saw the number "4" as the world number, and the number "3" as the divine number. The number "7" showed earth crowned with Heaven. In a divine, spiritual sense, "7" came to express completeness through union of the divine with the earthly, or the perfect number of the world with the perfect number of Heaven. Keep the thought of completeness in mind as you study the seven spirits, seven churches, seven golden candlesticks, seven stars, seven seals, seven trumpets, seven thunders, seven bowls, and seven sections of the book. The very sacred "70" is a multiple of the complete number "10" and the sacred complete number "7." If the reader is prone to question this, then consider the significance of seventy x seven used by Christ to show complete forgiveness when a believer had offended another, or the complete power to overcome the devil as seen in the seventy who returned witnessing that the devil was subject to them.

Another number that should be treated before leaving this type symbolism is "3½." When the perfect number "7" was cut in half, the "3½" was used to express incompleteness or the imperfect. This resulted in it coming to signify, in Apocalyptic writing, restlessness, turmoil, or the unfulfilled. John in viewing men in much despair used "3½." Various forms of this incomplete figure are used by the seer: "3½," "forty-two months," "1,260 days," "a time, times, and a half time." These terms all have the same meaning. Without exception the "3½" (regardless of its form) stood for incomplete, dissatisfaction, that which is indefinite. The figure is used by John to signify the indefinite time the two witnesses preached, the trampling of the Temple, persecution of the saints, and the time of the church in the wilderness.

One further note should be observed: Is the book to be taken literally or symbolically? All interpreters take a large part of the book symbolically. For instance, there is no one who thinks the dragon of chapter twelve is a literal dragon, for all hold the dragon to be a symbol of something else. Amillennialists hold that not only some of the figures in the book are symbolical, but unless there is a clear indication to the contrary, all are symbols.[8] Revelation belongs to a peculiar type of literature known as "Apocalyptic." The nature of this particular form of writing is that it portrays truth in terms of symbols.

C.F. Wishart's warning, "Let him who is without his favorite speculation cast the first stone,"[9] should be kept in mind as an approach is made to interpret Revelation.

No attempt will be made to deal with every verse in Revelation, but on the other hand, no key verse will be slighted. Verses that weigh heavily in differences of interpretation will be given greater attention.

2

Prologue

1. Revelation, Revelation 1:1-3
2. Salutation, Revelation 1:4-8
3. Tribulation, Revelation 1:9
4. Manifestation, Revelation 1:10-18
5. Observation, Revelation 1:19, 20

Study Text: Revelation 1:1-20

Hopscotch was a child's game played on the sidewalks in North Carolina when this writer was a youngster. Children entertained themselves hours without end hopping, skipping, and jumping, being governed somewhat by the toss of a small piece of glass.

Strange as it may seem, some would-be Bible interpreters have tried to play a kind of mystical hopscotch with the Word of God. Too often the anxious expositor hastens on to a favorite Scripture that he might show his expertise in exegesis. Wanting to delve into the "meatier matters," he rushes by the key to the meaning. Such is the case of Revelation 1:1. Trying to give that never-heard-of explanation to that never-been-explained mystery, the first statement of the book is overlooked or ignored by the "let's-look-at Revelation-20 expert." The opening statement and the following three verses shed enough light to guide the serious student of Revelation through the difficult places.

Note: The opening statement is "The Revelation of Jesus Christ," not "The Revelation of St. John the Divine" as printed in the title of some versions. The Greek word is "apocalypse" (unveiling), and for that reason the book is sometimes called by that name. God authorized the unveiling to be shown unto His servants (persecuted saints of Asia Minor). Christ employed an angel who signified it (this shows the symbolic nature of the message) unto His servant John.

Two other significant statements in verse 1 pertaining to the unveiling are "The Revelation . . . which God gave" and "things which must shortly come to pass." Harry Buis states in reference to "which God gave": "In other words, the Father said to the Son, 'Go to John and bring him these visions.'"[10] Summers says, "This is a message which God gave to Christ to show or demonstrate to His servants."[11] God-given unveilings are not nonsensical. Always, a close study of that which God has given will bring a clear meaning. This God-given uncovering, to be shown by signs and symbols, was about "things which must shortly come to pass." The argument that this phrase means no more than "certainty" is untenable. Immediate, necessary, hasty action is called for in this statement. To dilute the meaning to "certainty" is to weaken the case for the first century Christians who were undergoing great persecution at the hands of Domitian. Telling them that the "things" would surely come to pass gave little comfort. But to tell them that God was going to do something soon helped them to bear persecution even if it meant death. And in most cases, it meant just that. They needed assurance of immediate help, not some by and by millennium in a far removed uncertain future. John was assured, and thus wrote, "Help's on the way, it will be here soon" (paraphrased). John bore record of the Word of God, which always makes sense, and the testimony of Jesus Christ the which the Holy Ghost will teach us (John 14:26). He recorded all things that he saw (Revelation 1:2), but not all things that he heard (Revelation 10:4).

There is greater significance in regard to the unveiling in the statement "the time is at hand," than some would like to admit. This is a restatement of the very truth that the message is a revealing of events that must of necessity take place soon. This in no way dictates that every minute detail of the book is to see fulfillment immediately. The time between the beginning of relief until the consummation was not revealed to John. It was not necessary for the saints to see that, but they did need to be assured about present relief and ultimate victory.

The Book of Revelation, written in the form of a letter, was addressed to "the seven churches which are in Asia [Asia Minor]." In all probability, it was written for a greater readership, yet it was written to the seven specified churches. Why these particular churches were chosen is not made known as there were other organized churches in the region at the time of the writing. Morris has suggested that John may have had special relations with the named churches.[12] He further suggests that if the seven were visited in order, one would travel in a circle. Since this is a figure of completeness and the number seven is the number of perfection, such cannot be considered without significance. Dr. Summers has written that the use of the number "7," which is the symbolical number of completeness, indicates that the book was for all churches of Asia Minor.[13] Possibly, these were representative of all the churches. There is no hint whatsoever that these churches represent seven periods of church history. It strikes this writer a bit comical for the dogmatic literalist who cries, "Revelation must be interpreted literally!" to then suggest that the seven churches should be viewed in a symbolic vein. John shows his close relationship to the churches by mentioning himself by name five times in the book–1:1, 1:4, 1:9, 21:2, and 22:8. It is as though John were staking his apostleship on the message as he nowhere mentions himself in any other of his writings. Striving to show Heaven's concern for their present plight, John tells the Christians that grace is pledged and peace is promised by the Trinity. God had not abdicated the throne; Christ was still alive, and the Spirit was still at work. The saints needed to hear that and "that right early." "And besides," John seems to be saying, "the faithful witness, the first begotten of the dead, the prince of the kings, hath made us a kingdom of priests that we might share with Him in His dominion forever." (Compare Revelation 5:10 and 1 Peter 2:9; in connection, also study Colossians 1:13.)

The apostle, being so caught up in the hope of early help and anticipating Christ's intervention into the present state of affairs, glances all the way to the final triumph and cries, "Behold, he cometh!" If only he could get the persecuted to look beyond it all to the coming "with clouds" (judgment), his mission would be accomplished.

Banished to the Isle of Patmos "for the testimony of Christ," John had already felt the oppressing hand of the emperor. The recorder wanted his readers to know that he was a brother (spiritual brother), a companion in the kingdom, with patience, facing the tribulation which had broken forth upon all Christians. The term "in tribulation" must not be passed over lightly. One must see the tribulation bearing heavily upon the churches and understand that this is why John is writing. He did not allow himself to be dominated by the inevitable threat that some far distant persecution would arise later and again affect the church.

"In the kingdom" means just that. John was in the kingdom– ...that comes not by observation (Luke 17:20); . . . is within man

(Luke 17:21); . . . is not of this world (John 18:36); . . . is not meat and drink (Romans 14:17); . . . is righteousness, peace, and joy in the Holy Ghost (Romans 14:17); . . . is at hand (Matthew 3:2); . . . that shall be delivered up, not established when Christ comes again (1 Corinthians 15:24); . . . the kingdom, the throne of which, Christ was raised to sit upon (Psalm 89:34-36; Acts 2:22-36). His reference was to Christ's Kingdom which is declared to be spiritual rather than materialistic.

Pieters suggests that the futurist should reckon with the rendering "He made us to be a kingdom" (verse 6).[14] Verses 6 and 9 are then in agreement, for in verse 9 John announces to the saints, "I . . . am your brother . . . in the kingdom." A singing cherubim in Revelation 5:10 vocalizes agreement with John's doxology–"Thou madest them to be unto our God a kingdom" (verse 6). Believers have been translated into the kingdom, echoes Paul in Colossians 1:13. So, since we have been translated into that kingdom, Christ is assuredly upon the throne of the kingdom.[15] First Corinthians 15:25 certifies the fact: "For he must reign, till he hath put all enemies under his feet." In the light of this clear statement of Scripture, it is annoying that some would turn it around to mean the exact opposite. Christ "must reign" until all enemies are put under His feet, not "begin" His reign when this takes place. In fact, He is to deliver up the kingdom to God the Father when He comes again at the end of His reign (1 Corinthians 15:23-28).

Consideration should be given to the following outline on this subject.

Christ is reigning and must reign until:

1. He comes again, verse 23
2. The end, verse 24
3. He shall have put down all rule and all authority and power, verse 24
4. He delivers up the kingdom, verse 25
5. He hath put all things under Him, verse 25
6. Death is destroyed, verse 26
7. He subjects Himself to God the Father, verse 28

John, in all that he says and sings in the two verses, declares Christ is King, He has a kingdom, we are in it, and He reigns.

Israel was told in Exodus 19:6, "Ye shall be unto me a kingdom of priests, and an holy nation." Though this was the stated purpose of their calling, it was never realized in them (Matthew 23:37, 38). That which was not realized in them is realized in those who believe in Jesus Christ. John speaks with all assurance that the fact is accomplished, "He made us to be a kingdom." Only those who will not see fail to grasp the truth of the spiritual kingdom (the very Kingdom of Christ) to which John had reference.

Two facts are significant concerning John's first vision: (1) He was "in the Spirit" and (2) it was "on the Lord's day." Mauro writes, "He was 'in the Spirit,' that is to say, he had passed out of the state of condition or normal consciousness, into the supernatural state wherein spiritual things are perceived."[16] Acknowledging that John was in the Spirit, one cannot help but believe that the manifestation to follow is to have a spiritual (symbolic, perhaps?) meaning.

Knowing that John was a pastor and realizing that he was exiled from his churches, it seems not unreasonable to assume that about the time of worship on the mainland, the apostle, though alone, began a worship service on Patmos. It was the Lord's Day–the day of worship. Some futurists hold that the statement "on the Lord's day" really means "the day of the Lord." John, according to them, was carried forward in the Spirit into some future time in order to see things that were to happen in the end. This writer holds with Mauro when he says that to interpret "the Lord's day" as meaning "the day of the Lord" the construction is strained; and the expression is a different one from that used to designate the day of the Lord everywhere else.[17] A quick glance at verses 5 and 18 should give a more precise understanding to the statement "the Lord's day." In verse 5 Christ is called "the first begotten of the dead," and in verse 18 reference is again made to Christ's resurrection. Resurrection day of Christ is the Lord's day. As one writer has stated, "It was so named not because of what the church should do on that day, but because of what the Lord did on it."[18]

A trumpet-like voice gaveled the service to order by declaring, "I am Alpha and Omega, the first and the last." Christ manifested Himself first in speech, then in person. He wanted the churches to know "I started it, I'll finish it. I had the first word and will have the last word." Having heard the voice behind him, John turns to see, and being turned he saw seven golden candlesticks with Christ the priestly King in the midst. One stands aghast at what various interpretations men may have given the candlesticks had not God's symbolic interpretation been given showing them to represent the churches.

Four phrases in these verses are illustrative of the manifestation of Christ.

(1) The word *golden* describing the candlesticks. With persecution rampant, tribulation breaking out on every hand, and their spiritual father exiled to Patmos, the believers were beginning to wonder, "Are we forsaken?" By using "golden," Christ was assuring them of their worth, their preciousness. He had not forsaken them for they were of great value.

(2) "In the midst of the seven candlesticks." In this Christ assures, "I am with you." It is as though He were reminding them of His promise, "Lo, I am with you alway" (Matthew 28:20), and of the fact of divine presence as seen in Mark 16:19, 20. Though in His kingly position in verse 19 (upon the throne), He was yet with the apostles (all of whom suffered martyrdom later) in their apostolic activity.

(3) "Out of his mouth went a sharp two-edged sword." That two-edged sword of course is the Word of God (Hebrews 4:12). The way that Christ was to wage war was "in righteousness" (Revelation 19:11). The implement of war to be employed was a sword; a very sharp sword that was to proceed out of His mouth (Revelation 19:15, 21).

(4) "And have the keys." With a touch from his Lord who had asked the question many years before, "If I will that he tarry till I come, what is that to thee?" John (and the reader as well) is told "Fear not . . . I am alive." Authority even over death and Hades were in the hands of Christ; He had conquered both through His resurrection. Because He was alive and well the churches could take hope.

Consider the symbolism employed in this manifestation of Christ. Our Lord was "clothed with a garment down to the foot, and girt about the paps with a golden girdle." His was the clothing of a priest and king. The writer of Hebrews points out in Hebrews 6:20 that Christ was " . . . made an high priest for ever after the order of Melchisedec." Luke informs us in Acts 2:30-33 that Christ was raised . . . to sit on his [David's] throne." That there be no miscalculations in the time of the raising to sit on the throne, Luke, in quoting Peter, wrote "He seeing this before spake of the [His] resurrection." When Christ became the High Priest after the order of Melchisedec, He likewise assumed His kingship. Melchisedec was "king of Salem . . .

and . . . priest of the most high God" (Genesis 14:18). When He served as priest, He ruled as king. To be after that order Christ must of necessity be both priest and king at the same time! The subjects of the kingdom (persecuted saints of Asia Minor) needed to know that Christ was still mediating their cause and holding dominion over the kingdom. A central thought rings out to them, "He lives, He lives!" He was raised–that makes Him alive; He was raised to sit on David's throne–that makes Him in authority. That was good news for the churches.

"His head and his hairs were white like wool, as white as snow," thus symbolizing His holiness. They needed to know that the holiness which demanded Calvary, saying "sin must be punished," was still in evidence. To confirm the fact, His holiness was speaking out anew saying, "There will be a just recompense of reward to those who rule ruthlessly now." "His eyes were as a flame of fire," symbolic of His vision that penetrated every scene. Nothing had transpired without His notice. He who took note of the sparrow's fall (Matthew 10:29), was also viewing the whole scene of the persecution. They were worth much more than sparrows. Christ's feet were like "refined brass," symbolic of His omnipotence. There was no stronger metal known to John's readers in that day. The Almighty strength (strength above all strengths) was portrayed. John wanted them to be assured of the final outcome. "Greater is he that is in you, than he that is in the world" (1 John 4:4). The "voice . . . of many waters" signifies His authority over all peoples. Oft in the Scriptures a multitude of people or mankind is spoken of in the symbol "water." In His right hand He held the stars which are interpreted to be the angels (pastors, messengers) of the church. Here divine protection, not so much for the messenger as for the message is seen. The messengers were protected in that they bore the message. In reality, the protection of the Word is seen. "Till heaven and earth pass, one jot or one tittle shall in no wise pass from the law, till all be fulfilled" (Matthew 5:18). One need not strain to hear the divine message coming from "in His right hand seven stars." The clarity of that message cannot be improved. The testimony that has exiled John to Patmos and brought the strong hand of the emperor in persecution upon the believers will be protected; it is in God's hand.

Out of the mouth of "one like unto the Son of man" went a two-edged sword. Having dealt with this previously, all that need be said now is that the sword is symbolic of His judgment. Summers points out that some interpret this to mean Christ's ability to protect His own.[19]

The countenance of the Lord was bright as the noonday sun. The "Almightiness" of God was being pledged for the support of His followers. Shining in full strength reminds us of His majesty and majesty of His Kingship and Kingship of His Reign!

John is commanded for the second time to write. He is told to write "the things which thou hast seen" (the vision depicting Christ as King/Priest in the midst of the seven golden candlesticks); "the things which are" (the seven churches and their various conditions); and "the things which shall be hereafter" (all that was to come to pass that would finally see the triumph of Christ and His Kingdom over all the opposing forces). Any doubt as to the division for "the things which must be hereafter" on the part of the student should be made clear upon reading Revelation 4:1b, for there John is invited, "Come up hither, and I will shew thee things which must be hereafter." Though he states it differently, Jay Adams holds to practically the same line of thinking.[20]

Long debate is unnecessary for the demise of the theory that the seven churches represent seven periods of church history. John was not invited to see "the things which must come to pass hereafter" until after the church letters were written. Thus, God Himself was announcing to John that the messages to the seven churches were not prophetic. If they were not prophetic, then by divine order the scheme to make the church represent seven distinct periods of history collapses. The point need be labored no further as God's Word is final on the issue.

By using the word "mystery" (and then giving explanation), Christ was informing John that a certain rule had been employed (in interpreting "the things which thou hast seen") for the true meaning of the vision to be understood. Also, Christ was giving hint to how "the things which are, and the things which shall be hereafter" should be interpreted. In clearing up the mystery, Christ showed that figurative language had been employed to bring forth a truth. Such was to be the case throughout the writing.

In summary, chapter one of Revelation shows the Living Lord in the midst of the churches, holding their destiny in His hand, calming their fears, and showing His authority through His kingly role.

3

The Letters

1. Ephesus, Revelation 2:1-7
   a. Action
   b. Analysis
   c. Assurance
2. Smyrna, Revelation 2:8-11
   a. Resurrection
   b. Resume
   c. Reward
3. Pergamos, Revelation 2:12-17
   a. Method
   b. Martyr
   c. Manna
4. Thyatira, Revelation 2:18-29
   a. Justice
   b. Jezebel
   c. Jubilation

Study Text: Revelation 2:1-29

The message of Revelation in its entirety was written for the seven churches mentioned in Revelation 1–3 (Revelation 22:6). Seven individualized messages, one for each of the seven churches addressed through their pastors, were written in chapters two and three. The messages are not a series of forecasts, predicting weather in the political arena of the world through the progress of history, but rather, a series of symbols and visions set forth in forms dear to the original readers–members of the local churches. A study of the seven churches will reveal why the particular things mentioned in the individualized letters were relevant to the churches addressed. Though the epistles were to be shared (as was the case of the Pauline Epistles), each carried a definite message to the church named. So much so that it is futile for an interpreter to make the personalized letters predictive. The view that these letters represented in prophetic forecast periods in church history was not found in the ancient church but was suggested by Joachim of Floris about the year 1200.[21] No serious exposition of this view is found among Protestants until Vitringa (he died in 1722) wrote a commentary in which he spelled out the church age scheme.

Archbishop Trench denounced the system with the following words, "The multitude of dissertations, essays, books, which have been written and are still being written, in support of this scheme of interpretation, remain a singular monument of wasted ingenuity." [22] Such men as Elliott, Swete, and Zahn said it was untenable, perverse ingenuity, and false.[23] This study is presented from the viewpoint that the seven churches listed by John were in fact seven, local, tangible, organized churches that were situated in the cities whose names they bore. Each letter is best understood when "presented against the historical background of the cities of the day."[24] The very conditions in the cities are reflected in what is said in the letters about the churches.

In dealing with the letters, not every statement will receive treatment as has been stated previously. Neither will space be given to elaborate descriptions of the cities where the churches were situated. The purpose of this study would not be served by such. Again, be assured that no Scripture bearing significantly upon the Amillennial view will be without exposition.

Paul organized the Ephesian church and remained there longer than at any other place, approximately three years (Acts 20:31). He later wrote an epistle to them in which he sheds light on some of the conditions existing in Ephesus at the time. Also, Tychicus delivered a message to the congregation on the behalf of Paul (Ephesians 6:21; 2 Timothy 4:12). Other outstanding leaders serving the church were Timothy, Apollos, and John.

When Paul spoke to the elders from Ephesus at Miletus (Acts 20:17), he warned that grievous wolves would enter in among them not sparing the flock. Continuing his warning, Paul prophesied that false prophets would arise from among the Ephesian Christians speaking perverse things and drawing away disciples after them (Acts 20:29, 30). When Revelation was penned, Paul's prediction was receiving fulfillment (Revelation 2:4, 5).

With the wolves of Paul's prophetic message baying at the door and circling the camp, God had a message for them.

What a plight! And what a time to be without a pastor! Wolves from without, false prophets from within, and first love gone–what were they to do? Or would more doing on their part turn the tide? Hardly. Even Heaven had taken note of "their works" and "labor," yet there was a threat of removal. The condition called for repentance, not more works on their part, and divine intervention.

Christ's action is seen in three areas:

(1) "He that holdeth the seven stars in his right hand" (symbol of strength). In the vision that John saw, Christ had in His right hand seven stars, but now He is depicted as holding the seven stars. Majestic action is symbolized. To be in His hand is protection–to be held in His hand is security. The message was coming through, "You are secure in divine protection." But neither the protection nor the security were to be viewed without conditions. "Remember–Repent–Return," or else.

(2) "Who walketh in the midst." Again the reader's attention is called to the vision in the first chapter. There John sees Christ "in the midst" (very present), but here he presents Him as active, "walketh in the midst." If "holdeth . . . in his right hand" symbolizes strength in protection and security for the believers, then "walketh" may very well symbolize judgment upon His enemies. The figure of God treading upon His enemies in judgment is found both in the Old and New Testaments. Such a thought surely blessed the Ephesians.

(3) "I know thy works." Christ had pledged His omnipotence–"right hand," His omnipresence–"in the midst," and now He speaks of His omniscience. But in speaking of His knowledge, He makes the church aware of the facts about themselves and the evil forces. Fervently caught up in works, orthodoxy, and burdens, the Ephesians were warned about the loss of "first love." Certainly He knew about the evil ones, the false apostles, and the Nicolaitans (against whom He would bring judgment), but He also knew the Christians. Even so, Christ pledged Himself.

A divine analysis of the church is given. Having observed their hard work, genuine patience, hatred for sin (evil), and orthodoxy (and all of this for His namesake), Christ still had "somewhat against them"–they had left their "first love." They had "not fainted," but they had left the love that they had in the beginning of the church. In calling this to their attention He may have very well brought to their minds Paul's teaching on love in 1 Corinthians 13, particularly those statements that bring out "and have not charity, I am nothing . . . and have not charity, it profiteth me nothing." Remembrance, repentance, and return are recommended as a three-fold remedy for their dilemma. Failure on their part to meet the requirements would bring the Lord quickly upon them in His wrath and judgment for He said, "I will come . . . quickly, and will remove thy candlestick." But note, please, He said, "Except thou repent." The renewed call to repentance is followed by commendation which surely must have encouraged them to hear what the Spirit had to say. In the sayings of the Spirit there was much assurance. Anticipating their repentance, they are assured, as overcomers, of eating of "the tree of life, which is in the midst of the paradise of God." With the pledge of life in the paradise of God, Ephesian Christians were strengthened to overcome.

In all likelihood, Christianity came to this city while Paul was preaching at Ephesus (Acts 19:1, 10). Paul may have established the church himself. Only Philadelphia held with Smyrna the distinction of not being censured in the letters. Polycarp, one of the church fathers and a disciple of John, was consecrated bishop of the church. Allusions to persecutions and the call for faithfulness unto death suggest that difficulties were facing them. Even so, such were to come from without, not from within.

Before exposing to the church all of the calamities that would befall them, Christ assures them of His "aliveness"–"These things saith the first and the last, which was dead, and is alive." Paul spoke of "the power of his resurrection" in Philippians 3:10. He also in that same verse connects "the fellowship of his sufferings" and conformity "unto his death." Power of the resurrection is promised in the address, but an awareness of suffering and death comes in the content. Being reassured of His resurrection, though approaching great stress, no thought but "faithfulness unto death" occupied their minds. Unmistakable persecution, distress, and affliction would be thrown in opposition to the Christian faith, but the church was not to think for a moment that God does not know or care what is happening. Poellot wrote, "'The first and the last, which was dead and is alive' literally 'became alive,' is the only, eternal, and everliving Savior, Jesus Christ."[25] Jesus died that all might live and lived that they might never die. Comfort was found.

A resume (more prophetic than actual) of the church is documented. Though brief (only four verses in the King James Version), it is complimentary where it deals with the church, rather than accusative. Actually, only two statements are made of the church in its present condition, but several events are dealt with prophetically; not to be fulfilled in a far distant future, but soon. God had taken cognizance of their works as in the case of all the churches, but in Smyrna "works" must have been in proper perspective and acceptable, else divine criticism would have been leveled. Alluding to their faithfulness, Christ said, "Be thou faithful unto. . . ." Faithfulness on their part was evident. Now they are challenged to remain faithful.

Tribulation and poverty were twin problems for the faithful. Perhaps martyrdom was as yet unknown in the local congregation, but it was just ahead. In time, their "angel" Polycarp was to suffer a martyr's death. How many others met like fate is not known. Poverty could have been better endured if tribulation had not struck at the same time. These contemporary menaces were to try their faithfulness, but the "Alive One" had said, "I know thy . . . tribulation, and poverty." Poverty in material substance was a constant companion. Very possibly, the Jews of "the synagogue of Satan" taunted the Messiah followers with their state of poverty. The membership roll was filled with those drawn from the lower rung of society. Refusing to worship the emperor, some had their property and "belongings" confiscated. All of these factors combined to make the church poor, literally. In all probability it was difficult for the members to secure gainful employment. Observing the church from God's viewpoint (same view held by the saved), Smyrnans were rich.

Blasphemy of the Jews along with the threatening persecution of Rome had caused some alarm, but He who could calm every fear said, "Fear none of those things." Suffering was to be their lot when thrown into prison for trial, but the tribulation was to be of short duration. Reward for unrecanting faith, "I will give thee a crown of life"—no emptiness here. Everything promised was as sure as His resurrection. He who had promised "I will arise the third day," was now saying, "I will give." He had introduced Himself as alive from the dead. Seeing He had arisen, they could rest assured He would give. These were ever consoled by the thought, "Our God raised Himself from the dead; no problem, regardless of the nature, is too great for Him." Escape from the second death and crowned with life was the greater goal that kept them steadfast in tribulation, poverty, prison, and suffering.

A royal city, Pergamos, like Ephesus, challenged Smyrna's claim to "first city" appellation. The first religious provincial temple built for emperor worship was in Pergamos. Temples and shrines built and dedicated to Athena, Zeus, and Aesculopius helped make it quite a "religious" city. Even though the Roman proconsul had been moved to Ephesus, its magnificent library relocated, and much of its ancient glory departed, the influence of that city had not come to an end by the time John penned the letters. She was the official capital of the province. Roman authority was even in evidence. Satan's seat (altar for emperor worship) was there constantly threatening adherents to the Christian faith. Life for a Christian in the Pergamos community was trying.

Romans knew one power–the power of the sword. Christ, the "Captain of the host," stood in readiness to battle with all of the opposing forces–Romans, Jews, and Satan. Brandishing a "two-mouthed," sword that was whet for action, Jesus appears on the spiritual scene to make war on the offenders. Implements of His warfare, like those of the Christian, "are not carnal, but mighty through God to the pulling down of strong holds" (2 Corinthians 10:4). Verse 3 of the same chapter, as well as verses 5-7, should be read carefully. A vivid picture of Christ alert for the fray may have caused the saints to rest their case in the promise of Isaiah 54:17, "No weapon that is formed against thee shall prosper; and every tongue that shall rise against thee in judgment thou shalt condemn. This is the heritage of the servants of the LORD, and their righteousness is of me, saith the LORD." The sword of His mouth (His Word–Hebrews 4:12; Ephesians 6:17; Hosea 6:5; John 12:48), not a "bloodletting instrument," was the weapon drawn. How contrary to all that He taught to picture Christ engaging in a literal "blood bath" war. Never did the Lord contradict Scripture by conducting Himself contrary to His teaching. While on earth, He proclaimed, "All they that take the sword shall perish with the sword" (Matthew 26:52). In the same Scripture one reads, "Put up . . . thy sword." As beleaguered troops pinned down by the enemy would welcome reinforcements, Christian citizens of Pergamos cheered at the thought of Christ wielding the sword.

A comrade in arms had fallen. Antipas, singled out for faithfully witnessing and called by name, had already been slain. Attention was called to their works, their dwelling, their loyalty, and their faithfulness. Willing to suffer martyrdom for the name they had held fast, but allowing Balaamites to remain in their fellowship, the church was called upon to "repent; or else." The "else" was spelled out to mean, "I will fight against them with the sword of my mouth." The same sword pledged for their support could quickly be turned upon them. This thought alone should dispel all ideas of Christ going into battle leading the saints with literal swords unsheathed. Remember, the sword is designed to cut both ways.

"Hidden manna" (figure for divinely provided, spiritual food with which loyal souls are nourished)[26] brings to mind the Lord's statement to His disciples, "I have meat to eat that ye know not of." Morris, on the subject of the promised manna, wrote, "The meaning is simply the believer who overcomes will receive celestial food not available to the world."[27] Linked with this promise of "bread from heaven," is a "white stone" upon which is inscribed, "a new name." Several suggestions have been offered as to the symbolism of the "white stone": (1) acquittal, (2) stone in the breastplate of the priest, (3) happy day, (4) a ticket for bread, (5) to reckon, (6) a good luck amulet, and (7) precious stone associated with manna. Some writers have admitted that they simply do not know what the white stone signifies. This writer believes that it conveyed some assurance of blessing.

Probably the best view is that the white stone (pebble) stood for acquittal and the black stone (pebble) for condemnation. Since white signifies holiness, ideally one would like for it to mean acquittal on the basis of holiness.

As to the new name, Isaiah 62:2 reads, "Thou shalt be called by a new name, which the mouth of the LORD shall name." New names in the cases of the Biblical characters suggested a change in standing or character. An overcomer was to be given a name that "no man knoweth." Here people have what is termed "pet names" for one another. Pet names are not in common usages because they are names of intimacy. Between the believer and God exists an intimacy which is of such a mystical nature that it is impossible to properly describe it to another. It is rather useless for the would-be interpreter to speculate what name will be on a stone, since it is stated no one knows except he who receives it.

Thyatira lay a little south of Pergamos. The hometown of Lydia, the seller of purple, was well known for purple dyes, other dyed goods, and its works in bronze. It was the smallest and least important of all the cities in which the seven churches were located.

Lydia was probably the individual used of the Lord to carry the gospel message into Thyatira. She had been converted under Paul's preaching at Philippi. Just when the church was established is not known. Neither do we know the size of the congregation. The longest letter of the seven was sent there. The message is weighty.

Christ is identified as "the Son of God, who hath his eyes like unto a flame of fire, and his feet are like fine brass." He is infallible (as God's only Son), omniscient (piercing eyes like flames of fire), and strong (feet as brass refined in service).[28] He was qualified to speak judgment; justice would be meted. For them to know He knew helped. For if He knew, they knew judgment would be measured.

Jezebel dominates the scene. In the main body of the letter, two verses (19 and 25) actually deal with the church. Had verses dealing with "that woman Jezebel, which calleth herself a prophetess" been deleted, the letter would have been cut in half and the reader would have considered the church ideal. But as one can see, the letter does not close when the Lord has completed His commendation in verse 19. Evils are present in the membership and must be condemned.

"Thou sufferest that woman Jezebel" was the divine indictment against them. Shielding one guilty of heresy was tantamount to condoning the evil. Several views have been fostered as to the woman Jezebel and her sin. Some interpreters have held that she was the wife of the local pastor! Others have taught that this is an allegory presenting the heresy which was persisting. Probably the better view is that there was a corrupt woman who held membership in the church. She was teaching and also claiming a kind of special revelation with mystic powers from the Lord. Jezebel, possibly, was the name given to the woman because of her activities which reminded those who observed Ahab's wife by the same name. In all probability, she was guilty of spiritual fornication rather than actual, because the statement "to seduce my servants to commit fornication" is connected with "and to eat things sacrificed unto idols."

Some might contend for the argument of actual fornication because of the Gnostic teaching. Whichever the case may be, she was seducing His servants and making them "her children" (followers). God announced that He was not going to permit her to continue with the evil practice in His church. Destruction was forthcoming upon Jezebel and her converts. Proof that God was still in charge of affairs and judging the works of men was the design in it all. No portion of the Scripture dealing with Jezebel can be misconstrued to mean the Roman Catholic Church as futurists would have one to believe.

"The rest of Thyatira" (those who had not known the heretical doctrine and the depths of Satan) were told that no greater burden would be put upon them. Christ then challenges them to hold fast until He arrives. Holding fast called for overcoming and the keeping of His works unto the end. McDowell states it simply, "His words are a reminder to the church of the ever-present possibility of the Lord's return. The reward for faithfulness is a share in the authority of the victorious Christ."[29] Other possible meanings to "till I come" and "unto the end" could be "until I come in judgment upon your enemies bringing aid in your plight" and "unto your personal end." "Unto the end" reminds one that the Christian life is not a battle but a campaign. Perseverance is important in the life of every believer.

The statements, "I will give power over the nations" and "he shall rule them with a rod of iron," should be given a spiritual interpretation. This writer agrees with *The Wesleyan Bible Commentary* writing on these statements: "The meaning can be seen as the final victory of truth of the gospel over evil and evil forces, with the saints as the chief agents of Christ in the decisive results."[30]

Jubilation must have reigned–Christ had promised them "authority over nations" (including Rome) and a "rule with a rod of iron." He further promised "the morning star." The "rod of iron" was the shepherd's rod, which was tipped with iron, used by the shepherd to guard his flock. Messiah rule is symbolized here. All faithful believers in Christ participate in the reign. Believers will share in all that the Father has apportioned to the Son. McDowell has suggested this possible meaning: "the morning star, brightest of the heavens, is a symbol of the greatness and glory of the Christ in which all those who love Him to the end will share."[31]

4
The Letters
(Continued)

5. Sardis, Revelation 3:1-6
   a. Control
   b. Caution
   c. Clothed
6. Philadelphia, Revelation 3:7-13
   a. Sovereignty
   b. Strength
   c. Signature
7. Laodicea, Revelation 3:14-22
   a. Witness
   b. Wretchedness
   c. Worth

Study Text: Revelation 3:1-22

Situated astride a mountain, Sardis lay about thirty miles southeast of Thyatira. Claiming the invention of the art of wool dying, it was a center of wool trade. Licentiousness and luxury were two of the things for which the city was noted. Past glory, rather than future promise or present accomplishment, seems to be the unstated theme illustrated so powerfully in the letter. The favorable geographical location proved to be her eventual downfall. A false sense of physical well-being because of the steeps brought the city under siege twice. Among the cities of Asia, none presented a more deplorable contrast–past greatness and present decline. Religious history of Sardis, like its civil history, belonged to the past.

The letter does not contain condemnation for immorality or heresies, but rather a denunciation for laziness and carelessness. The very character of the city of Sardis is seen in the church. Evidently, it had conformed to the world around it rather than being the transforming influence in the world it should have been. Like a careless man with an inherited fortune living only to revel in that which has been received, without any sense of responsibility or obligation to the community and attempting to make no investments or real security for the future of the estate, Sardis has been called "The Church of the Dead." And, so it was.

Christ is pictured in the salutation as being in full control–"He that hath the seven Spirits of God, and the seven stars." The expression "seven Spirits" tells of the plenitude of the divine spirit. His holding the seven stars is another reminder that the church belongs to Him. Sardis had conducted herself as if she had no obligation to higher authority.

Members of the congregation were called upon to be watchful. Even though outside disturbance had not reached through to them as yet, they were not to think that the position of the city would give them protection. Taking things easy and becoming slack would only further endanger them. "Strengthen the things which . . . are ready to die," He commanded. Their works had been found imperfect. Challenging the believers to "hold fast," Christ calls for remembrance of things received and repentance. Failure on their part to conform would bring swift judgment upon them. A warning is sounded, "If therefore thou shalt not watch, I will come on thee as a thief, and thou shalt not know what hour I will come upon thee." Twice, the city of Sardis had fallen to invading enemies. The city was situated on a high plateau over against steep walls. Thinking themselves secure, Sardians failed to watch every point on the wall. Because of their carelessness, the enemy scaled the wall and overran the city. Christ may have used this warning to remind the church people of those incidents. Failure to watch would bring Christ in special judgment upon them. His coming in judgment upon a careless church would be as unexpected as His visible Second Coming. Jesus employs language (which in the fullest sense describes the Second Coming) to describe a special coming in judgments on nations and churches. An example is to be found in the language applied by Christ in describing the judgment of God to be brought upon Jerusalem (Matthew 24). Though they were to be ever mindful of His coming and judgment day, this particular warning had to do more with a special judgment which would come upon them. Mute testimony, vindicating God's Truth in this warning, is found in the remains of the Christian church at Sardis. Spiritual watching on the part of the congregation at Sardis would have averted the sudden judgment.

The controlling Christ was cautioning them of careless conduct. Possibly the few in Sardis who had not "defiled their garments" had the same staying effect as the ten would have had, had God found ten righteous in Sodom.[32] Walking with the Lord in white is the promised outcome for the worthy. Whether "in white" means victory, purity, or festivity is not so important here. What counts is "they are worthy." Morris suggests, "For they are worthy does not mean that they have merited justification (some believe that white stands for justification), but that they have done nothing to forfeit it."[33] The worthy walkers in white, being overcomers, will not have their names blotted out,[34] but rather, confessed. Approaching persecution threatened their physical existence; the end of which would call for the removal of their names from the citizens' roll of the city. But their names would remain on God's roll as they would be confessed by Christ before the angels (Luke 12:8). Death to the Christians at Sardis possibly would come by the denunciation of their names, but real life (spiritual) would not be terminated as Christ would confess them. When Christ speaks up for a man, he is accepted.

The last stroke of the pen to Sardis is of hope and encouragement. Communication from God could still be received. One need only to open his ears to hear. John had recorded in his epistle (John 16:13) that the Spirit would guide into all truth. Here the church is once again assured that Heaven is still able to get a message to man when man is but willing to hear.

The city of Philadelphia (dating back to 159 B.C.) received its name from Attabus II, who won, because of his love for his brother, the epitaph Philadelphus–"brother-lover." Established as a center for the spreading of the Greek language, manner of life, and culture, it was from its beginning a "missionary city" for the promotion of loyalty and spread of the Hellenistic way throughout the land. Missionary enterprise of a Christian nature is found in the letter.

Smyrna was the "rich poor" church and Philadelphia was the "strong weak" church. The authority of King Jesus based upon His truth and holiness is pledged for their open door opportunity. That door stood ajar because of strength ("thou hast a little strength"), Scripture ("hast kept my word"), and steadfastness ("hast not denied my name").

The missionary enterprise in which they were to engage, backed by the authority of the king, was to be successful. Isaiah prophesied in Isaiah 22:22 that Christ would receive the authority of David, "And the key of the house of David will I lay upon his shoulder; so he shall open, and none shall shut; and he shall shut, and none shall open." How similar John's wording here, "He that hath the key of David, he that openeth, and no man shutteth; and shutteth, and no man openeth." Pay special attention to the fact that the prophet said, "He that hath [already in possession of] the key [authority] of David." For this reason, Christ could declare with all authority and assurance, "I have set before thee an open door." That door of evangelization was divinely set ajar because the church had but "little strength." Consciously aware of her weakness, she became the fitter object for witnessing power. Hers was to learn the lesson of Paul, who in 2 Corinthians 12:10 said, " . . . for when I am weak, then am I strong." Also, in 2 Corinthians 13:4 he stated, "For though he was crucified through weakness, yet he liveth by the power of God. For we also are weak in him, but we shall live with him by the power of God toward you." God's power, His Word, and His name always make for success.

Since God had left desolate the house of the Jews (Matthew 23:37, 38), those claiming kinship with the Lord other than by faith (Galatians 3:29) were to be branded as being of the synagogue of Satan (Romans 9:6). In that city at least some were to be converted—"I will make them to come and worship before thy feet." The missions opportunity was among the Jews in particular. Success crowned their efforts because the Jews were divinely made to know and to worship. But their conversions, though divinely wrought, were not apart from the faithful witness of the church which had kept the word of Christ (patience), that is, the Word of the passion and death of the suffering Messiah.

Because they had "kept," the Lord would "keep." The hour of temptation from which they were to be kept is not to be confused with the great tribulation of Matthew 24:21, the destruction of Jerusalem in A.D. 70, because Revelation was not written until A.D. 95 or 96. Fulfillment of Revelation 3:10 came during the persecution under the Roman emperors. A note of interest: The church at Philadelphia continued through the centuries surviving even the Ottoman invasion. It is said that the town still has a bishop and about one thousand Christian inhabitants. "I come quickly" was a great incentive to faithfulness and perseverance. It also offered consolation during the temptation. A double meaning has been suggested—"live in hope of my return" and "I am going to come suddenly in help and judgment." Probably the second thought is the clearer meaning here. He had promised, "I will keep thee," thus assuring them of His presence and power. Keeping them, in all probability, called for judgment upon the enemy. Anticipating His return, they were to hold fast what they had (a successful soul-winning enterprise) and "hang on" to the crown.

Pillars in the Temple of God were to be made of those who overcame. Upon those pillars were to be written the name of God, the name of the city of God, and the new name that Christ would have. The language employed here certainly is symbolical, and no contradiction is to be sought when considering Revelation 21:22, which tells that no temple will be in Heaven. John's point is that the overcomers will be forever, permanently situated in the presence of God. Philadelphia was subject to devastating earthquakes which plagued always the stability and security of its inhabitants. No greater promise could be made to the faithful than permanency in God's spiritual house and association with His name, not that of Caesar. "Go no more out" suggests protection as well as permanency. The elect safely shut up forever and the enemy shut out forever. No friend will ever depart from the city and no enemy will ever have entrance.

The name of God, the name of the city of God (which is the new Jerusalem), and Christ's new name were all to be written upon the overcomer. Many times the names of believers had been dropped from the rolls of the cities. No longer were they recognized as citizens. But no longer were they to be concerned about their names being removed from the rolls. Roman officials disclaimed the believers; not so with Christ. Their names were not only written down in Heaven, but Christ's name was to be written upon them. When Domitian's name would no longer strike fear and mean authority, the overcoming saints would be claimed by the Source of all authority and would bear His name.

Prosperity was the thing for which Laodicea was noted. Being situated at the junction of the Valley of the Lycees and the Maeander, and where three important roads intersected, the city of Laodicea more or less commanded the approaches to Phrygia. It was among the richest commercial centers in the world. Banking, manufacture of clothing from local black wool, and a medical school were boasted by the city. The church was probably established by the preaching of Epaphras (Colossians 1:7 and 4:12, 13). Archippus has been named as being the angel (bishop) of Laodicea. Some thirty odd years previously, Paul had admonished him about his ministry. It is supposed that he was the son of Philemon. Further mention is made of the church by Paul in his Colossian letter: "Salute the brethren which are in Laodicea . . . And when this epistle is read among you, cause that it be read also in the church of the Laodiceans; and that ye likewise read the epistle from Laodicea" (Colossians 4:15a, 16). Conditions in the city had greatly deteriorated in John's day. Of the seven churches addressed by him, Laodicea received the most severe condemnation. God had no words of praise for this church. Sardis had a few that had not defiled themselves, but no such redeeming fact is found here. Somehow the spirit of the city made its ways into the church. In each letter, things characteristic of the city were used to bring the message to the church. This is seen so clearly, thus making a church represent an age impossible.

Christ identifies Himself to the believers in the church of Laodicea as "the Amen, the faithful and true witness, the beginning of the creation of God." Just how this may have struck the minds of the members is not known, but this writer feels Christ was saying, "I will have the last say." Amen in this case is equivalent to the Truth. It is reminiscent of John 14:6–"I am the way, the truth, and the life." Summers writes,

> To Laodicea, an example of abject failure, He addresses Himself as One incapable of failure. The word "Amen" came from Hebrew to Greek to English untranslated. In its original meaning it carried the idea of nursing or building up. The derived use which has come down to us is that of something which is established positive.[35]

"Amen" was used by the saints at the conclusion of prayers and in giving assent to God's Word, but the Son only used "Amen I say unto you." This is language peculiar to the Lord, who being the Truth avers by Himself alone. "Amen I say unto you" is the New Testament equivalent to the Old Testament, "As I liveth, saith Jehovah." Christ's unchanging faithfulness (Hebrews 13:8) as the "Amen" stands in vivid contrast with the wavering of the "neither cold nor hot" Laodiceans. The stability of Christ (Truth) is held up before a weak church. Christ is shown to be the faithful and true witness because of His stability. Here in the beginning–here in the end–stable all the way seems to be the total picture. Christ created all things and by Him all things consist, "In the beginning was the Word, and the Word was with God, and the Word was God. The same was in the beginning with God" (John 1:1, 2). And also, "For by him were all things created, that are in heaven, and that are in earth, visible and invisible, whether they be thrones, or dominions, or principalities, or powers: all things were created by him, and for him" (Colossians 1:16). Though the church might cease and its witness fail, Christ would ever remain a true witness. Those concerned with the continuance of the truth could take hope.

Indifferent, but not altogether heartless, would best describe the membership of the church. There was no burning zeal for the cause of Christ; only warm affection–lukewarmness. Had they been cold it would have been easier for Him to have dealt with them. Also, in a cold state they would have come nearer discovering their real needs. Having stated their true condition and His intention to spew them out, the "Amen" points to the cause of the lukewarm condition–ignorance of their true condition. Thinking themselves to be rich, they were poor; thinking themselves to be clothed, they were naked; thinking themselves to have vision, they were blind. Laodicea, as has been pointed out, was well known for its banks, clothing, and medicine. Christ used the terms familiar to the people (this was characteristic of His earthly ministry also) to bring spiritual truths.

Calling for repentance, Christ rebukes them, yet assures them of His love. He then pictures Himself as being outside the church seeking entrance. The picture of Divine Concern–"Behold," Divine Condescension–"Behold I," Divine Patience–"I stand . . . knock . . . call," Divine Respect for the human will–"If any man will," Divine Entrance–"I will come in," and Divine Communion–"will sup."

Overcoming, even in the Laodicean church, was a possibility. Overcomers were promised positions with Christ upon the throne. Their coveted seats, if they overcame, were just as sure as His position upon the throne–"even as I also overcame, and am set down with my Father in His throne."

> Which he wrought in Christ, when he raised him from the dead, and set him at his own right hand in the heavenly places, Far above all principality, and power, and might, and dominion, and every name that is named, not only in this world, but also in that which is to come: And hath put all things under his feet, and gave him to be the head over all things to the church (Ephesians 1:20-22).

Christ's promise pertaining to the saints reigning with Him is reminiscent of 2 Timothy 2:12, "If we suffer, we shall also reign with him: if we deny him, he also will deny us." A definite change in the spiritual temperature would of necessity have to be effected if any of the membership overcame. Christ "outside the door" gives hint to their spiritual condition, but His standing, knocking, and calling speaks of their spiritual possibility.

During the earthly, personal ministry of Christ (before His death, burial, and resurrection), He told Zebedee's wife in regard to seats in the kingdom, "It is not mine to give" (Matthew 20:23). But now He says, "Will I grant to sit with me." The difference may lay in the fact that the mother of James and John requested that one sit on the right side and the other on the left (Matthew 20:21). On the other hand, Revelation 1:18 may hold the answer, "I am he that liveth . . . I am alive . . . Amen; and have the keys. . . ."

5

The Throne

1. The Open Door, Revelation 4:1-11
   a. Invitation, 4:1a
   b. Explanation, 4:1b
   c. Revelation, 4:2-11
      (1) Enthroned Sovereignty, 4:2, 3a
      (2) Emerald Sign, 4:3b
      (3) Elders Seated, 4:4
      (4) Eternal Spirit, 4:5
      (5) Enlightened Symbols, 4:6-10
      (6) Exalted Singing, 4:11
2. Closed Book, Revelation 5:1-14
   a. Held, 5:1-6
   b. Handled, 5:7, 8a
   c. Heralded, 5:8b-14

Study Text: Revelation 4:1—5:14

Another studious look at Revelation 1:19 is essential before going into an in-depth study of these chapters. "Write the things which thou hast seen, and the things which are, and the things which shall be hereafter." "The things which thou hast seen" has reference to John's first vision–Christ in the midst of the seven golden candlesticks; "The things which are" speak of the seven churches and their conditions; "The things which shall be hereafter" announce the beginning of the prophetic portion of Revelation.

"After this" simply means when the letters had been written. "After this," according to Buis, means "after Christ had finished dictating the seven letters, John sees this done."[36] Those who hold to the theory that the seven churches represent seven periods in church history (this theory was refuted earlier in this writing) would have one to believe that John meant at the end of the church age. Since chronological order cannot be successfully established in the Book of Revelation, one would do well to seek the true meaning apart from such systems. Chapters five and twelve will not fit into a chronological mold. Chapter five tells of a divine search (to be dealt with more fully in the chapter) for one who was able to loose the seals. That search at least in part was made before Paradise was moved from beneath. Otherwise, the statement "under the earth" would be without meaning. Chapter twelve deals with the birth of Christ and other significant happenings in His life, which will be explained when that chapter is taken up for exposition. So, without much difficulty the reader can readily see the futility of the chronological scheme. There are those who would object and would say, "Yes, but John saw (when called up to Heaven) 'things which must be hereafter.'" Bear in mind, John is seeing the Drama of the Ages unfold before his very eyes. Having seen an open door in Heaven, and having been called by a "trumpet-like" voice to come up, John arrives "immediately" in the spirit. Upon arrival, John sees the stage set. That which first unfolds when the action begins is a prelude to the "things which must be hereafter." Quite often this course is followed in modern play production. It is a kind of "filling one in" on what has transpired in order for the person viewing to understand the full drama. At any point in the drama, a "looking back" (in order to establish a scene) is in order. There are several such places in the drama as will be seen later. To begin the breaking of the seals, which in fact begins the "things which must be hereafter," without some background would confuse the understanding of the original readers. Chapters four and five serve as that background.

Up until now everything has been preparatory. At this point the main part of the "unveiling" begins. John, seated in the front row as a one-spectator audience, is about to witness the one and only showing of the drama. Before being called up to Heaven, John had been prepared on earth, though in the spirit, for the viewing. The vision of the living Christ in chapter one has helped in preparing John. The people for whose benefit the production is given have been described in chapters three and four. It is now time for the curtain to rise revealing the set stage.

John has already taken courage. While on Patmos his vantage point was not too good. A dark picture met his eye when he looked across the waters back to the mainland. But just prior to leaving Patmos for the Heavenly Theater, he was given a "sneak preview" of the happenings in Heaven—"a door was opened in heaven." Being called Heavenward, John realizes that he is going to see things from God's viewpoint. "Immediately . . . in the spirit," John is set for the duration of the special feature.

John's spiritual experience was intensified when he saw the throne and Him that sat upon it. The earthward vision had strengthened him somewhat because in many ways he and his readers were reassured that God still reigned and under no circumstances had God's throne been shaken by the threat of Domitian and others like him. But now "in the spirit," and in Heaven itself, John beholds his Lord on the throne; the victory is guaranteed. If there were intensity when John beheld the occupied throne, that intensity was intensified when he saw the holiness and righteousness symbolized by the jasper and sardius stones. Jasper stones are pure white and the sardius is blood red. But that is not all. There was a rainbow around the throne, in sight like unto an emerald. As the rainbow of promise in Genesis 9:12-17,

> And God said, This is the token of the covenant which I make between me and you and every living creature that is with you, for perpetual generations: I do set my bow in the cloud, and it shall be for a token of a covenant between me and the earth. And it shall come to pass, when I bring a cloud over the earth, that the bow shall be seen in the cloud: And I will remember my covenant, which is between me and you and every living creature of all flesh; and the waters shall no more become a flood to destroy all flesh. And the bow shall be in the cloud; and I wilt look upon it, that I may remember the everlasting covenant between God and every living creature of all flesh that is upon the earth. And God said unto Noah, This is the token of the covenant, which I have established between me and all flesh that is upon the earth.

The rainbow gave hope and symbolized God's mercy to Noah. It now serves the same purpose for John, his readers, and every believer. Rainbows, when viewed by man on earth, reach from earth to earth and speak only of an earthly promise, but the one beheld by John was "round about the throne"–there is no end. Eternal promises backed by throne authority are suggested by the unending Heavenly "emeralded" display. The awesome splendor of the holy, righteous God, arrayed in such dashing colors is seen as a reassuring token of hope and mercy in the midst of severe judgment. Punitive righteousness will deal with the enemies of God's cause, but "His own" can count always on His mercy and grace ever present, "The Lord is not slack concerning his promise . . ." (2 Peter 3:9). Also, "I have sworn by myself, the word is gone out of my mouth in righteousness, and shall not return . . ." (Isaiah 45:23).

Clothed with white raiment, wearing crowns of gold, twenty-four elders sat upon twenty-four thrones (seats) around the throne. They represent the twelve apostles of the New Testament and the patriarchal fathers of the Old Testament. Combining the redeemed of both periods into a common bond, declaring the destiny of triumph and God's glory, the twenty-four in all that they symbolize certainly signify victory. Such a scene speaks to John and the addressed. Twice during Christ's ministry among His apostles He thrilled them with the promise that they would reign with Him (Matthew 19:28; Luke 22:30). Here it is symbolized for all overcomers. This brings to mind the statements, "They lived and reigned with Christ" (Revelation 20:4) and ". . . They shall reign for ever and ever" (Revelation 22:5). Did Zebedee's wife know something about this when she asked, "Grant that these my two sons may sit, the one on thy right hand, and the other on the left, in thy kingdom" (Matthew 20:21)?

The awesomeness of the scene is heightened yet again when "lightnings and thunderings and voices" proceed from the throne. God's almighty power and His right to speak (judge) with full and final authority are symbolized. "Out of the throne proceeded" suggests that judgment was already in motion. There were seven lamps burning before the throne. They were "the seven Spirits of God"—the seven-fold Holy Spirit. Here once again the fullness and plenitude of the Spirit is symbolized. The picture portrays the Spirit as being ever watchful in heavenly happenings. God's people are pictured in verse four, and what God will do on their behalf is seen in verse five. The transcendency of God is symbolized by the "crystal sea." As viewed by John, the sea separated the transcendent God from His own, who through the blood of Christ had been redeemed. God wanted them home and they wanted to be home.

John wanted so much to be with his people. God showed the apostle that their situations were somewhat similar. But before the book closes, the sea is no more (Revelation 21:1), and God's people are in direct fellowship with Him. Another picture is yet seen. Persecuted Christians were separated from the Lord, but this would not always be the case. They could look forward to a grand home going.

"Four beasts" is better interpreted as living creatures, not "beasts" as in Revelation 13:1. The word is entirely different. Some interpreters see the four living creatures as representing attributes of God showing eternal vigilance for His own. They further suggest that together they symbolize God's eternal watchfulness. In Ezekiel 1:5 they are called living creatures, and in Ezekiel 10 the same beings are called cherubims. The better interpretation seems to be that the four symbolize the whole creation, wild animals, domesticated animals, man, and fowls of the air. Each of the creatures has six wings as did the winged seraphim of Isaiah 6:2. In that case one pair showed reverence, a pair signified humility, and a pair symbolized swift obedience. The viewer is to understand from this picture that God is sovereign and will bring all things in submission to Himself. Domitian may have by force and authority those who will worship him, but God in contrast will have all at His feet. The view that some hold in respect to the reign of Christ pictures Him as ruling by force. Force (other than through the Word and Spirit) is never applied by Christ in order to bring men in obedience unto Himself. This writer rejects any system of interpretation that shows Christ in a dictatorial authoritative position. Even where the Scriptures speak of Christ ruling with a "rod of iron" (Revelation 2:27; 12:5), one is not to see Him ruling through force, but rather should see Him as the Shepherd-King. This view will be dealt with in the discussion of chapter twelve.

The throne vision concludes with the doxology sung first by the creatures and then by the combined voices of the creatures and elders. What a choir! All creatures and all humanity joining to sing "glory and honour and thanks" to the ever-living Sovereign. Domitian would not live forever. Even the forced praise would cease. Mankind is seen in verse 10 as being capable of sharing a more meaningful worship relationship with God. The interpretation that beasts and elders represent all creation receives support in the closing words of the song, "for thou hast created all things."

A vast contrast exists between chapters two and three where the churches for the most part are described as being sinful, weak, and persecuted and in chapter four where a description shows the glory of God's dwelling place. Let it be said again, the purpose of the revelation is that the suffering saints might see "the unseeable" and take great encouragement.

God's sovereignty is the overshadowing theme of chapter four, and redemption through the blood of Christ is the main thought of chapter five. Chapter four shows us the Reigning Lord and chapter five the Redeeming Lamb.

The Patmos seer observes a book in the right hand of Him upon the throne (a roll of papyrus) written within and without and sealed with seven seals. "Upon the throne" shows the authority behind that which is written in the book. "In the right hand" signifies how well the message is guarded and how important it is. "Written within and on the backside" symbolizes the fullness of the message. "Sealed with seven seals" shows how securely the writing was sealed. The seven seals also suggest the complete secrecy of the contents of the roll. When considering the fact that the book was securely sealed, one cannot help but feel that the sealing indicates the impossibility of any person giving an explanation without divine help. There is no hint as to what was written, but there is reason to believe that the scroll was a full and complete statement of "the things which must be hereafter."

"A strong angel." Though he was strong, he did not attempt to break the seals, and there is reason. Opening of the seals did not have so much to do with strength as with worthiness. "Who is worthy?" is the lusty cry of the strong messenger; not "Who has strength?" A search had been made in Heaven, among the inhabitants of earth and beneath the earth. None were found able (worthy). History's greatest search had been made; "no man" was found. This brings to mind two Old Testament passages that tell of a divine search for a man, "I sought for a man . . . but I found none" (Ezekiel 22:30) and "Run ye to and fro through the streets of Jerusalem, and see now, and know, and seek in the broad places thereof, if ye can find a man . . ." (Jeremiah 5:1).

The duration of the search is not given. However, since no man preceded Christ into Heaven, "And no man hath ascended up to heaven, but he that came down from heaven, even the Son of man which is in heaven" (John 3:13) and "Whither the forerunner is for us entered, even Jesus, made an high priest for ever after the order of Melchisedec" (Hebrews 6:20), it is only reasonable to assume that that part of the search was not made until after the resurrection of Christ,

> Thy dead men shall live, together with my dead body shall they arise. Awake and sing, ye that dwell in dust: for thy dew is as the dew of herbs, and the earth shall cast out the dead.
>
> Isaiah 26:19

> And the graves were opened; and many bodies of the saints which slept arose, And came out of the graves after his resurrection, and went into the holy city, and appeared unto many.
>
> Matthew 27:52, 53

> Now that he ascended, what is it but that he also descended first into the lower parts of the earth? He that descended is the same also that ascended up far above all heavens, that he might fill all things.
>
> Ephesians 4:9, 10

If this be true, then that part of the search that concerned beneath the earth had to take place before His resurrection. Those who died in faith prior to Christ's death, burial, and resurrection, received not the promise:

> These all died in faith, not having received the promises, but having seen them afar off, and were persuaded of them, and embraced them, and confessed that they were strangers and pilgrims on the earth.
>
> And these all, having obtained a good report through faith, received not the promise: God having provided some better thing for us, that they without us should not be made perfect.
>
> Hebrews 11:13, 39, 40

If at death the Old Testament saints did not obtain the promise, that heavenly better country, the prepared city (Hebrews 11:16), then where were they until "God . . . provided some better thing for us, that they without us should not be made perfect" (Hebrews 11:40)? The answer is found "here . . . and there" in a "line upon line" process (Isaiah 28:10).

When the believing thief was dying on the cross, he requested, "Lord, remember me when thou comest into thy kingdom. And Jesus said unto him, Verily I say unto thee, To day shalt thou be with me in paradise" (Luke 23:42, 43). On the morning of Christ's resurrection He told Mary, "Touch me not; for I am not yet ascended to my Father..." (John 20:17). If He had not ascended, then He must have descended.

> Now that he ascended, what is it but that he also descended first into the lower parts of the earth?
>
> Ephesians 4:9

> For Christ also hath once suffered for sins, the just for the unjust, that he might bring us to God, being put to death in the flesh, but quickened by the Spirit: By which also he went and preached unto the spirits in prison.
>
> 1 Peter 3:18, 19

Remember, He told the thief, "To day shalt thou be with me in paradise." Paradise was below (Hadean world) until the resurrection. Study carefully the story of Lazarus and the rich man in Luke 16:19-31. Only a great gulf was between (Luke 16:26). All of these Scriptures will be treated more in detail when Revelation 20 is explained. At some point in history God searched the earth for a man. Suffice it to say, John in the vision saw the search whenever and wherever it was made and "no man . . . was able to open the book." Asia Minor's distinguished prophet yearned to know the secrets of the book. He must have sensed that in the book the destiny of man was penned. His burdened soul could bear no more; he wept. Crowding his mind must have been thoughts like, "Here is the message so desperately needed by the oppressed churches," but "no man was found worthy to open and to read the book, neither to look thereon." That was cause for weeping! John (as they would say in North Carolina) did not just tune up for crying, but bawled! He wept much. One of the elders knew the next scene and for that reason told John, "Weep not: behold, the Lion of the tribe of Juda, the Root of David, hath prevailed to open the book, and to loose the seven seals." Looking through his tears, the prophet sees in the midst of the throne a Lamb who had overcome death. What? The elder said, "The Lion of the tribe of Juda," but John sees a "Lamb." What significance is to be seen in this symbolism? The Lion represents bravery and strength. That He is standing suggests readiness for action. Having overcome death, He is ready to take on every foe. The Lamb represents meekness and goodness. But let there be no mistake about the Lamb in regard to His power and ability. Power is signified by the horns. Seven denotes that all power (Matthew 28:18) was given unto Him. Already interpreted for us, "seven eyes" represent the seven spirits which signify the Holy Spirit. Two Scriptures are of interest: Prophetically–"The Spirit of the Lord God is upon me . . ." (Isaiah 61:1); Vindicative– " . . . for God giveth not the Spirit by measure unto him" (John 3:34). Perfect omniscience (all-knowing) is also symbolized in the seven eyes.

Who but Christ could approach the throne and take the book?! Every living thing "in the midst" had a part to play, but only the "worthy" could assume this all important role; no stand-in here. Only the two-titled person (Lion-Lamb) could perform now. Dramatically, with an unhesitant attitude and a strong spirit of determination, all of a sudden the Worthy takes the book right out of the hand of the throne occupant. Man's destiny was sealed in that gesture. How fitting the carrying forward of God's judgment upon the wicked and the ultimate victory of the saints in the nail-scarred hands. At the moment the book was lifted, Heaven's reaction was manifested by the living creatures and the elders. Again Heaven was made to ring with singing. A new song entitled "Worthy is The Lamb" was introduced. Each singer came off his throne to take position at the harp which he played as he sang. Listen closely. Pick up those words that compose the anthem of redemption,

> Thou art worthy to take the book, and to open the seals thereof: for thou wast slain, and hast redeemed us to God by thy blood out of every kindred, and tongue, and people, and nation; And hast made us unto our God kings and priests: and we shall reign on the earth.
>
> Revelation 5:9, 10

"Out of every kindred, and tongue, and people, and nation" gives credence to the view that the elders in fact represent all of the redeemed from both testamental periods. Here is just another example of the book interpreting its own symbolism.

Worthiness of the Lion-Lamb Savior is seen in His redemptive work in the words of the song. Summers suggests that the redemptive work is described by four terms:

1. It is for God, primarily–"thou didst purchase unto God."
2. It is through Christ's blood–"thou wast slain . . . thou didst purchase with blood."
3. It is unlimited–"men of every tribe, and tongue, and people, and nation."
4. It makes the redeemed a kingdom–"and madest them to be unto our God a kingdom and priests; and they shall reign upon the earth." As men partake of the redemptive work of Christ, they become parts of God's kingdom; they become priests to serve Him here in the world.[37]

Of "and they shall reign upon the earth" Poellot says, "Millennialism? No! This does not mean that the Church will exercise a physical rule over this present earth with Christ for 1,000 years. A thousand years are not mentioned in this passage, and we should not read them into it."[38] He holds that "shall reign" points beyond even the spiritual reign which the saints exercise on the present earth, to the more glorious rule which shall be theirs on the new earth of Revelation 21:1. At any rate, no physical reign for a spiritual people.

Angels, living creatures, elders, and a numberless host blend their voices loudly to sing the second verse. When the third stanza is sung, "every creature" from all over creation reaches close harmony. Honor, glory, and power are accorded Heaven's authority and the Lamb. Without ability to restrain themselves longer, the beasts shout, "Amen!" and the twenty-four elders become prostrate.

This scene brought new courage and new hope to the hearts of John's original readers, the persecuted Christians of Asia. Such has brought cheer to the hearts of Christians in every age. Three things were made perfectly clear: (1) God is mightier than all His foes. He has never scheduled defeat on His agenda; (2) God had not laid aside His scepter; (3) God had not abandoned the throne.

6

The Seals

1. First Seal—White Horse and Rider
   Symbolism—Conquest, Revelation 6:1, 2
2. Second Seal—Red Horse and Rider
   Symbolism—Warfare, Revelation 6:3, 4
3. Third Seal—Black Horse and Rider
   Symbolism—Hunger (Famine), Revelation 6:5, 6
4. Fourth Seal—Pale Horse and Rider
   Symbolism—Pestilence, Revelation 6:7, 8
5. Fifth Seal—Martyrs
   Symbolism—Persecution, Revelation 6:9-11
6. Sixth Seal—Earthquake
   Symbolism—Judgment, Revelation 6:12—7:17
   Protection, Provision, Promise for 144,000
7. Seventh Seal—Silence
   Symbolism—Transitional, Revelation 8:1

Study Text: Revelation 6:1—8:1

Keen of hearing, sharp of vision, Prophet John misses nothing. He states, "I saw when the Lamb opened one of the seals." Thereupon he heard one of the beasts in a thunderous voice say, "Come and see." Ancient manuscripts have variation on this reading. According to some authorities the better rendering would be "come." It would appear that this would better suit the scene. "Come and see" seems to leave one with the idea that the "living creature" was calling upon John to action and sight. However, John was already beholding the action. In all probability the call was for the rider to "come" across the stage of action that he might portray his message in pantomime. There were no lines spoken and no action engaged other than riding across the stage. That it makes much difference is doubtful, but the latter suits the case.

At the signal, a man with a bow rode a white horse into view. He was forthwith crowned and rode victoriously. Identity must be found in the color of the horse and the description of the rider. Three popular views of the first horse and rider are held among Amillennialists. Some hold that the man on the white horse represents Christ, or at least the cause of Christ. To them the color of the horse would suggest purity, the crown royalty, and the bow represents the instrument to be employed in warfare. There are two weaknesses in this theory. This horse marches the same direction as the others–an odd position for Christ. And too, it would be crude to have the Lamb breaking the seal (drawing the curtain) and then quickly changing into the garb of what appears to be that of a Parthian soldier.

Another view is that the "horse, rider, and what is said of him, are a composite symbol," in which is set forth "the whole Word of God as Jesus speaks of it in John 12:48."[39] Those holding this persuasion see Christ the incarnate Word playing the role of drawing the curtain while the inspired Word rides.

The third view, held by this writer and others, sees the first horse and rider representing conquest through military strength. White, the color of the horse, signifies victory. White horses were ridden by a conqueror on the returning, victorious march. One of the forces to be used by providence against the Roman strength is symbolized in this horse. Rome had no enemy she dreaded more than the Parthians. Crowns, being hated by the Romans, were not worn by her emperors. Coins have been discovered that pictured riders wearing a crown, holding a bow. God's method of destroying mighty Babylon (Rome) was manifold, but one sure instrument was outside military conquest. Victory was coming and the persecuted could see it when they had the privilege to read John's inspired writing.

War and bloodshed are symbolized by the fiery red horse and his rider who are summoned to ride. Naturally, the red horse (war and bloodshed) follows the white one (militarism). Again, no words are spoken by the rider. The color of the horse, the power of the rider, and a sword help in identification.

"To take peace from the earth" was the power given the rider. Peace is taken from the earth when men "kill one another." The "great sword" given unto him when added to all of the other details gives the identity as war.

The third living creature speaks and a silent rider astride a black horse moves into the view of the seer. He holds a pair of balances (strange equipment for a horseman) in his hand. This horseman represents famine. As he rides, from out of the midst of the four beasts rises a voice saying, "A measure of wheat for a penny, and three measures of barley for a penny; and see thou hurt not the oil and the wine." Prices announced were not starvation prices, but were famine prices. At the time, the very necessities (wheat and barley) of life would be almost out of economic reach of the poor; the luxuries (oil and wine) of the rich would be in abundance. Just as naturally as war and bloodshed follow militarism and conquest, famine follows war. Various commentators have called attention to the fact that during the reign of Domitian, emperor of Rome, an attempt was made to curtail the production of oil and wine. Vineyards were uprooted in order that more wheat and barley might be planted. Pressure by popular demand caused the emperor to change his policy. Wine was to be in abundance but bread was to be scarce and expensive. Domitian's attempt in the face of God's decree was futile. One of the things that helped bring about the downfall of Rome was drunkenness.

The voice of the fourth living creature called for the next rider just off stage to ride. There should be no speculation about this man; his name is death. See the parade of horsemen–militarism, war, famine, and death. Hell followed close behind. To the rider of the pale horse was given power over a fourth part of the population. A fraction of the people were to die. Death was to come by the sword, starvation, pestilence, and wild animals. By announcing the fraction of the population that would experience death through the designed calamities, God was saying in effect, "I set the limits; I draw the lines of boundary." David's words in Psalm 76:10 fit well the above, "Surely the wrath of man shall praise thee: the remainder of wrath shalt thou restrain."

When the curtain is drawn on the next scene, the "slain for the word of God" are seen under the altar crying loudly. With the opening of the fourth seal the symbolism changes. Horses and riders showed the means of judgment; this scene gives the reason for that judgment–martyred saints. These martyrs are from the persecution of Domitian in particular, and Rome in general. Antipas, a faithful member of the church at Pergamos, was called by name in Revelation 2:13. How many died under Domitian's reign is not factually known, but history records many. "How long, O Lord, holy and true, dost thou not judge and avenge our blood on them that dwell on the earth?" Critical commentary has been written about the cry of the souls under the altar. Please notice that the souls are crying from under the altar. That is where the blood of the sacrifice was poured out. Could it be that each crying soul had not so much himself in mind, but maybe the other martyr when crying, "How long . . . dost thou not judge and avenge our blood"? A careful study will reveal that the cry for revenge rests upon God's holiness and truth. The holiness of God demands that wickedness be judged. This fact was well known to the crying saints. Also, they were saying, "God, you speak truth, and your truth proclaims judgment upon wickedness." The inevitable was to come. These wanted to know when. Receiving a well-deserved rest, the martyrs in white robes of purity learned that others would soon be joining their ranks. Here again the Apocalyptist, as in every series of sufferings, introduces encouragement for the believers. God's vindication of the right and His punishment of evil were not to be affected by the pleadings of the slain. As they had intimated in their supplication, God's holiness and truth would accomplish judgment. Earthlings as well as Heaven's citizenry may sometimes feel that God will not judge because of the lapse of time. But wait! What is written? "Because sentence against an evil work is not executed speedily. . . . " This partial Scripture (Ecclesiastes 8:11) gives us to know that sometimes judgment is not soon coming according to man's time, but it will come. A promised disciplinary action delayed by the writer's father only tended to make the judgment more dreaded. Those on earth's side yet to be martyred could see in time, upon reading John's account, just what they could expect beyond death.

Typical apocalyptic language is employed when the sixth seal is opened. Symbolism is not to be swept aside here in favor of a literal interpretation. Old Testament passages predicting judgment and great events by use of the same symbolism abound. A well-known example:

> And it shall come to pass afterward, that I will pour out my spirit upon all flesh; and your sons and your daughters shall prophesy, your old men shall dream dreams, your young men shall see visions: And also upon the servants and upon the handmaids in those days will I pour out my spirit. And I will shew wonders in the heavens and in the earth, blood, and fire, and

> pillars of smoke. The sun shall be turned into darkness, and the moon into blood, before the great and the terrible day of the LORD come. And it shall come to pass, that whosoever shall call on the name of the LORD shall be delivered: for in mount Zion and in Jerusalem shall be deliverance, as the LORD hath said, and in the remnant whom the LORD shall call.
>
> Joel 2:28-32

Pieters makes this comment on the above Scriptures:

> These are familiar expressions for great and terrible events. St. Peter said that the prophecy of Joel 2:28-32, from which the forms are partly taken, was fulfilled on the day of Pentecost, (Acts 2:17-21). Although on that occasion there was no blood or fire, or vapor or smoke, neither was the sun turned into darkness, nor the moon into blood. So we see that they are not to be taken literally, but as symbolizing the overturning of all that hitherto has been considered most firm and unshakable.[40]

Christ employs similar language in Matthew 24:29-31 when He tells of the judgment that will be brought upon the Jewish nation,

> Immediately after the tribulation of those days shall the sun be darkened, and the moon shall not give her light, and the stars shall fall from heaven, and the powers of the heavens shall be shaken: And then shall appear the sign of the Son of man in heaven: and then shall all the tribes of the earth mourn, and they shall see the Son of man coming in the clouds of heaven with power and great glory. And he shall send his angels with a great sound of a trumpet, and they shall gather together his elect from the four winds, from one end of heaven to the other.

Marcellus Kik states,

> The above portion of Scripture employs such strong and vivid language that many think it can be descriptive of nothing else than the end of the world and the Second Coming of Christ. These descriptive terms would seem to indicate a catastrophic end of the earth. And yet, when this passage is studied in the light of prophetic language and pronouncements, it can readily be seen that it is descriptive of the passing away of Judaism.[41]

Apocalyptic language was used in the Old Testament Scriptures to describe national disasters. When disaster hung low over Idumea,

Egypt, and Babylon, the prophets employed this type of language (Isaiah 13:10; 34:4, 5; and Ezekiel 32:7, 8).

Some hold that this is symbolical of the final judgment. Others see each vision complete in itself and covering the field of activity. That particular idea is called "The Recapitulation Theory." The writer holds somewhat to this idea, yet cannot help but see judgment being brought to bear upon certain enemies and in a way sweeping the reader along to thoughts of final judgment. As John sometimes hastened on to say "He is coming," he also rushed on to show judgment. Judgment is pictured however one may view the total scene. Arguments can be propounded against this being literally the final judgment. For instance, time marches on as one can very well see when the seventh seal is opened. Also, there will be no hiding place at the Second Coming and judgment. The idea, "the great day of his wrath is come" comes from those calling for the rocks to fall upon them, not John. Such calamity was to be of such nature that those caught up in it would think for sure the end had come and judgment was set. The judgment pictured in the symbolism when the sixth seal was opened does not bear fully the character of final judgment. Here the kings of the earth and others hid themselves and pleaded for death. The judgment is characterized by the resurrection of the dead and their appearance before the judgment seat. History is still in process when the seventh seal is opened.

Though the Scripture does not deal with it, a question must have been raised in John's mind. "What about the saints, when judgment is poured out?" The prophet had seen militarism, war, famine, pestilence, and natural calamity move against God's enemies; he could not help but wonder about the believer. Of course, he knew some were yet to die for it had been said "that they should rest yet for a little season, until their fellowservants also and their brethren, that should be killed as they were, should be fulfilled" (Revelation 6:11).

It has been seen that there were times when a scene swept the thoughts of the reader to the end of symbolical language. It has also been seen that there were times when the scene opened that there was a bringing up to date; a fill-in; a calling to remembrance that the particular scene might have proper background. Just such a thing is now employed in order that the question, "What will happen to the saints?" be answered. God could best show what would happen by showing what had happened. The 144,000 were to be the example. This called for a looking back. When one looks back, he sees judgment being held back until something is done for the servants of God. One could then see just what was going to be when judgment was unleashed upon the wicked. As God had done something for the Old Testament saints (represented in the number sealed of the twelve tribes), He would do something for those on earth during the day of His wrath.

In this vision, John sees four angels standing on the four corners (points of the compass) of the earth holding back the winds which symbolize retribution. Old Testament Scriptures picturing wind as judgment are numerous (Job 38:24; Isaiah 41:16; Jeremiah 4:11, 12; 18:17; 49:32, 36; and Ezekiel 5:2; 12:14).

Another angel came into the prophet's view crying to the four, "Hurt not the earth . . . till we have sealed the servants of our God in their foreheads." He ascended from the east and bore the seal of the living God. One hundred and forty-four thousand were sealed in their foreheads; twelve thousand out of every tribe. McDowell wrote, "It is possible, of course, that he is describing in apocalyptic imagery here the safety of the Jews who have 'come out from their tribes' to be the elect of God."[42] Sealed with God's seal, they are protected and secure, not from physical injury, but are rather secure in the protection they have received for their immortal souls from God's hands. The number 144,000 suggests completeness. In Jewish religious thought, the figure 12 was the symbol of organized religion in the world. There were twelve apostles, twelve tribes, and twelve gates. When the writer of the Apocalypse wanted to picture the security of the perfect number sealed, the number 12 was reduplicated to 144,000.

With the picture of the sealed from the past well-fixed in his mind, John looks again and this time sees a great multitude which no man could number. These came out of every nation, kindred, people, and tongue. A definite distinction can be seen between the two groups in that the 144,000 were from the tribes, and the multitude was from all nations. John was now seeing that host that would make it all the way to heavenly victory. They "stood before the throne, and before the Lamb, clothed with white robes, and palms in their hands" (Revelation 7:9).

"Salvation to our God which sitteth upon the throne, and unto the Lamb" (Revelation 7:10) is the song sung by the multitude. Two things are made evident in the song: They knew from whence came their salvation, and they knew the whereabouts of their Savior.

Christ was not seen upon the throne in some far-removed future, but was presently upon the throne. Angels, living creatures, and elders prostrated themselves and worshiped while the choir sang of salvation. Furthermore, they broke forth into praise saying, "Blessing, and glory, and wisdom, and thanksgiving, and honour, and power, and might, be unto our God forever and ever. Amen" (Revelation 7:12).

At this point, one of the elders asks John about those arrayed in white robes. Since the prophet gave no concrete answer, he was told by the inquiring elder that "these are they which came out of great tribulation" (Revelation 7:14). When one sees them before the throne with no adversity, but rather Christ in their midst leading them unto fountains of living waters, he is prone to sing, "Heaven will surely be worth it all."

What tenderness is seen in the statement, "God shall wipe away all tears." God had seen them in great tribulation; He knew their hunger, thirst, and suffering. Much controversy has been gendered over the term "great tribulation." But when it is understood that the tribulation brought to bear upon the Jewish nation was "such as was not since the beginning of the world to this time, no, nor ever shall be" (Matthew 24:21), one looks for a meaning other than some supposed great tribulation to be before the end. Josephus, the reputable Jewish historian, when speaking of the destruction of Jerusalem, gave testimony of suffering at the time as being unbelievably horrible. Others believe that since the innumerable host represents all Christians, the "great tribulation" spoken of symbolizes what every true believer must pass through. It is the earthly personal experience of the people of God–all of God's people. "We therefore take the expression 'the great tribulation' in Revelation 7:14 to mean the suffering through which the children of God in all ages pass before they enter into the eternal kingdom of God."[43] "Yet if any man suffer as a Christian, let him not be ashamed; but let him glorify God on this behalf" (1 Peter 4:16). "Yea, and all that will live godly in Christ Jesus shall suffer persecution" (2 Timothy 3:12).

7

The Trumpets

1. Introduction to the Sounding Trumpets, Revelation 8:2-6
2. First Trumpet, Revelation 8:7
3. Second Trumpet, Revelation 8:8, 9
4. Third Trumpet, Revelation 8:10, 11
5. Fourth Trumpet, Revelation 8:12
6. Flying Angel (eagle), Revelation 8:13
7. Fifth Trumpet, Revelation 9:1-12
8. Sixth Trumpet, Revelation 9:13-21
9. Intermission, Revelation 10:1-11

Study Text: Revelation 8:2—10:11

Seal number seven when opened brings silence in Heaven. It is transitional. Zephaniah gives the command to be silent in the face of God's judgment, "Hold thy peace at the presence of the Lord GOD: for the day of the LORD is at hand: for the LORD hath prepared a sacrifice, he hath bid his guests" (Zephaniah 1:7).

Literalists have trouble at this point, for here is an illustration of the impossibility of a literalistic interpretation of Revelation. In a previous passage it is stated that in Heaven they never cease to praise the Lord, but here it is said, "there was silence." A dramatic effect is the purpose of this silence. The half-hour signifies a comparatively short period of time. This "holy hush" is brought about because of the expectancy on the part of all wondering what now shall take place when the remaining contents of the scroll are revealed.

A new series of visions begins with the seventh seal. Seven (ready-for-action) angels appear and to them were given seven trumpets. When every possible meaning is expounded, one cannot help but see the full message of God's judgment signified in the symbolism. Before the seven "prepared themselves to sound," another angel claims John's attention. There seems to be a singular purpose in the appearance and activity of this angel. The prayers of all the saints had been heard and God was now going to answer. That God had received their prayers is seen in the expression, "and filled it with fire of the altar, and cast it into the earth." All that was going to transpire when the seven trumpets sounded may be foreshadowed in the vivid symbolism of verse 5. Anxious saints wanted an answer, Revelation 6:10. As if in one angelic gesture, God says here is the answer. With full confidence that God will pour full judgment upon the wicked, John listens to the sounding of the trumpets and observes the activity.

Just as there was a definite relationship between the first four seals, there is a noticeable connection between the first four trumpets. Verse 13 of chapter 8 makes the distinction between the first four trumpets and the last three. "And I beheld, and heard an angel [eagle] flying through the midst of heaven, saying with a loud voice, Woe, woe, woe, to the inhabitors of the earth by reason of the other voices of the trumpets of the three angels, which are yet to sound!"

When do these judgments occur? The method of interpretation followed by this writer would dictate that they fell upon the Roman Empire initially. Rome was persecuting the church at the time John beheld these visions. Waiting in silent expectation, the heavenly host has this question in mind, "What will the trumpets announce?" Trumpets were generally used to give an order to charge, announce things, and summon armies. Whatever the purpose of the silence, whether it symbolized delayed judgment (rest yet a little season until . . .), or dramatic effect, blasting trumpets broke it.

Hail, fire, and blood followed the sounding of trumpet number one. As is illustrated in the prelude to the sounding, these three elements as though they were one are cast upon the earth. A third part of the trees was burned and all of the grass of that third part was burned likewise. Just here, Summers cautions against looking upon these events as a prediction of literal events which are to take place and destroy one-third of everything.[44] In no way is this to be looked upon as final judgment. Only one-third of everything touched is destroyed. Partial judgment to warn wicked and perverse men is the true meaning here. One-third was simply a conventional way of saying a large part. "The hail and fire and blood are not to be taken as symbols of separate disasters, spiritual or material. Taken together they symbolize destruction wrought by nature upon the earth."[45]

A volcanic eruption takes place when the second angel sounds. A series of natural calamities causing disaster over the Roman

Empire was one of the reasons the empire was broken down. There were earthquakes, volcanic eruptions, and floods. History records a devastating eruption that took place at Mount Vesuvius in August, A.D. 70. Pompeii and many other villages were engulfed. It is said that ashes from the burning mountain (volcano) fell on ships at sea and upon the shores of distant nations. Avalanches of fire were sent down the mountainside into the sea. John had remembered these things. God possibly had already begun His judgment against Rome even at that early date. Other similar eruptions had taken place. Fiery blasts had destroyed vegetation and the sulphurous vapors had killed fish. The water had been described as like blood. Such things were in the minds of John's readership. Judgment at the sound of the first trumpet fell upon land. At the sounding of the second trumpet judgment is seen to fall upon the sea. Again the term "third part" is used. A third part of the sea became blood (the flow of lava into the sea brought about this discoloration of the sea), a third part of sea creatures died, and a third of the ships were destroyed. Once more the judgment inflicted is partial, but nonetheless, covers a large portion.

The third angel sounded and a great star fell from Heaven. As the salt water was affected by the second blast, so the fresh water is touched by the third sounding. "Wormwood" (bitter) is the name of the star that fell polluting the water. In Deuteronomy 29:18, wormwood is mentioned, "Lest there should be among you man, or woman, or family, or tribe, whose heart turneth away this day from the LORD our God, to go and serve the gods of these nations; lest there should be among you a root that beareth gall and wormwood." Also, it is spoken of in Jeremiah 9:15, "Therefore thus saith the LORD of hosts, the God of Israel; Behold, I will feed them, even this people, with wormwood, and give them water of gall to drink." Poellot declares the main thought to be "increasing and expanding destruction."[46] Some would look for a person as the administrator of this judgment since the star is named. Not all fresh water is affected, and not all men die. Once more a large portion (one-third) is mentioned as being affected by this plague.

Land was affected by the first trumpet, the salt water was touched by the second blast, fresh water was polluted by that which followed the third sounding, and now the heavenly light-giving bodies are affected when the fourth angel blows. To a people already full of fear this type experience could easily be understood as being another sign of God's wrath. An unusual eclipse, blacking out one-third of the sun, one-third of the moon, and one-third of the stars, is pictured. With the first four trumpet blasts and the following activity still vivid, this interruption with the natural shining of the heavenly luminaries called attention to the fact that these judgments are from above–from God. Destructive natural forces are represented in this series of four plagues announced by the trumpets. Special, and not common demonstrations of nature, are pictured in the parade of the electrical storm, the volcanic eruption, the falling meteor, and the eclipse. They symbolize when viewed together the results of God's wrath in the spiritual realm.

A flying, loud-crying eagle announces a triple woe upon earth's inhabitants. This interruption could signal the severity of the three trumpets which were yet to sound. It is as though the eagle were saying, "If you think the judgments in the first four plagues were rough, just wait until the other three have sounded." "By reason of" has been interpreted as, "the worst is yet to come."[47] Eagles, quite often, in the Old Testament depicted judgment. They were considered to be bad omens.

When the eagle has cleared the scene, the fifth trumpeter sounds–a star is seen by the seer. There is some question as to whether he saw the star fall or saw it after it had fallen. Summers writes, "A huge star becomes personified and, having fallen, exposes a yawning abyss."[48] Morris pens, "When the fifth angel sounded, John saw a star fallen to the earth (so rather than fall as the tense is perfect; cf. Moffatt, 'a star which had dropped')."[49] McDowell says, "When the fifth angel sounds the seer sees 'a star from heaven fallen unto the earth.'"[50] Buis,[51] a writer of *The Wesleyan Bible Commentary*,[52] Poellot,[53] and others hold to the same view.

Blaney holds that the fallen star-angel is the same as the wormwood star of Revelation 8:10, 11.[54] Most other writers do not personify the wormwood star, but do see the "fallen star" in Revelation 9:1 as a person. Most hold with Morris who said, "Unlike the star in Revelation 8:10, this one was in some sense a person. Angels were sometimes called stars (cf. Revelation 1:20) and it seems likely that this star was an angel."[55] Interpretations of identity are multitudinous.

> The most diverse identifications of the star-angel are given. He might be Nero (Weymouth), a fallen angel (Simcox, Love), an

> evil spirit (Kiddle), or even Satan himself (Hendriksen, Atkinson; Swete thinks 'possibly Satan'). On the other hand he is seen as the Word of God (Torrance), an angel, possibly Uriel (Charles), our Lord Himself (Berkeley).[56]

Who would dare be dogmatic in the face of the fact that the "experts" are so divided! Since the viewer himself does not identify the star, no one else has sufficient evidential information to speak with certainty. Remember, symbolical language is employed. Understand that this is pageantry, and the details are given in order to make the drama more impressive. Still, there is the question, "Who is this fallen person, and just what does fallen imply?" But just before answering those two questions, some other statements should claim one's attention. They are, "from heaven," "unto the earth," and "to him was given the key."

Regardless of his identity, the personified star was from Heaven. Whether this means he was "from Heaven" in the sense no longer a resident, or whether it means dispatched (Heaven sent him) "from heaven," is not made totally clear. One's view at this point would be governed by his identification of the star. From Heaven does suggest at least that his mission was directed to serve the purpose of the Divine. "Unto earth" causes some students (this writer seldom uses the word scholar) to feel that the star-person was no longer associated with Heaven but was rather assigned to earth or "in the earth." The better meaning seems to be that he, being dispatched by Heaven, had a mission to perform which affected earth. Authority to open the "pit" was his by presence–"to him was given the key." God dispatched the star (from Heaven); directed the star (unto the earth); delivered the key (to him was given the key).

If "to him was given" means he was allowed to perform the action that released the evil forces, then the star could very well be a personality of evil. If, however, "to him was given the key" is interpreted to mean authority was given this person, one must conclude that the person (angel) is not evil. "Fall" or "fallen" must of necessity be interpreted in the light of which of the two views is held by the would-be interpreter. To hold to the word "fall" rather than "fallen," and to see the star-person as a personage of good rather than evil, brings one to the conclusion that "fall" had reference to the speed of the heavenly person dispatched to execute the action of judgment. On the other hand, if "fallen" is held to be a correct rendition, then a condescended person of good with Heaven's authority to act is pictured. Then what does "fall" or "fallen" mean to those who hold that the star is an evil person or spirit? "Fall" to them would mean that some heavenly person fell from his original estate as John beheld the calamity. "Fallen" to those who hold to the evil person theory would suggest that some person of good had in time past fallen, but now in the fallen state was carrying on a work of evil.

Now, a summation needs to be drawn. Those who hold that the star represents a personage of good see such a one dispatched quickly (fall) or condescended (fallen) with authority to unleash the hellish forces in judgment. Others holding to the differing view see an evil person "fall," or having "fallen," given the power to release evil which is used of God to bring judgment. "Where does this writer stand?" someone may ask. Believing what Christ said in Matthew 28:18, "All power is given unto me . . ." and what He said in Revelation 1:18, ". . . I am alive for evermore, Amen; and have the keys of hell and death," there is but one "Scripture-sense" conclusion that can be reached. In all probability, Christ is the star. Revelation 20:1 reveals Christ as an angel of authority (having the key) coming down from Heaven with a great chain (His Word–the gospel) in His hand for the purpose of binding Satan. Three Scriptural references testify that Christ has been given the key–the authority (Isaiah 22:22; Revelation 1:18; and 9:1). Two or three witnesses will Biblically establish. The case is rested.

Smoke as of a great furnace rises from the bottomless pit when opened. Enough smoke to blacken the sun and the sky arises. Smoke signals judgment. Darkening of the sun and polluting of the air signifies the magnitude of the judgment. The locusts with scorpion powers symbolize what kind of judgment that is coming–frightening, devastating, fast, and painful. Forces of evil usually move against the saints, but in this case the locusts act contrary to their nature: "They should not hurt the grass of the earth, neither any green thing, neither any tree." Only those men which have not the seal of God in their foreheads are tormented. The tormented would not die though they would seek death, because of the pain inflicted. Vivid description of the locusts is given only to show the horribleness of the wrath poured out and experienced. Five months was the lifespan of a locust (this type locust). A short period (certainly a limited period) is signified by the five months. Solomon tells us that locusts have no king but go forth in bands (Proverbs 30:27). Unusual is a word that could well be employed to describe these locusts in much of their activity and appearance, and the fact they have a king makes them even the more unusual.

Evil usually goes against good, but in this case evil moves against the evil. "Hellish rottenness" is the term employed by Summers when speaking of the judgment brought to bear upon Rome.[57] He further pointed to the internal decadence in the Roman Empire (rulers and leaders) and said such helped bring about the downfall.

"One woe is past; and, behold, there come two woes more hereafter." A trumpet blast by the sixth angel announces the impending second woe in the series proclaimed by the eagle. Woe number three will follow the sounding of the seventh trumpet.

At the sounding of the sixth trumpet, from the four-horned altar, a voice gave divine direction to the sixth angel, "Loose the four angels which are bound in the great river Euphrates." Being loosed and prepared, these evil angelic commanders led the immense cavalry from the Euphrates. Dana states, "These invaders from the Euphrates were the dreaded Parthian cavalry, the constant menace to the eastern border of the Roman Empire. They were among the few that the Romans ever failed to conquer."[58] The horsemen symbolized external opposition. Morris, in dealing with the description of the horses and horsemen, writes, "Some see a reference to the habit the Parthians had of twisting their horses' tails so that they looked like snakes. They recall also the Parthian skill in shooting arrows behind them as they rode."[59] Summers calls our attention to the fact that three great things combined to bring about the overthrow of the Roman Empire–natural calamity, internal rottenness, and external invasion.[60] These three instruments used of God against the forces of evil can be traced easily through the work of Gibbon, *The Decline and Fall of the Roman Empire.* Invincible Rome fell as Daniel had foretold. Poellot, reflecting on this vision, states "The entire vision is a prophecy of a frightful, supernatural judgment."[61] Buis suggests, "Two hundred thousand thousand, or two hundred million, would signify a vast host."[62] Futurists, with their literal interpretations, have trouble here. What modern nation has a cavalry of such magnitude–200,000,000? Some, realizing the dilemma, have suggested the combined horsepower of the modern vehicles used by the invading army would total 200,000,000. Such scheming would put the interpreter in the "symbolic camp." The better meaning seems to be that the number is a great host, a number of completeness. Again the details are added for the purpose of the vision being made more dramatic and have no known prophetic or doctrinal significance. The judgment was not on the Christians, but rather on the world power, verses 20 and 21. None would argue that the Christians would not be affected by the judgments, but their trials since they mixed with the world in their pilgrimages would be increased. One must conclude with some of the better known authorities that the vision is given as a means of reassurance to the Christians. They needed reassurance that Rome would never triumph over Christianity. Even though a large portion (one-third) of wicked mankind was killed by the invaders, "the rest of the men" did not repent of their idolatry or wickedness.

No sooner had the impenitence of wicked men been announced than another great radiantly clad angel from Heaven was observed by the seer. Support for the view that this particular angel is Christ is lacking. Clothed with a cloud (a garment of majesty); crowned with a rainbow (a sign of hope); countenanced by the sun (signifying wisdom, knowledge); cordoned (feet encircled) with fire (denotes judgment); carrying an open book (symbolizing pertinence); crying a lion's roar (great, loud, striking fear); causing a storm (seven thunders, warning); couched on land and sea (an announcement for all), the angel proclaims no further postponement–"that there should be time no longer." Taken out of context, one might take this to be "taps for eternity!" When studied in context, however, the end is not seen that clearly. The meaning is simply "there should be delay no longer." Retribution would be visited without further delay or postponement. That this is the true meaning can be seen in the fact that John was not to write the warning of the seven thunders. Those warnings must have been for the prophet's benefit. At any rate, there were to be no more warnings and no more delays. Unrepentant (verses 20 and 21) men were to be divinely warned no more. Though "that there should be time no longer" does not primarily have reference to the end, "the mystery of God should be finished" does carry with it the idea "the mystery of God performed to the fullest, even to the end." This is made perfectly clear when the student realizes that in the days of the voice of the seventh angel the mystery is finished. A close reading of Revelation 11:15-19 reveals such. (A more complete exposition of these verses will be given later in this writing.) John, on previous occasions, has ushered his readers all the way to the climax only to bring them back again in history to reveal the mystery step by step.

Commanded by a heavenly voice to take the "little book" from the angel, the Revelator requests the book. Upon orders by the angel, the apostle takes the book (mere scraps of papyrus) knowing that it will be sweet to taste but bitter to devour. To attempt to improve on what John has said about the "little book" would put one on dubious ground, since he does not specify to what it refers with any precision. At this point this writer is thankful for convictions that call for a symbolical interpretation rather than a literal one. Sweet was the revelation but bitter was the judgment contained therein. Dana has stated,

> It is a joyful experience to the seer that he is honored by becoming the recipient of Divine revelation. In this respect of the experience he sees high privilege, and it is gratifying–it is "sweet." But in the thought of the dreadful consequences of the revealed retribution, when finally it befalls sinful man, there is bitterness.[63]

When addressed again the elder was to learn of his return to the mainland and to the pulpit. What a joy John must have experienced when told, "Thou must prophesy again." Banished to Patmos for the Word of God and for the testimony of Jesus Christ, John is promised a new and fuller lease on his ministry–"prophesy again before many peoples, and nations, and tongues, and kings" (Revelation 10:11). Just how this was going to be accomplished is unknown, but know of a surety that every church touched by that famous apostle of love had cause to rejoice. He was unusually good before being exiled, but now that he had had that experience, plus a trip to Heaven–what preaching!

8

The Trumpets
(Continued)

1. Intermission (continued), Revelation 11:1-13
   a. Temple Measured, Revelation 11:1-3
   b. Two Witnesses, Revelation 11:4-12
   c. Great Earthquake, Revelation 11:13
2. The Seventh Trumpet, Revelation 11:14-19
   a. Heavenly Voices, Revelation 11:14, 15
   b. Worshiping Elders, Revelation 11:16, 17
   c. Angry Nations, Revelation 11:18
   d. Open Temple, Revelation 11:19

Study Text: Revelation 11:1-19

Divine authority, to measure with a rod-like reed the Temple (sanctuary), the altar, and the worshipers, was given to John. Something new is represented in this command. A spectator of visions only, now he must take an active part. In all likelihood the church is being referred to for elsewhere it is described as God's sanctuary (1 Corinthians 3:16; 2 Corinthians 6:16; and Ephesians 2:21). Since the *temple* (sanctuary) refers to the church, the *altar* must signify the sacrificial nature of the Christian service, and *them that worship* stands for the worshiping community. Measuring symbolically means two things: preservation and destruction. No indication is given as to how the measuring would be accomplished. Morris has stated that probably Moffatt's "numbering the worshippers" is the sense of it.[64] *Wesleyan Bible Commentary*, quoting Charles, states "but the temple of which he spoke represents the church, and the measuring, like the sealing in chapter seven . . . denotes the preservation of the faithful."[65] The church, the true Israel, is the sanctuary in the vision and John may mean there is a reversal here: Judaism may be represented as the outer court and under control of the Gentiles.

Mankind is divided into two camps, Christians and Gentiles (cf. 1 Corinthians 5:1; 1 Thessalonians 4:5). The Temple is measured for special care and preservation. The meaning of the symbolism is that the true spiritual Israel will be protected and preserved. The greater part of the Gentile world dominated by persecuting Rome will suffer. All of this is symbolized in the fact that the Gentile court was not measured for protection. "Leave out" literally means cast out. These in contrast to true believers are those who stand outside the true church though they may be said to associate with it.

Forty-two months (3½ years) is the duration of this particular period of distress. Three and one-half was an indefinite number and signified uncertainty, restlessness, and turmoil. Here God's protection over His people during an indefinite time of great stress and turmoil is symbolized. Seven is considered to be the number of absolute perfection, so half of seven represents incompleteness or indefiniteness.

Scholars foremost in the field of interpretation have held that since in Oriental symbolism the number two carried the idea of strength, the two witnesses appear to symbolize a powerful witness. John gives a hint to the interpretation when he records, "These are the two olive trees, and the two candlesticks . . . ." When the two witnesses are viewed in their place in the structure of the book, they are a part of an interlude between the sixth and seventh symbols. They constitute one of four figures of which the other three are without question apocalyptic images. Some call the two witnesses the Law and the Prophets; others call them the Church; and still others say they were Christ's witnesses, the Word, or the Christians with the Word, the two ground-forms of witness: the Church communion and Christians . . . morals and manners, or the people of God.

This writer has a tendency to be inconsistent here and call the *two* two (instead of seeing two as powerful), and declaring them to be (sticking yet with the symbolical) the Word of God–Old and New Testaments. But even so, the two make one, and that one is powerful because God has given His Word power. Make a comparison between John's statement about the witnesses being lampstands and olive trees with that which is written in Zechariah 4:3-7 and 11-14. Note the interpretation given by the angel to Zechariah when he stated that he did not understand the figures of the lampstand and olive trees: "He answered and spake . . . saying, This is the word of the Lord . . . These are the two anointed ones, that stand by the Lord of the whole earth." Terms like "the word of the Lord" and "the two anointed" certainly cause one to think of the inspired Word of God. They have an indefinite period of time (3 1/2 years) to "finish their testimony" (declare the whole counsel of God). When the above statement is considered, one is prone to want to declare the two witnesses to be the Word and the church. Of course, all understand that either is ineffective without the other. Viewing "finished their testimony" as declaring the whole counsel, one cannot help but see the "finished" as brought to fruition, meaning the Word had done its job. (Not all the job as it would relate to all time, but had most definitely accomplished its task in establishing the church, the organism that would never die.) Note carefully that the work of the witnesses is finished (has accomplished something) before Rome (the emperor) makes war.

Summers believes that the vision naturally divides itself into three parts. First, there was the period when the gospel was preached with remarkable success, verses 4-6. Second, there was a time when a power arose which attempted to crush the testimony of the gospel, verses 7-10. Third, there was the period of the progress of the gospel, which proved that Rome had not considered the power of God, verses 11-13.[66]

The persecuting power that makes war is called the "beast," which as Dana has stated must be in anticipation of chapter thirteen where the beast most clearly represents the Roman government.[67] Rome is meant by "the great city, which spiritually is called Sodom and Egypt, where also our Lord was crucified" (Revelation 11:8). When this is accepted, another thought is made evident. The two witnesses are the Word of God, the beast is Roman government; the two were killed and their dead bodies lay in Rome. This brings to mind the thought that Roman government was able to stop the witness in Rome (the capital) for a period of time, so much so that it was dead as far as the city was concerned. But at no time was the work of the Word completely stopped (killed) everywhere. Some will object to Rome being called the site where the dead bodies lay. The objection will come because of the statement "where also our Lord was crucified." Believing that John, the Jewish apocalyptist, would not refer to Jerusalem as Sodom and Egypt, consequently, Rome must be considered. Pontius Pilate, by the power of Rome, had a large share in crucifying Jesus. Ultimate responsibility lay upon the courts of Rome. Galilean churches, in the second quarter of the first century, put the blame primarily upon the Jewish enemies. But to an Asiatic Christian languishing on Patmos under Rome's cruel hands during the Domitianic persecution, another aspect of the crucifixion appeared. The aged apostle's natural resentment had led him to see Rome's part in the crucifixion of his Lord more clearly, and for that reason he assigns the chief responsibility there. John's fourth Gospel gives Pilate a much larger place than is to be found in the synoptics.

Bodies not buried were most usually objects of much scorn and ridicule. Gaiety seems to be the order of the day on the part of earth-dwellers (those of this world). In all probability, the government sighed with relief when the church in Rome was silenced. Of short duration was that sigh; had they known the meaning of Daniel's writings, they would have seen the little stone pounding away at the feet (foundation) of the image (world system) (Daniel 2:39-43). Festivity was cut short because "the Spirit of life from God entered into them [the witnesses], and they stood upon their feet" (Revelation 11:11). When this took place, "great fear fell upon them which saw them." Heaven's attentiveness had been captured. Divine intervention, aid, and preservation are symbolized. Also, the resurrected witness reached Heaven, and yet that same witness was observed on earth by "their enemies." Christ the Living Word, God's witness to mankind, was, after being resurrected, caught up in a cloud. Even so, Mark declares He was still active on earth though in Heaven (Mark 16:19, 20).

> So then after the Lord had spoken unto them, he was received up into heaven, and sat on the right hand of God. And they went forth, and preached every where, the Lord working with them, and confirming the word with signs following. Amen.

Now God's witness, the written Word (being resurrected), reaches Heaven's portals anew by resounding praise of the newly saved and those whose lives would be yet terminated because of the implanted Word. Among those enemies who beheld fell both judgment and salvation. God's Word always works both ways (Hebrews 4:12). Some fell to destruction and others were brought to the point of praise.

Two woes are past and "the third woe cometh quickly" (suddenly). The pause (between the sounding of the sixth trumpet and the blasting of the seventh) had brought to view the little book and the two witnesses. With those two visions past, the seer is informed, "the third woe cometh quickly." He understood from this that there would be no further delay in regard to the seventh angel sounding. It is as though John were told, "Stand by in readiness–the seventh trumpet will blow suddenly."

Much has been said about the announcement of an impending woe with the sounding notes of the seventh trumpet for when the seventh blew, "great voices in heaven" were heard. "Great voices in heaven" singing the "Anthem of the Kingdom" was a far cry from what had transpired when the other trumpets had been blown. Some question, "Where is the woe?" Trying to find what they would recognize to be a woe, they look beyond the remaining verses of chapter eleven. However, when one takes into consideration the fact that the woes previously viewed by John were upon the enemies of the Lord, he will look for the carrying out of the seventh woe in context. A woe as has been seen time and again can be effected two ways. To bring outright destruction and hardship upon an enemy is a woe, but on the other hand, a blessing brought upon those attacked by the enemy is likewise a woe to the enemy. Heaven's rejoicing! And the reason for the rejoicing proclaims with certainty that the enemy has been greatly affected in some way. Look no further. The answer is to be found in "the kingdom of this world is become the kingdom of our Lord, and his Christ; and he shall reign for ever and ever" (Revelation 11:15). Attention is directed to the fact that in the above quotation the word "kingdom" is not pluralized. Every scholarly work points to the fact that the better manuscripts have "kingdom of this world" and "kingdom of our Lord" rather than "kingdoms of." It is most unfortunate that the word kingdom, though found in the singular, was pluralized. Their doing so reveals a misconception on their part that has troubled the minds of many in developing a concept of the term. *Kingdom* in the English conveys the idea of territory or in some cases a political entity. Because such an interpretation has been put upon the word, that connotation has dominated the efforts of writers who have sought to give the meaning of *kingdom* and of the *kingdom of God.* No informed interpreter would argue that the Greek term *Basileia* does not carry with it the connotation of territory and political entity with a king ruling. But even so, there is another meaning, and that is "rule or sovereignty." However, the English word *kingdom* fails to carry over this meaning; therefore, it is incapable of representing the prominent usage of the word in the New Testament. A careful study of the usage of the word *kingdom* reveals that its most common meaning is the idea of sovereignty, rule, or dominion. Jesus frequently gave that meaning to a kingdom when speaking of "the kingdom of heaven" and "kingdom of God." In the great proclamation (Revelation 11:15), revealed by the seventh sounding, the meaning of the word is rule or sovereignty. Thus, the statement "the kingdom of the world" means dominion, rule, or sovereignty over the world. Know also that the kingdom of God is the dominion or rule of God. Some may call the following a paraphrase, but this writer chooses to call it a proper translation of the great proclamation of the heavenly voices: "The rule over the world became our Lord's and His Christ's; And He shall reign for ever and ever." Declaring the above to be a correct translation calls for an explanation of "are become." This question arises, "Is the action to be understood as having taken place already, or is one to understand it as a future action that is conceived as already having taken place?" Good authorities have stated that in a projected series of events the would-be interpreter cannot make a decision on the basis of the Greek tense. There are those who would make an appeal to the Hebrew prophetic perfect. Their interpretation would be that that which is to take place is represented as having already taken place. It seems only right to this writer that the action is to be interpreted upon the basis of John's purpose and the full context of the book. God the Father has always exercised sovereignty over the world (Daniel 4:34-37; 5:18-21; Romans 13:1-6). But the thing that must be understood here is that at some point in time sovereignty and dominion over the world became the possession of God and His Christ. The voices of Heaven were proclaiming affirmedly that the dominion over the world had come to God and Christ. Joint rule is affirmed. Plainly stated, it is God's reign in history through Messiah, God's anointed. "He shall reign for ever and ever" speaks of the everlasting kingdom (Daniel 2:44; 7:13, 14; 2 Samuel 7:13, 16; Psalm 89:29; Isaiah 9:7; Micah 4:7) reigned over by God through Christ. Prophecy, both in the Old and New Testaments, spoke of Christ coming into a position of authority (kingship, rulership). Psalm 89:34-37 declares,

> My covenant will I not break, nor alter the thing that is gone out of my lips. Once have I sworn by my holiness that I will not lie unto David. His seed shall endure for ever, and his throne as

> the sun before me. It shall be established for ever as the moon, and as a faithful witness in heaven. Selah.

Christ declared His authority in Matthew 28:18 and Revelation 1:18. His authority is further declared in Revelation 9:1 and Revelation 20:1 in the symbolical key. Christ was in a position to exercise that authority when He ascended up on high (Ephesians 4:10). This truth is born out in Revelation 12:5, "And she brought forth a man child, who was to rule all nations with a rod of iron: and her child was caught up unto God, and to his throne." More evidence is seen in Revelation 12:10, "And I heard a loud voice saying in heaven, Now is come salvation, and strength, and the kingdom of our God, and the power of his Christ: for the accuser of our brethren is cast down, which accused them before our God day and night." When Christ was in Heaven on the throne as Priest-King making intercession (Hebrews 7:25) and reigning (Revelation 12:5), it was declared "now is come salvation [Christ's intercession for the believers], and strength, and the kingdom of our God [Christ reigning], and the power [authority] of his Christ." Note carefully at this point a portion of the praise accorded Christ by the elders in Revelation 11:17, "because thou hast taken to thee thy great power [authority], and hast reigned."

Scriptural evidence bears out that when Christ was raised to sit on David's throne (Acts 2:30), He was invited by the Father to sit on His right hand (Acts 2:34). Verse 36 declares that God made Jesus both Lord and Christ. The only conclusion that can be drawn is when Christ took His rightful place upon the throne, He began to rule over the spiritual kingdom, and at the same time entered into a joint membership with His Father in sovereign reign. There is no denying that Christ is at the Father's right hand upon the throne. Remember it was declared of Christ, "The Lord sware and will not repent, Thou art a priest for ever after the order of Melchisedec" (Hebrews 7:21). While calling that to mind, remember also that Melchisedec was both priest and king. He was not priest and then king, but was both at the same time. With that in mind, one should look closely at Hebrews 10:12, 13, which in speaking of Christ states, "But this man, after he had offered one sacrifice for sins for ever, sat down on the right hand of God; From henceforth expecting till his enemies be made his footstool." According to 1 Corinthians 15:25, "For he must reign, till he hath put all enemies under his feet." Christ is Priest until His enemies become His footstool and He is King until all enemies are under His feet. At that time He will deliver up the kingdom to God the Father (1 Corinthians 15:24). That is, He will surrender the spiritual kingdom to the Father and will subject Himself to God that God may be all in all.

Where the Old Testament speaks of Messiah's coming, it does so in connection with the kingdom, and this kingdom is always spoken of as "everlasting." The New Testament tells of the kingdom being taken away from "Israel" in Matthew 21:43, "Therefore say I unto you, The kingdom of God shall be taken from you, and given to a nation bringing forth the fruits thereof." But never a word is said about its restoration to that ancient covenant people. Peter, in 1 Peter 2:9, after having told of the rejection of Israel, applied to the church all the epitaphs once used to describe the covenant people, "But ye are a chosen generation, a royal priesthood, an holy nation, a peculiar people; that ye should shew forth the praises of him who hath called you out of darkness into his marvelous light." Simon virtually states that the church in reality is now what Israel used to be. Mary was told by the angel, "The Lord God shall give unto him [Christ] the throne of his father David: And he shall reign over the house of Jacob for ever; and of his kingdom there shall be no end" (Luke 1:32, 33). Isaiah speaks of Christ in this role in Isaiah 9:6, 7–

> For unto us a child is born, unto us a son is given: and the government shall be upon his shoulder: and his name shall be called Wonderful, Counselor, The mighty God, The everlasting Father, and The Prince of Peace. Of the increase of his government and peace there shall be no end, upon the throne of David, and upon his kingdom, to order it, and to establish it with judgment and with justice from henceforth even for ever. The zeal of the LORD of hosts will perform this.

Jesus vindicates the truth of His kingship in John 18:37, "To this end was I born, and for this cause came I into the world." Christ had been asked by Pilate in John 18:33, "Art thou the King of the Jews?" to which He had answered, "Sayest thou this thing of thyself [Pilate, do you know the truth of the statement?], or did others tell it thee [did others tell you the truth about me being King]?" "Pilate answered . . . Thine own nation and the chief priests have delivered thee unto me." Jesus then replied, "My kingdom is not of this world: if my kingdom were of this world, then would my servants fight, that

I should not be delivered to the Jews: but now is my kingdom from hence" (John 18:36). The "Man of Authority" who spoke "with authority" made a definite distinction between His "servants" and the "Jews." At the same time He was stating that the "Jews" ("thine own nation," as Pilate had put it), were not the kingdom over which He was "born king." His kingdom was constituted by "servants." Romans 6:22 sheds light on how one becomes a servant, and by so doing becomes a part of Christ's kingdom, "But now being made free from sin, and become servants to God, ye have your fruit unto holiness, and the end everlasting life."

There is a bit of irony in the voice of Christ when speaking of His kingdom to Pilate for He states, "Thou sayest that I am a king. To this end was I born . . . Every one that is of the truth heareth my voice." Just here the Lord made His speech very plain. Paraphrased it reads, "Everyone who understandeth the truth about my kingdom and heareth what I have to say about it knows that my kingdom is not of this world. The Jews are not my kingdom; my servants are the subjects of the spiritual kingdom. I am born king, my kingdom was the cause for my coming, and I bear witness that the kingdom is from hence."

Before leaving this particular thought, attention should be given to Daniel 7:13, 14, a passage which in the early Christian community was interpreted messianically.

> I saw in the night visions, and, behold, one like the Son of man came with the clouds of heaven, and came to the Ancient of days, and they brought him near before him. And there was given him dominion, and glory, and a kingdom, that all people, nations, and languages, should serve him: his dominion is an everlasting dominion, which shall not pass away, and his kingdom that which shall not be destroyed.

The one like the Son of man came with clouds of Heaven to the Ancient of days (cf. Acts 1:9). Upon His arrival, with the clouds, the Son of man had dominion and a kingdom. Both the reigning of Christ over His servants and His joint sovereign reign can be seen as has already been stated. The elders fell from their thrones (seats) upon their faces in thankful praise unto God. They knew their king and were blessed when He was shown in the vision to John as having come into His authority and reign. As they continued to express themselves, they spoke of the angry nations (cf. Psalm 2:1-6); and in a similar vein (as the souls under the altar) called for the wrath of God to be poured out upon the dead (dead as used in 2 Timothy 4:1) and for their judgment to be executed. They also called for the rewarding of the servants, prophets, saints, and them that feared the name of God both small and great. Before concluding their message, they asked for the avenging of those who had set about destroying the earth.

In answer to the elders, God's people (symbolized by the Temple, 2 Corinthians 6:16; Ephesians 2:21) were shown to be in His very presence as more judgment (signified by the natural happenings and voices) was yet to come. God's majesty is also portrayed in the lightnings, voices, etc.

The Patmos prophet has once again shown that Christ is King of Kings and Lord of Lords, and though His sovereignty is challenged by an earthly sovereign, Christ will triumph. What comfort this must have brought to the Asian saints facing persecution during the challenge.

9

The Signs

1. The Woman, the Child, and the Devil, Revelation 12:1-6
2. The Angels and the Dragon, Revelation 12:7-12
3. The Dragon on the Earth, Revelation 12:13-17
4. The Beast from out of the Sea, Revelation 13:1-10
5. The Beast from out of the Earth, Revelation 13:11-18
6. The Lamb on Mount Zion, Revelation 14:1-5
7. The Seven Angels, Revelation 14:6-20

Study Text: Revelation 12:1—14:20

Seven prophecies are constituted in the seven visions of this section. United, they describe the supernatural conflict between good and evil, God and the devil.

The first wonder represents the very issue, which actually furnishes the occasion for the great conflict. Images two, three, and four present the forces arrayed against the Lord Jesus Christ. Forces of righteousness, which defend the cause of Christ, are clearly seen in the fifth and sixth signs. As in the case of the seventh seal and the seventh trumpet, the seventh sign is transitional.

The nature of the conflict in chapters twelve through fourteen is spiritual. These chapters describe the fight waged between the forces of evil and the church here on earth.

John called the next scene made visible a great wonder in the sky. He saw a radiantly clad pregnant woman standing with the old garment under her feet. She was wearing the crown of the conqueror. Differing views about the identity of the woman are held by the scholars. Some, in identifying the woman, use the term *church* in the sense of the spiritual community out of which Christ was born. If in fact one can use the term *church* in the sense of the people of God, and not in the strictest sense, the sun dress can be seen as grace and the discarded garment at her feet as law. Even so, the twelve stars in the royal diadem need not change. When the moon (law, the lesser light) was her garb, the twelve stars represented the twelve patriarchs, and when the sun (grace, the greater light) became her dress, the stars signified the twelve apostles. This thought is better understood when one studies the deeper meaning of Christ's statement in Matthew 9:16, "No man putteth a piece of new cloth unto an old garment, for that which is put in to fill it up taketh from the garment, and the rent is made worse." Also, one should give consideration to Hebrews 8:6-9, which deals with a faulty first covenant and the establishing of a new covenant. Further light is shed on the true meaning in Hebrews 8:13, "In that he saith, A new covenant, he hath made the first old. Now that which decayeth and waxeth old is ready to vanish away." It is a well-known Scriptural fact that the people of God in the New Testament did not wear the "garb" of the people of God of the Old Testament.

John did not see the change of dress for that was not important at this point. He was not endeavoring to convince the Jewish people of a distinct connection between the "people of God under law" and the "people of God under grace," but was rather showing to the Christians, Christianity from its beginning. Of course it began with Christ. Through the series of seven wonders the scribe reveals the triumph of Christ beginning with His birth. A woman great with child, pained, travailing, crying, and ready to be delivered, is rather defenseless. But note carefully, even though the dragon (no need for argument here, for John in verse 9 calls the dragon old serpent, devil, and Satan) stood in readiness to devour the child at birth, he made no move against the woman to abort the child. Even the devil knows his limitations when he moves against God. God the Father like a faithful father was protecting her who was to bring forth His child (Luke 1:32, 33, 35). The color of the dragon speaks of his destructive blood-thirsty character. "Seven heads" is symbolic of the wisdom of Satan. Beasts that naturally have horns use them to defend themselves, destroy, or demonstrate a show of strength. Here, the ten horns represent the great destructive power of the devil. Crowns always denote authority. "Seven crowns" would suggest full or complete authority. In the matters of evil, Satan has such authority. This awesome, awful "wonder" drew a third of the stars from Heaven and cast them down to the earth.

When the devil "was kicked out" of Heaven, originally he marshaled one-third of the angels. Just when this action took place is not stated. So, why speculate? This writer has long believed that couched in the language of Isaiah 14:12-15 one can see the original standing of Satan and get a hint as to why he and the angels were expelled. Another portion of Scripture giving light on the subject is Ezekiel 28:13-19. Mention is made now of the fact that the devil, like a warrior flexing his muscles, might show his strength and bring fear. It is almost as if he were saying as he stood before the woman lashing his tail, "one-third of the angelic beings are with me in this assault." No sign of fear on the part of the woman is detected. She delivers in spite of the threatenings on the part of the fierce dragon. Though John does not here write of the life of Christ (the manchild), one cannot help but think of the threat Herod was to Christ (Matthew 2:13-18) and of the crucifixion where no doubt Satan thought he would win the victory. But if John had dealt with the early life of Jesus, he would have in all probability made mention of the many times Christ cast out devils. Also, he would have included statements of Christ that predicted the casting out and binding of Satan (Luke 10:17; John 12:31, 32; Matthew 12:22-30).

The devil was not successful in his attempt at the birth of Christ (Jesus escaped, Matthew 2:16), during the ministry of Christ (the devils were subject even to the seventy, Luke 10:17), or in His death ("He arose the third day," 1 Corinthians 15:4). When Christ arose He not only came alive but came into His power (Revelation 1:18; 3:7; 5:12, 13; 9:1; 11:15, 17; 12:5, 10; and 20:1) and sat down on His Father's throne (Acts 2:30-35; 1 Corinthians 15:25).

Much ado has been made by the futurists over the statement "rule all nations with a rod of iron." Christ is pictured by some of that camp as an iron-fisted tyrant who is nothing less than a dictator. How unlike everything the Lord had to say of Himself while among men. Such word pictures are drawn of Christ because those interpreters have a misconception of the term "rule with a rod of iron." The true picture here is that of a shepherd-king. Recall, He was promised the throne of His father David (Psalm 89:34-37; Luke 1:32) and David was a shepherd-king. Just as it has been observed that Christ is Priest-King it is now observed that He is Shepherd-King. His disciples (His church was established in the top of the mountain, Isaiah 2:2; Micah 4:1; and Mark 3:13-15) were called a flock by Him and they were promised the kingdom (Luke 12:32).

"And the woman fled" symbolizes the dispersing of the early Christian community by persecution. "A thousand two hundred and threescore days" (three and one-half years) are symbolic of a persecution of limited duration. An indefinite period of time is signified since three and one-half is a number of incompleteness in Hebrew numbering.

The war that raged between the forces of good (Michael and his angels) and the forces of evil (the devil and his followers) had to be fought out in Heaven as well as upon earth. Evil forces prevailed not and certain limits were placed upon them—"neither was their place found any more in heaven." The "Christ event" had put God in human flesh and the God-man had come off victorious from the conflict with Satan. Your attention is called again to Christ's statement in Luke 10:18, "I beheld Satan as lightning fall from heaven." And again a serious look should be taken at John 12:31, 32 where Christ makes a definite connection between Satan being cast out and His crucifixion. With this in mind, one should have no trouble understanding the cry of the loud voice in verse 10, "... Now is come salvation, and strength, and the kingdom of our God, and the power of his Christ...." The accuser of the brethren, which deceiveth the whole world, was cast out. In the matter of emperor worship, the devil constantly had them hailed into court. Regularly he flaunted his evil practices in the face of God by bringing railing accusations against Christians to those who enforced the worship of the ruler. His power was broken. No longer would he be able to deceive the nations in regard to the worship of himself through emperor worship. This will be dealt with again in Revelation 13 and Revelation 20, where more is said in reference to the worship of the emperor during Domitian's reign.

Brethren accused by the old serpent overcame him. They would not recant, but rather chose to die the death of a martyr. Three things enabled them to be overcomers: (1) the blood of the Lamb, (2) the Word of their testimony, and (3) they loved not their lives unto death. That an end had come to accusations in this regard called for Heaven to rejoice. Those souls under the altar that had been told to rest awhile until their brethren had been killed could now rejoice. But at the moment Heaven broke into joy, "the inhabiters of the earth" were warned yet of other practices of Satan.

Realizing his predicament, the dragon turns his attention to the woman (God's people) that had escaped at least for a season (three and one-half years, verse 6) much of that hurled at her because of dispersal. The persecution that drove the woman into the wilderness may have been that brought by the Jews against the "true people" of God (Acts 8:1). Persecution brought upon the woman as described in verses 13 and 14 may have been that brought to bear by Rome. When the center of church activity shifted from Jerusalem (Jewish center) to Antioch (Gentile center), the persecution brought by the Jews against Christianity became less effective. There was a period of time in which the church had peace.

> Then had the churches rest throughout all Judaea and Galilee and Samaria, and were edified; and walking in the fear of the Lord, and in the comfort of the Holy Ghost, were multiplied.
>
> Acts 9:31

This could account for the statement, "where she hath a place prepared of God, that they should feed her." Also, some thought should be given to the fact that no Christians died in the destruction of Jerusalem, A.D. 70. Nero had had some Christians killed during his reign, but Rome moved against the Jews in the siege of Jerusalem and not against Christians. Food gives nourishment and nourishment gives strength. It was some time before Rome began to persecute the church. When the Roman persecution broke out, wings (signifying the strength of God, Isaiah 6:2) were given the woman (Revelation 12:14). Again she is able to escape despite the fact that the serpent sends a flood (mass of people turned against the people of God) after the woman. The persecution is of indefinite duration. As shall be seen in chapter 13, the sea (verse 1) and the earth (verse 11) are both used as symbols of people. John seems to rush the reader on to a time when the earth (signifying common man's acceptance of Christ) opens up and stops the flood (signifying government evil practice of forcing emperor worship). If this seems somewhat confusing, think of the contrast in Rome's attitude toward Christianity under Domitian and Christianity under Constantine. From henceforth the devil had to settle with making war with the seed of the woman wherever he found them. Of course, that brings one's thoughts all the way up to the present and unto the end.

The remnant of her seed does not refer to the Jews in the flesh, but rather to a spiritual remnant–those "which keep the commandments of God, and have the testimony of Jesus."

There is a degree of controversy over the statement, "I stood upon the sand." Representatives of the two views are Morris and McDowell. Morris writes, "We should read 'he stood.'" And adds, "The words refer to the dragon . . . ."[68] McDowell agrees with the statement as found in the King James Version.[69] There seems to be no reason for the argument. The evidence seems to indicate that it was in fact the seer who was standing upon the sand. John is positioned variously throughout the drama. It should not be thought strange that the prophet joins an earth scene. He sometimes is pictured as being in Heaven and then again on earth. When one reads "I stood upon the sand of the sea, and saw . . ." he cannot but help understand that he who stood upon the sea also saw. Strange that there is no dispute over the one who saw. A beast was seen coming up out of the sea. Futurists have no hesitation about injecting a non-Revelation term (Antichrist) and applying it to "the beast." Mankind is pictured figuratively as water (Ecclesiastes 11:1), flood (2 Samuel 22:5), and as the sea (Revelation 13:1). Sometimes evil men are described as the "troubled sea" (Isaiah 57:20, 21). Evil has long been associated with the sea because the contents of its mysterious depth could not be fully known. Had some inexperienced viewer held John's coveted position, he may have thought the dragon himself was rising from the water. His description certainly calls to mind the vivid word picture given of the dragon in Revelation 12:3–"seven heads"–great wisdom, "ten horns"–great power, "seven crowns"–great authority, "upon his heads the name of blasphemy"–names associated with the beast are blasphemous. Further description, however, distinguishes the water beast from the serpent. Features about the sea creature caused John to say he was like a leopard with bear feet and a lion's mouth. Such a description is symbolic of a fast-moving, unchanging ("can a leopard change his spots?" Jeremiah 13:23), heavy-footed, loud-voiced individual. The man signified was brought to his position, prestige, and power by the dragon (devil, forces of evil). Distinguishing marks of this image take away the difficulty of determining who he is. He was guilty of blasphemy, both because of the names he ascribed to himself and the things he spoke against God (verses 1 and 6). The beast was sovereign over all the known world (verse 7). Except for the Christians who would not recant, all worshiped him (verse 8). Images of the beast were set up throughout the land (verse 14). Persecution even unto death was brought to bear upon those who refused to worship the beast. When one considers the facts as he observes the Emperor Domitian of that day, the identity of the beast is unmistakable. Observe: Domitian applied to himself titles of deity, communication directed to him had to be prefaced with "Supreme Lord God." Correspondence sent to him was refused unless this appellation was used in the salutation.

He was worshiped by all under Roman domination except for the faithful in the Christian community. Images of him were made and set in various places throughout the empire. Those refusing to worship him were persecuted unto death. Ostracism was one weapon used against those who would not worship the beast. Those who would not worship did not bear the prescribed mark that would permit them to buy and sell. Over a long period of time many were brought to death by this method. Of course, the sword and nearly every known weapon was used in bringing to death those who would not adhere.

Nero had been the most wicked of all Roman emperors prior to Domitian. When he died, a myth was started that he would be reincarnated. This gave rise to what is called the *Nero-redivivus* myth. According to the myth, Nero would come back to life and perhaps would lead an army of Parthians into battle and reestablish himself as emperor. Nothing is said of John believing the myth, but he does make use of it as he did many other images and expressions borrowed. When Domitian became so terrible, many accepted the *redivivus* myth believing that in Domitian, Nero had come back alive. All of this is symbolized by the statement, "one of his heads as it were wounded to death; and his deadly wound was healed." Great wonderment on the part of the people spurred them to worship. When adored by the people, the beast spoke great things and blasphemies. He was given power for forty-two months (an indefinite period of distress and turmoil). Blasphemies were hurled against God, His name, His tabernacle, and against those who had made it to Heaven. Speaking against those "tabernacled in heaven" might suggest that Domitian knew he was somewhat defeated by the Christians who chose martyrdom over emperor worship because they had made it to Heaven. His wisdom was from the dragon, and he knew full well the whereabouts of the saints that had died. Power to make war against the saints was one of the gifts given the beast by the dragon. The saints are admonished not to fight back with the sword. They were instructed to be patient and faithful. God promised that the captor would be captive and the killer would be killed.

Following the first beast is a second who is like the first in power. "He exerciseth all the power of the first beast before him." This second beast came from among the people (earth). His sole responsibility was to cause the citizenry to worship the beast. Let it be understood that to worship the beast was to worship the dragon. Note in verse 4: "They worshipped the dragon which gave power unto the beast: and they worshipped the beast." Both the priesthood and the *concilia* have been named as the second beast. "Two horns of a lamb" give the beast religious significance and speech "as a dragon" signifies allegiance to the dragon. "And he doeth great wonders, so that he maketh fire come down from heaven on the earth in the sight of men, And deceiveth them that dwell on the earth by the means of those miracles. . . ." Though one might see the concilia in the enforcement of emperor worship, he cannot but see the priesthood of emperor worship when viewing the magical tricks performed. The magic of these can be clearly seen in the fact that they deceived the people into believing that it was the beast come alive that was speaking. It appeared that the live image was pronouncing the sentence of death upon those who refused to worship the beast. Those worshiping the beast were given a mark in their right hand or in their foreheads. Individuals were not permitted to buy or sell unless the mark, the name of the beast, or the number of his name was evident. Very possibly "a mark in their right hand, or in their foreheads" signified they had in their minds the thoughts of the beast and did his work with their hands. The philosophy of the beast and the labor of his work were seen clearly in them as they came to worship. A registry was kept of those conforming and those failing to yield. Christians would not worship the beast because they had the mind of Christ (Philippians 2:5) and did His work. They also bore the mark of the Lord.

Many, when speaking of the badge of identity that enabled the emperor worshipers to buy and sell, deal only with the mark of the beast. But the Scripture mentions "the mark, or the name . . . , or the number of his name." "The mark" of the beast/man was evil. "The name of the beast" was Domitian (the very mention of his name was suggestive of blasphemy, Revelation 13:1, 5, 6). "The number of his name" was 666. "Count the number of the beast" is the instruction given to the wise and those who understand. One can understand when he counts the number. The number is six (evil), six (evil), six (evil). Six is one short of seven which is the symbol of perfection. When six has been added to six, and six added to six, it is still not seven. Regardless how many sixes are added in a string of sixes, the number will never reach seven (perfection). People of that day understood six to symbolize evil and 666 to represent extreme evil.

Up until that time Domitian had proved himself to be the very personification of evil. John's original readers understood that the prophet was indeed speaking of the evil emperor when dealing with the number of the beast. Applying what has been written, one has no trouble seeing the number 666 to represent evil, evil, evil. The man is a trinity of evil.

In chapter seven the 144,000 are named but no action is seen on their part. There they are revealed to give John the assurance by example of what God would do for His people. Here they are shown with the Lamb as a force of righteousness in opposition to the forces of evil. Isaiah prophesied of these in chapter thirty-five, verse 10, "And the ransomed of the LORD shall return, and come to Zion with songs and everlasting joy upon their heads: they shall obtain joy and gladness, and sorrow and sighing shall flee away." No question should arise as to the true meaning of this symbol. Certainly it refers to Christ and His triumph. This scene follows two dark and threatening chapters. When the curtain is drawn, the Lamb is revealed on Mount Zion with a perfect number of the redeemed. Their appearance just now causes the hearts of the Christians to be joyous. Such a force of righteousness gives courage, but more than that, to see the redeemed with the Lord gives even more hope. Championing their cause, the Redeemer-Lamb marshals a complete army of righteousness on Mount Zion. A new song is sung by that vast number–a song of victory, the meaning of which is known only to them. Undefiled "with women" is symbolic of the fact that they had not committed spiritual fornication. They had been faithful. In their faithfulness they followed the Lamb wherever He went. And, they were truthful. Never did they deny the supremacy of their Christ. The outcome of the battle was never in doubt. A perfect number with the Lamb on Mount Zion spelled victory.

Another symbol of the victorious is revealed when an angel is seen flying in the midst of Heaven preaching the gospel unto them that dwell on the earth. Men are called upon to fear God the Creator who will bring judgment. The success of the gospel bringing both salvation and condemnation can be clearly seen. Doom of Imperial Rome (Babylon) is announced by the second angel. Identification of the city is not difficult due to the description given. "She made all nations drink of the wine of the wrath of her fornication." Rome's fall was so certain in the mind of God that it is represented as having taken place already. Destruction of those who worshiped the emperor is pictured by the third angel's announcement. God's unmixed wrath consisted of fire and sulfuric burning. The language employed gives a picture of torment not soon over–"the smoke of their torment ascendeth up for ever and ever." Verse 12 calls to mind the statement, "Vengeance is mine; I will repay." Those who are patient, faithful, and obedient are assured that those who worshiped the beast would be punished by the Lord though they escaped in life because they had worshiped the emperor.

A voice with divine authority instructed the seer to write a beatitude pertaining to the dead who die in the Lord. Blessings of the beatitude are cited in the statements, "rest from their labours" (work under adversity) and "works do follow them" (reward for labor is promised).

A second force of righteousness employed by the Lord in opposition to the forces of evil is shown in the sickle. Divine judgment is symbolized. Christ here makes an appearance as King (on His head a golden crown) and Judge (in His hand a sharp sickle). At a divine signal, a sickle is thrust into the ripe grain. A second signal is given and the sickle is thrust into the grape cluster. It is generally agreed that both "thrusts" represent judgment. Disagreement, however, has arisen over the two symbols. There are those who hold that the gathering of the grain represents the judgment of the righteous and the grapes represent the judgment of the wicked. Some view both as symbolic of judgment upon the wicked. Though there is some evidence on either side of the argument, it seems that the latter is the better position for one to take. Futurists favor dividing the two symbols as they find room for many judgments. No well-known authority holds to a differentiation, but rather holds to the fact that both symbols picture the judgment in God's hands as instruments of defeat. Futurists and literalists have trouble getting a 200-mile river in Palestine. The thoroughness of the judgment is to be seen in the statement that speaks of the enormous flow of blood.

10

The Vials

1. Introduction to the Seven Plagues, Revelation 15:1
2. Interlude of Thanksgiving, Revelation 15:2-4
3. A Transition, Revelation 15:5—16:1
4. The First Bowl Brings a Plague Upon the Land, Revelation 16:2
5. Contents of the Second Were Poured Out Upon the Sea, Revelation 16:3
6. The Third Bowl Brings Judgment Upon Rivers and Fountains, Revelation 16:4-7
7. Bowl Four Is Emptied Upon the Sun, Revelation 16:8, 9
8. Plague Five is Poured Out Upon the Very Seat of Government, Revelation 16:10, 11
9. Pouring Forth of the Sixth Bowl Dries up the Euphrates River, Revelation 16:12-16
10. The Seventh Is Poured Out Upon the Air, Revelation 16:17-21

Study Text: Revelation 15:1—16:21

A marvelous sign appears in the vision–Heaven, seven angels having the seven last plagues–"in them is filled up the wrath of God." A close resemblance to the seven seals and the seven trumpets is seen in the judgments symbolized by the pouring forth of the vials of wrath. Chronology is not to be sought when examining the three specific areas of events depicted in the seals, trumpets, and vials. A close examination will reveal that each cover about the same time span but appears to be much like three different angled pictures of the same setting. Thus, various aspects of the total picture receive varying degrees of emphasis. It is almost as though John were saying, "Let us look at the scene from another angle," as he moves from one set of symbols to another. Pieters quotes Dr. William Milligan as having said,

> Nothing can more clearly prove that the Revelation of St. John is not written upon chronological principles than the scenes to which we are introduced in the fifteenth and sixteenth chapters of the book. We have already been taken to the end, as we have seen, in chapter fourteen, the Son of Man upon the throne of judgment, the harvest of the righteous, and the vintage of the wicked. Yet we are now met by another series of visions setting before us judgments that must take place before the final issue. This is not chronology; it is apocalyptic visions, which again and again turn around the kaleidoscope of the future, and delights to behold, under different aspects the same great principles of the Almighty government, leading always to the same glorious results.[70]

This wrath of God is the sign for the complete avengement of the subjects of the Kingdom of Heaven on the persecuting powers. The souls under the altar had cried out for it. This "throne news" creates in Heaven unusual demonstrations of joy. John sees a "sea of glass mingled with fire," and on it standing those who had gotten the victory over the beast, and over his image, and over his mark, and over the number of his name, having the harps of God. Dana sees the splendor of "the sea of glass mingled with fire" as an apocalyptic representation of the beauty of the triumph of the redeemed.[71] Having crossed martyrdom's fiery sea, the saints begin to sing. In this song of jubilee the saints of both the Mosaic and Christian dispensations sing. What is the song of Israel's leader? Commentators have pointed to the song sung by the children of Israel after they had crossed the Red Sea. Some would hold that the song Moses taught the Israelites just prior to his death (Deuteronomy 32) was probably what they sang.[72] The one celebrated the justice and the other the mercy of God. And, the music was so arranged that they were responsive one to the other. The combined choir sang the song of Moses and the song of the Lamb. What singing! The Old Testament saints chanted, "Great and marvelous are thy works, Lord God Almighty," and the New Testament martyred saints responded, "Just and true are thy ways, thou King of saints!" The grand chorus sang in concert, "Who shall not fear thee, O Lord, and glorify thy name? for thou only art holy: for all nations shall come and worship before thee; for thy judgments are made manifest."

As antecedent to God's judgments to be visited upon the evil forces, John is presented with a view of the spiritual agencies intimately interested in their infliction. A new order of angel-agents appeared coming out of the open heavenly temple. John does not distinguish between the temple and the throne as God's abode. Angels were said to "stand before God" (Revelation 8:2), were "standing round about the throne" (Revelation 7:11), standing "over the altar" (Revelation 8:3), and coming "out of the temple" (Revelation 14:17). They had been in the tabernacle of testimony. These had been in the very presence of God and were entrusted with the responsible mission of destroying the persecuting powers. Commissioning for the task came from one of the four living creatures. "Seven angels" and "seven golden vials full of wrath" represented the message and execution of God's enduring judgments. "Full" indicates that the avengement so long awaited has come. These bowls are emblems of the prayers of the saints. The bowls came from God. He was very present in the temple, as was evidenced from the fact that the cloud of God's glory filled it. This is reminiscent of the cloud coming down upon the tabernacle (Exodus 40:34), the temple (1 Kings 8:10, 11), and upon the Mount of Transfiguration (Matthew 17:5). John, being well acquainted with Old Testament Scriptures and having been present at the transfiguration, was familiar with the glory cloud–which always signified God's immediate presence. He had brought the bowls (prayers of the saints) which He had received for ages. They are now filled with judgment (answer to their prayers–vengeance). God continued in the temple to give the judgment-angels audience when necessary to their work until the seven plagues had effected their purpose (that this is true is indicated by "no man being able to enter the temple" during that period) and was executing judgment which was coming in answer to the prayers of His people who are represented by the "man." Therefore, there was no longer a need of them coming to the mercy seat with grievances. He had heard. He was answering. No more need for the prayer, "How long, O Lord, holy and true, dost thou not judge and avenge our blood . . . ?" (Revelation 6:10). An easy transition to the pouring out of the seven vials of wrath is afforded by the foregoing.

From the very beginning of the drama John has heard voices of almost every description. Now a "great voice" (evidently the voice of God) commands the seven messengers, "Go your ways, and pour out the vials of the wrath of God upon the earth." In vindication of God's justice, seven bowls of wrath are viewed being poured out in this vision. One will want to take note of the fact that these arrange themselves in three groups, and that there is a striking comparison between them and the seven trumpets. Woes upon nature and man are presented. An outstanding contrast should be observed between the bowls and the trumpets. Whereas only a third part was affected at the blast of the trumpets, these woes affect the objects afflicted in their entirety. The last bowl of wrath, like the last symbol in each of the other series, is transitional. It introduces the series, which depicts the kingdom in final triumph.

Summers has written a statement that might well introduce the pouring out of the bowls of wrath. "No attempt to determine the special meaning of the objects thus visited by the wrath of God–land, sea, rivers, sun–has yet been or is ever likely to be successful."[73] Speaking similarly on the subject, Pieters records,

> . . . general meaning is plain; but so far as detailed exposition of the separate bowls and their happenings is concerned; the confession of ignorance made in connection with the trumpet series is again in place. It is possible–indeed, very likely–that to the mind of the apostle, as he saw the visions, each one had relation to some definite event in history or fact of experience; but if so, these meanings have not come down to us by any trustworthy tradition and remain undiscovered to the satisfaction of the most earnest and intelligent students. Literalism is here hopeless. How could any one put the wrath of God in a bowl and pour it out on the sun?[74]

An attempt to give what seems to be a reasonable interpretation to the symbols will be attempted by this writer. Though some scholars give some explanation, most choose to simply say that the symbolic language employed cannot be made to "walk upon spiritual all fours," thus knocking out the idea of a literal interpretation. To be dogmatic here is not a sign of wisdom regardless of the school in which one may claim fellowship. More important than an interpretation for "land, sea, rivers, and sun," is the general effect of the wrath of God when poured out without mixture. Observe the groups before mentioned. They are four, two, and one. This is the same procedure seen in the execution of the seals and trumpets. There is quite a similarity between the vial plagues and the ten plagues poured out upon the Egyptians. Here, as in the case of the Egyptian plagues, there is a wicked ruler, and his subjects are the recipients of God's wrath poured out of the bowls. Plagues upon the Egyptians failed to produce repentance and the bowl plagues also fail to bring about repentance. "We may regard these plagues, poured out of the seven vials upon the earth, as the last warnings God gives the unbelievers," wrote Poellot.[75] Differing somewhat with his brethren who hold basically with his views, Poellot continued by stating,

> The seven angels are good angels, strong servants of God. The figure seven is a symbol of God's dealing with man. We do not take the figure seven literally here, as if these last plagues (judgments, punishments) were exactly seven in number. Nor do we identify the seven plagues with seven events or periods in the history of the world. They are the sum total of the remaining expressions of the wrath of God as seen in His righteous judgments, dramatized in some detail before the eyes of John as the vision unfolds.[76]

Very probably Poellot is correct in viewing the seven plagues as representing the sum total of judgment to be poured out upon the enemies of the church. Also, one might consider the number seven as signifying the full and complete judgment to be meted upon the oppressors and persecutors, though at the same time hold that the seven is in fact seven.

The first bowl brings a plague upon the land. This calls to mind the plague of boils, which was brought upon the Egyptians as recorded in Exodus 9:8-12. Its contents struck the men who had the mark of the beast (emperor) and those who worshiped his image, and caused sores, which were exceedingly painful and annoying to come in the flesh. This first bowl of anger suggests very readily examples of moral corruption. Having given themselves so totally to the things of the flesh, it should not be thought strange that the judgment measured back to them would deal most drastically with things of the flesh. "Rottenness" is a term frequently found in the writings of those expressing the moral conditions in Rome and throughout the Roman Empire. "Grievous" would suggest great pain, and "noisome" would signify the crying out because of that pain. Men (wicked men marked by the beast) had great affliction brought upon them when the first bowl was emptied.

Contents of the second judgment bowl were poured out upon the sea. As has been shown several times before, the sea (waters) represents mankind in general, but at other times evil men in particular. Though the seven bowls are called the last plagues, it is evident that the reference is to the final grouping of judgments to be brought upon Imperial Rome bringing about her downfall. To see them as the last plagues (judgments) period, raises all kinds of questions when one reads "every living soul died" (verse 3), and yet read in verse 9 that some men are still around to be "scorched." "Sea," as used here, must represent evil men, men who trusted in man and by the shedding of blood lived. Through the death of others (in this case the saints) the evil corrupted officials and the evil corrupted supporter remained in power and kept things pretty well intact. This is reminiscent of Revelation 13:10,

> He that leadeth into captivity shall go into captivity: he that killeth with the sword must be killed with the sword. Here is the patience and the faith of the saints.

All of those who depended upon man in the wicked sea died. The blood (letting of the martyr's blood) which they had counted on to keep them in authority and power was but to bring blood upon them. Mortal conflict is seen in the statement, "blood of a dead man." They trusted in the sword; now they by the sword must die. A look to verse 12 will show the truth of this statement, "the way of the kings of the east might be prepared." One of the outstanding instruments used to destroy Rome was invading armies, thus, conflict. All in the sea of governmental wickedness who had trusted in the sword died.

"The rivers and fountains of waters" which flowed into the sea became blood also. Those forces that kept alive the sea were killed. Symbolized here is the very system that kept the sea in power. A general breakdown of the very life streams of the empire was affected by the pouring forth of the third bowl. Notice how the rivers and fountains take on personality when the water angel speaks of them in verse 6, " . . . they have shed the blood of saints and prophets, and thou hast given them blood to drink; for they are worthy." Had the angel not given this bit of commentary, one would be at a loss to give proper interpretation to the sources of fresh water mentioned in verse 4. Blood for blood seems to be the sentence. Having shed the blood of the "saints and prophets," their blood is shed. When the water angel declared God's righteousness in judgment, another voice was heard coming from the altar saying, "Even so, Lord God

Almighty, true and righteous are thy judgments." God needed no one to justify His action, but even so the "voice" gave testimony of God's right to pour out such judgment. If anyone had dared question, the answer was already pronounced. "Another voice" may have been the saints in unison speaking as one voice. They had cried out for vengeance. Now vengeance had come. God's righteousness was being vindicated both in the acts of judgment and the cry of the voice.

Bowl four is emptied upon the sun. It was like a world of oxygen poured into the sun of earth's firmament. Heat from the sun became so intense that men were scorched by it, but escape they could not. They became furious against providence. They blasphemed the name of Him who had power over these plagues, and they repented not to give glory unto Him. The sun is symbolic of the nation and government. Wanting to be a source of all kinds of natural blessings, it becomes a farce that only inflicts the deepest kind of misery upon the subject. Natural calamity, internal rottenness, and external invasion brought hard times upon the Roman government. Though very strong at the time John received the writing–she did crumble as predicted by Daniel,

> And in the days of these kings shall the God of heaven set up a kingdom, which shall never be destroyed: and the kingdom shall not be left to other people, but it shall break in pieces and consume all these kingdoms, and it shall stand for ever.
>
> Daniel 2:44

The benignant sun was changed to a fire of destruction as a plague on the men that had the mark of the beast and who worshiped his image. But they were not cured of their blasphemies.

Plague five is poured out upon the very seat of government. With this thought, the *Wesleyan Bible Commentary* is in agreement:

"This plague falls upon the seat of the evil government of the beast rather than upon his subjects as in the case of the first four. It is a plague of darkness, probably spiritual darkness."[77] Spiritual darkness was characteristic of the Roman kingdom prior to the angel's action in delivering the contents. When one reads the closing statement of verse 9, "and they repented not," he can better understand the meaning of "his kingdom was full of darkness." Pharaoh had a hard heart when Moses first began to insist that he should let God's people go. Each plague failing to bring repentance on the part of the

Egyptian ruler only served to harden his heart even more. (Count the times Pharaoh hardened his heart as God dealt with him through the plagues even as God had said He would do, Exodus 7:3.) That is exactly what happened when the bowl designed for the seat of government struck full impact. Darkness prevailed, but impenitence brought more. Conduct similar to that on the part of the Egyptian ruler is seen now in the actions of subjects of the Roman emperor. Again, like the Old Testament monarch, blasphemy issues and repentance are ignored.

Pouring forth of the sixth bowl dries up the Euphrates River. Drying up of the eastern boundary opens the way for military action and invasion by eastern monarchs. "Waters thereof dried up" symbolizes the removal of the barriers against invasion. A striking affinity can be seen between this scene and the sixth trumpet plague which brought into action the four angels in Euphrates. Destruction was released by them, and the way of military destruction is seen here. Being threatened by invading forces, the dragon, the beast, and the false prophets send out a communiqué calling for all forces to gather. John, "in the spirit," could see things in the spirit; therefore, no complications arise when the seer speaks of seeing "three unclean spirits like frogs." Thoughts of communication come to mind because the frog-like spirits came out of the mouths of the three forces of evil. Writing in regard to the frogs, Pieters said, "No doubt these frogs represent influences exerted through teaching or propaganda of some sort."[78] Satan made his call, the emperor made his call, and the false prophet made his call. That which is affected by the communication in the gathering of the forces was within itself miraculous. "That great day of God Almighty" had reference to a Day of Judgment, a day of reckoning. Such language is employed by many of the prophets of Israel when referring to a day when God would pour forth judgment. There are places in Scripture where the term does in fact have reference to the end, but not here. One's mind certainly is swept along to scenes of the end, but the end is not yet. Many would-be interpreters can see only the end when terms like "great day of God Almighty" and "I come as a thief" are used. Every event could in fact be the last, and not once would this writer imply anything to the contrary, but John was dealing with a situation that was to see its fulfillment in Rome and its conflict with spiritual forces (or forces enlisted by the Lord for a spiritual purpose). Systems of doctrine have been propounded upon the name

Armageddon. When all has been said about the name, let it be understood that it symbolizes a decisive battle. Many important battles involving Israel and her enemies were decided at Megiddo. Armageddon and Har-Magedon are to be found in various translations in the New Testament. Har-Magedon means Mountain of Megiddo and Armageddon means waters of the city of Megiddo. John's association with Megiddo was in all probability the fact that the Plain of Esdraelon or Megiddo had figured in many great battles of the Hebrews. Jeremiah 51:25 speaks of Babylon as "the destroying mountain." If this were in the mind of John, then Har-Magedon may stand for Babylon, which has been seen to symbolize Rome in Revelation 14:8, 16:19, and subsequent references. Even so, this symbolism is not to be taken to mean Rome as a place, but rather Rome–the embodiment of all evil in battle array against the church and Christ. Verse 17 gives hint to the fact that more emphasis is to be placed upon the spiritual aspect of the battle rather than anything else. This is seen in the statement, "poured out his vial into the air." Satan is called the Prince and Power of the Air. He is now attacked in a spirit-sense, even though invading armies are seen in the overall symbolism attacking also. At least some portion of the meaning lies in the fact that God used the eastern kings as He had used Assyria in battling Israel or as He had used other nations to accomplish His purpose.

"And the seventh angel poured out his vial into the air; and there came a great voice out of the temple of heaven, from the throne, saying, It is done" (Revelation 16:17). Affected especially was Babylon the great, Rome itself, the centralized authority and power which fostered evil in its perennial opposition and persecution of the church of God. God zeroed in on Rome. She became His target. Judgment unrestrained hit dead center and the greatest empire known by man to that day staggered like a drunk man, and of course in time, collapsed never to rise again. John beheld in the vision the "filled to the brim" fulfillment of Daniel's prophecy related to the effect of God's kingdom upon Rome. The weakened feet (part iron and part clay) were crushed, thus bringing down the image representing men's kingdoms and authority. The cry from God's presence, "It is done," meant the full judgment of God against Rome was done. That is, when the full impact of each bowl had done its due, God's judgment against Rome would have been carried through to the finish. More judgment is to be seen against the trinity of evil, but it is only the "filling full" of the announced judgment.

So mighty were the judgments that both heaven (the elements) and earth felt the effects. Babylon-Rome was divided and destroyed, for to her was given the "cup of the wine of the fierceness of his wrath." Great Babylon (Rome) had been brought into remembrance. These words were in all probability a source of much comfort to the saints earthward and Heavenward. John is saying, "God did not forget." In the midst of persecution there were times when, no doubt, all of those being oppressed wondered, "Has God forgotten?" Having seen the saints under the altar and having heard them cry for "revenge," hope is buoyed, for every indication now says "He has heard; He is answering." Whether the cry had caused God to bring judgment might raise questions, but the fact remains the saints cried and the very thing they hoped for came to pass. God, being God, will in every circumstance be God. He has declared, "Vengeance is mine, I will repay." Rome's payday had come. God remembered. When Rome lost its power, every city of the empire was weakened. The far reaches of the kingdom were touched. This is seen in the statement, "Every island fled away." Mountains (symbolical of power) were not "found" to be strong anymore. High places in the time of Israel wielded much religious-political power. Civic high places (mountains) and spiritual high places (places of emperor worship) were not to be found powerful anymore. Verse 21 uses such language as to convey the idea that the judgment was of God (out of Heaven), was severe (hail . . . the weight of a talent), and came because of continual impenitence.

11

The Whore

1. Description, Revelation 17:1-6
2. Delineation, Revelation 17:7-18
3. Denunciation, Revelation 18:1-20
4. Destruction, Revelation 18:21
5. Desolation, Revelation 18:22-24

Study Text: Revelation 17:1—18:24

Glenn G. Knight, a student of Professor H. E. Dana, permitted this writer to borrow his copy of *The Epistles and Apocalypse of John*, written by Dr. Dana, and used as a text when Knight was in his class. On page 99 of that title, not in the printed text but written in pencil by Mr. Knight, is a classroom statement of the author: "John was not trying to tell what the future was going to be, but that there was going to be a future." That statement should be kept to the forefront of the mind while endeavoring to discern the correct interpretation of the symbols employed by the Patmos prophet in chapters seventeen and eighteen. For that matter, care should be taken in the rest of the book that there is no attempt to weave the materials of the chapters into some eschatological scheme. One will find through diligent study that these chapters do not compose a program of connected happenings presented for the sole purpose of satisfying the curious mind that seeks to know the future. They are rather designed to set forth a great promise of ultimate and certain reality. Triumph of redemption over all evil forces and the redeemed's eternal peace is that reality.

A necessary interlude is formed between the seventh plague (bowl) and the allotment of rewards and condemnation. These chapters when taken together give a glance back at the latter portion of chapter sixteen. The story of the fall of Rome briefly sketched there is expanded here. Monumentally they stand to reaffirm the ancient prophetic principle of God's judgment–the destroyer shall himself be destroyed. At least on two occasions before (Revelation 14:8;

16:19) it was stated that Babylon would be destroyed but without certain identification or specific details. Those following the script had well guessed that Rome was meant. Here no room is left for any doubt. A new revelation is constituted on a familiar subject. One of the vial-angels invited John to view the judgment of "the great whore that sitteth upon many waters." Upon acceptance of the invitation, the Beloved is given spirit transportation into the wilderness. There he observed the woman "with whom the kings of the earth have committed fornication," and by whom "the inhabitants of the earth have been made drunk with the wine of her fornication." Astride a scarlet beast, bedecked with gold, precious stones, and pearls, holding a golden cup full of the evidence against her, she was arrayed in a garment of scarlet and purple. Her identification is given at least partially when the angel explains "the great whore that sitteth upon many waters." Further identification is given in Revelation 17:15 where commentary explains, "The waters which thou sawest, where the whore sitteth, are peoples, and multitudes, and nations, and tongues." Observe also, it is said that the harlot sat on seven mountains. Rome was built upon seven hills, but perhaps the better meaning of the symbol is (since a mountain represents power) seven mountains represent fullness of power. She was built upon supreme authority. This writer so interprets because the waters are symbolic. It stands to reason that if the waters are symbolic, the mountains are also. Another statement of identification is found in verse 18 where John is told, "The woman which thou sawest is that great city, which reigneth over the kings of the earth." Called to see the judgment of the "great whore," an unmistakable description is given of that "great city,"–Rome. Dana wrote, "This woman is quite clearly another representation of imperial Rome, intoxicating the Mediterranean world with her wickedness and in turn made drunken with the blood of Christian martyrs."[79] Description of the woman is suggestive of the riches and stateliness of the Imperial City. "Babylon the Great" is the symbolic name borne by Rome. Beyond all doubt her identity is discovered in verses 9 and 18. To identify the "great harlot" with the city of Rome certainly suits the circumstances of the time. To interpret this vision as the great apostasy of the papal system (or for that fact, earlier or later apostasies in which the professing but spiritually adulterous church is combined with the secular power to bring tribulation upon the true saints) is to suppose that the beloved apostle here speaks of some things that had no connection in anyway with the real needs of the addressed churches. The knowledge of such could be of no benefit whatsoever to the persecuted saints of Asia. It is difficult to imagine how the first readers of Revelation could possibly attach any other meaning to the explanation given in 17:9 and 18, except to think of the Imperial City.

"Kings of the earth have committed fornication" implies that the kings turned from alignment to the true God and Sovereign to bring themselves in subjection to the wicked sovereignty of this sinful harlot. It could also possibly imply that the kings turned from their true purpose in a position of authority to a "go along" attitude unresisting. Wherever these kings in obedience to Rome turned from protection of the people to persecution, the blood of the martyrs flowed. This answers to the statement, "The inhabitants of the earth have been made drunk with the wine of her fornication." John gives commentary on the subject in verse 6 where he states, "I saw the woman drunken with the blood of the . . . martyrs of Jesus." Rome's fornication drenched the kingdom with blood. Her wine was blood.

The prophet saw the badge of identity on the forehead of the harlot. It read, "MYSTERY, BABYLON THE GREAT, THE MOTHER OF HARLOTS AND ABOMINATION OF THE EARTH."

This reflects a custom practiced by prostitutes of the day who wore their names on their foreheads. Harlot of harlots, mother of harlots is the proclamation of the name. No far removed, apostate Roman church came to the mind of the original readers–they could think only of Rome. She was the Abomination of the Earth.

After the seer saw the blood-drunk woman, he was informed by the angel-guide that the mystery of the woman and the beast would be explained. Explanation of the mystery begins with the angel stating, "The beast that thou sawest was, and is not; and shall ascend out of the bottomless pit, and go into perdition" (verses 8a, 10 and 11). Similar language is employed by John four times. Identity of the beast is to be found in the expression "was, and is not, and yet is." Once again John appeals to the Nero legend (*Nero-redivivus* myth) as a means of identifying the beast. In no way is one to regard this as the apostle's sanction of the myth; he is only using it as a convenient tool to shun the persecutors while at the same time showing who is represented in the symbols. Domitian is pointed out as a reincarnation of the deceased, evil Nero. The Nero-redivivus myth held that Nero would return. As has been stated before in this writing, it was believed that he would return with his evil practices. Some held that he possibly would lead the armies from the east into battle. When Domitian became so cruel in his rulership, many held that Nero had in fact returned. Nero is indicated in verse 8. The one who "was, and is not, and yet is" became the eighth, but he who became the eighth was of the seven. Domitian was the eighth. He is spoken of as being of the seven because he, like Nero, persecuted the Christians. He was the first Roman monarch after Nero who did inflict cruelty upon the saints. Since all of this is true, Domitian could be apocalyptically represented as Nero reincarnated according to the legend. The seven heads represented seven mountains (previously discussed) and seven kings or rulers. Of all authorities consulted, Summers appears to have the best answer:

> They are also seven kings which have formed the basis of the great empire: Augustus, Tiberius Caligula, Claudius, Nero, Vespasian and Titus. There is an eighth, who is to have a part in history, but he is one of the seven already mentioned–he was and is the reincarnation of the evil, persecuting work of Nero.[80]

Power of the empire is represented in the ten horns. Rome's power was to be found in her many provinces so this symbol must be interpreted as the vassal kings (Rome's rulers in provinces). Authority of the rulers was delegated to them. They ruled only at the pleasure of and according to the dictates of central authority. Only one thought possessed them, and that was to be in obedience to the Roman Empire which was personified in Domitian. These made war with the Lamb. John, knowing the outcome, announced "the Lamb shall overcome them." It is then proclaimed why the Lamb was declared victorious–"He is Lord of lords, and King of kings." Gathered with the victorious Lord-Lamb are the "called," "chosen," and "courageous" (faithful). A very interesting development is prophetically observed in verse 16. The vassal kings were to come to hate the whore, and in time were to join the destructive forces against her. All of the hate for and destruction of Rome comes as a result of God putting into their hearts to fulfill His will. Actual development which eventually brought about the downfall of the Roman Empire harmonized with the remarkable description given by John in verses 14-17.

Chapter eighteen has been called "John's mosaic of doom" by Dana.[81] Doom of the allies of sinister Rome is revealed in this vision.

Denunciation rings loud and clear as the theme of the chapter. Drawing heavily from the language of several Old Testament prophets, John puts together a declaration of doom and desolation against cohorts of the Roman emperor. This chapter sounds much like a dirge or a song of doom.

An announcer-angel came down out of Heaven with great authority and the glory of God upon him. Having accomplished his purpose, the angel fades from the scene. His voice is mighty. All concerned could hear, especially the unrighteous. The emphasis of repetition is employed by the angel as he loudly proclaims, "Babylon the great is fallen, is fallen." "Mightily with a strong voice" suggests that the announcer was so confident of victory he wanted the whole world to hear the prophetic cry. No secret mealymouth announcement here! No soft spoken declaration coming out of unsurety! In the mind of God she had fallen, and the angel was speaking God's mind. Ugliness, corruption, and moral rottenness are pictured as being characteristic of the once fair lady. She has now become the harlot. She has "become the habitation of devils, and the hold of every foul spirit, and a cage of every unclean and hateful bird" (Revelation 18:2). Such a description declares the city to be ripe for judgment. Inhabitants of the city are symbolized as buzzards (desirous of filth) and hawks (preying upon the unwary). Babylon, though ripe for judgment, had not fallen at the time Revelation was written, but other cities of whose doom prophets had spoken had in fact been destroyed. So John, speaking with certainty that was born of prophetic tradition, knew that Rome was sealed for doom and destruction. An added feature to her identity is given in verse 3 along with a description with which the reader has now become familiar. The added feature is: "And the merchants of the earth are waxed rich through the abundance of her delicacies." John's certainty of Rome's fall came in a double measure. That her fall was predicted was sufficient for him to speak with assurance. In addition to that sure prophecy, however, was the fact of fulfilled prophecy. A case in point is that of Jeremiah prophesying against Babylon. Now that Rome is tagged "Babylon," John cannot help but rejoice and cause rejoicing on the part of the persecuted. For the contemporary saints there is also cause for rejoicing as one looks back. All evil symbolized by Babylon will be put down and God shall be all in all (1 Corinthians 15:28). "Come out of her," cried a heavenly voice. The reason for their departure is spelled out when the voice goes on to say, "that ye be not partakers of her sins, and that ye receive not of her plagues. For her sins have reached unto heaven, and God hath remembered her iniquities."

Before the destruction of Babylon, both Isaiah and Jeremiah issued like invitations and warnings. Isaiah 52:11, "Depart ye, depart ye, go ye out from thence, touch no unclean thing; go ye out of the midst of her; be ye clean . . ." Also,

> Flee out of the midst of Babylon, and deliver every man his soul: be not cut off in her iniquity; for this is the time of the LORD'S vengeance; he will render unto her a recompense. Babylon hath been a golden cup in the LORD'S hand, that made all the earth drunken: the nations have drunken of her wine; therefore the nations are mad. Babylon is suddenly fallen and destroyed: howl for her; take balm for her pain, if so be she may be healed . . . forsake her, and let us go every one into his own country: for her judgment reacheth unto heaven, and is lifted up even to the skies.
>
> Jeremiah 51:6-9

Much of what is being said sounds like a paraphrase of Scripture directed toward the city for which Rome is named in apocalyptic language. Babylon of old was a city. It may have also symbolized the embodiment of evil, for at times it was used in respect to Israel and even Jerusalem, but it was a city. Babylon in Revelation is Rome (a city), but there is that sense in which it stands for the forces of evil. Some interpreters would see Babylon as the representative of evil being finally overcome by the forces of righteousness. Not a bad view, but more is meant here than that. "The woman . . . that great city" is Rome (Babylon). God's people were called to sanctification lest they be partakers of her sins and receive her plagues. Verse 5 states, "Her sins have reached unto heaven, and God hath remembered." Some may have thought that God would not remember, but if nothing else (of course His righteousness would) had called Rome's wickedness to mind, the saints under the altar would have done so.

Judgment, in a double portion, is seen both in the cry, "Babylon . . . is fallen, is fallen," and in, "Reward her even as she rewarded you, and double unto her double . . ." "Reward her" seems to be directed more toward God than toward men. This is brought out more clearly in the statement "for strong is the Lord God who judgeth her." There is an air of recompense about the word "reward." Revenge is not denoted here, but rather requital. The expression "double unto her double" calls for a full measure of punishment. A feeling of tremendous depth is viewed in these statements against the guilt of the city. "An eye for an eye, and a tooth for a tooth" seems somewhat inadequate. A much more severe punishment is demanded. Phillips' translation has it, "mix her a drink of double strength." She had mixed a deadly portion for others, now God mixes one for her.

Rome's pride likewise figures into her judgment. "Pride goeth before destruction, and an haughty spirit before a fall." A glorified braggart, she sat disclaiming ever to know sorrow. Like a vain woman beholding herself, she calls herself a queen. Men of the world had caused her to view herself in this fashion, but God saw her for what she was–a harlot. Curious that she would say, "I am no widow," but old Babylon also saw herself in that light. "I shall be a lady for ever: so that thou didst not lay these things to thy heart. . . ." Her pride demanded her fall. If there had been no other corruption, pride would have brought her down. Her pride having been viewed (I sit a queen), a divine "therefore" releases swift (in one day) plagues of famine, mourning, and death. No partial judgment here, for it is written, "She shall be utterly burned with fire." Burning of Rome during the reign of Nero was partial, but God's scourge of burning would be complete. Devastating plagues of judgment would utterly bring Rome down to ashes and dust.

Standing afar off, unable to help because of the fear of her torment, kings of the earth bewail and lament her when the smoke of her torment ascends. They chant the first of the three dirges (verse 10) recorded in this connection–"Alas, alas, that great city Babylon, that mighty city! For in one hour is thy judgment." These kings had been aligned with, then against, and now cry for the city. It has been said that such action is consistent with vicious human nature. Dirge number two is sung by the rich merchants, for when Rome went down, wide traffic ceased. Twenty-nine different trade items are listed. As if in response to the kings, the merchants sing, "Alas, alas, that great city, that was clothed in fine linen, and purple, and scarlet, and decked with gold, and precious stones, and pearls!" They too saw the swift judgment that came upon Rome. Monarchs sang, "in one hour . . . judgment"; merchants sang, "in one hour . . . great riches . . . come to naught"; mariners sang, "in one hour she is made desolate." The third dirge sung by the mariners was, "Alas, alas, that great city, wherein were made rich all that had ships in the sea by reason of her costliness." Monarchs in every kingdom, merchants on every sea, mariners in every company weep not that they were so much in love with the harlot, but because the source of their riches was cut off. Every nook and cranny of the world felt the crashing fall of Imperial Rome.

When the double reward of verse 6 had been executed in the vision, all Heaven is called to rejoice. Holy apostles and prophets are told that the reward of the wicked has come that God might avenge them. God had in remembrance all the while those who had suffered for His cause. He, in His providence, had allowed time for "ripeness" before judgment. God rendered judgment according to the crime. Rejoicing on the part of the persecuted saints has Heaven's sanction. This situation is the reverse of Revelation 11:10; there the people rejoiced over the death of the two witnesses. Chapter seventeen records the actual rejoicing of Heaven's throng.

A millstone cast into the sea by a strong angel suggests the sudden fall of Rome and the rippling results. When a stone is cast into the sea, it sinks out of sight, but the waves created keep rolling until the farthest reaches are touched. Some may argue that the city of Rome exists today, and of course, that is true, but Babylon-Rome fell never to rise again. Crumbling stone and artifacts speak silently of a one-time great world capital city. No longer would it stand as the world center of pleasure, business, and domestic life. Thus, the three main attractions of Roman life were to be destroyed. Festivities and holidays occupied much of the time of the Romans. All such was to be banished from the life of that city for "the voice of harpers, and musicians, and of pipers, and trumpeters, shall be heard no more at all" (verse 22a). Industry was to be abolished, for there was to be no longer "craftsman, of whatsoever craft." "The sound of a millstone shall be heard no more at all" in the Imperial City (verse 22b). Home life of the city was to be blotted out though the domestic life had been preserved there more than any other place among the Gentiles (verse 23). Dana states, "With festivity, industry and domestic life destroyed, Rome could only lie a dismal waste."[82] Here is a most graphic picture of the destruction that befell Rome.

All nations had been deceived by Rome. Throughout the Roman Empire men bowed in worship to the emperor. When Rome fell, no longer were the nations to be deceived in this practice. A more detailed study on this thought will be given in chapter twenty when the binding of Satan is treated. Verse 24 is best understood when the student calls to mind why Domitian had the prophets and saints slain. They were slain when they defied the *concilia* in the worship of a man-god, the emperor. Blood of these outstanding spiritual giants was found in Rome. Someone may ask, "How can it be that the blood of all that were slain upon the earth was found in her?" For every saint slain, regardless where they were in the kingdom, Rome was held responsible. At her orders, death had been brought to those who failed to deny Christianity and embrace the worship of the beast. Again the attention of the reader is called to Revelation 13:10, "He that leadeth into captivity shall go into captivity: he that killeth with the sword must be killed with the sword. Here is the patience and the faith of the saints."

The text of the mighty angel, who before delivering his message illustrated it with the casting of a millstone into the sea, was "no more at all in thee." Prior to the delivery of this message, monarchs, merchants, and mariners had sung very similar dirges about the judgment (verse 10), riches come to naught (verse 17), and made desolate (verse 19). They had done so weeping. In the message the angel gives even more to weep about. No more music, no craft, no more grinding, no more light, no more weeping–everything in every area of life stopped. For all of that, Heaven's inhabitants had cause to rejoice, but there was more. Not given exactly under the "no more" text, but nonetheless a part of the message, three things were caused to cease: (1) no more traffic of the merchants, (2) no more deceiving of the nations through sorceries, and (3) no more the letting of the saints' blood in the city. If the "no more" prophetic message brought more weeping to the combined dirge singers, then the stopping of the merchants, deception, and murder brought more rejoicing to Heaven's choir.

12

The Victory

1. The Song—Hallelujah Chorus, Revelation 19:1-6
2. The Supper—Marriage Supper of the Lamb, Revelation 19:7-10
3. The Soldier—Christ Jesus, Revelation 19:11-14
4. The Sword—Out of His mouth (righteousness), Revelation 19:15, 16
5. The Summons—Supper of the Great God, Revelation 19:17, 18
6. The Slain—Beast, False Prophet, Remnant, Revelation 19:19-21
7. The Symbols—Key, Chain, Thousand, Revelation 20:1, 2
8. The Seal—Set upon Satan, Revelation 20:3
9. The Souls—Reigning with Christ, Revelation 20:4-6
10. The Sentence—Devil Cast Into the Fiery Lake, Revelation 20:7-10

Study Text: Revelation 19:1—20:10

Contrasts abound in Revelation, but none are more pronounced than the "Alas, alas" of the combined mournful choir of monarchs, merchants, and mariners (chapter 18), the fourfold "Hallelujah and Amen" of the "much people in heaven," and the "many waters" earthly choir. John had heard the lament of those who had profited through Rome's wickedness. Their dirge was sung not so much because they cared for Rome itself, but because she in a real sense was their livelihood. Rome's profiteers sang in despair beholding the destruction. Heaven's choir sang for two reasons: the destruction of "Babylon" and the triumph of Christ. "Alleluia" (hallelujah) is not found elsewhere in the New Testament. There are instances in the Old Testament, particularly in the Psalms, where certain forms are used that carry the same message, "Praise ye Jehovah," but even there the word "hallelujah" does not appear. It is as though God the Holy Spirit reserved the special word of high praise just for the Heaven-earth choir.

The "hallelujah chorus" is fourfold and should be studied from that viewpoint. Higher and higher the praise seems to rise until in one mighty voice they exclaim, "The Lord God omnipotent reigneth," which calls for rejoicing.

At the wafting of the first "Alleluia" words full of rich meaning reached John's ears–salvation . . . glory . . . honor . . . power. Heaven in full voice was saying, "Praise ye the Lord for he alone is the source of salvation and is worthy of glory and honor and power." Salvation rested just as squarely upon God's truth and righteousness as did His judgment. Though they were thrilled at the thought of thorough and complete destruction of Rome by God's judgment, they chose to sing first of their own deliverance (salvation) before singing of the enemy's destruction. Having had the privilege to view the vision (on the basis of truth and righteousness), and then know that destruction was inevitable, the Heavenly choir understood that the judgment befitted the evil. Judgment came upon the "great whore, which did corrupt the earth with her fornication" and had martyred the saints. That God had avenged "the blood of his servants at her hand" had also helped prompt the sounding of the first "Alleluia." Smoke arising "for ever and ever" shows how complete and final was the judgment. It was as if God were saying to them about their enemies what Moses said to the Israelites about the Egyptians, "Ye shall see them again no more for ever" (Exodus 14:13). Such a thought brought forth the second "Alleluia." Hardly were they rejoicing over the fact that so many had gone down in eternal destruction, but rather because their wickedness had ceased. The cessation had come about as God had taken the part of the saints because of truth and righteousness. When the finality of their judgment was announced by the second "Alleluia," the twenty-four elders and the four living creatures, who became prostrate before the Lord, sanctioned the choir by intoning the "Amen." It is somewhat difficult to understand if the "much people" were joined by the prostrate elders and living creatures when the third "alleluia" rang out, or if the elders and creatures sang this one alone. When reading the succeeding verses, one is inclined to believe that the "much people" choir was joined by elders, living creatures, and finally, by all the redeemed. Remember, this was a vision and as such could very well include all the saints in every age along with Heaven's host.

At the sounding of the third "alleluia," an authoritative voice (coming from out of the throne) called for all the servants of God to praise Him. Without hesitation every God-fearing voice on earth (a great multitude . . . voice of many waters) thunderously joins in to make both Heaven and earth resound with the fourth "alleluia," followed by exalted praise, "the Lord God omnipotent reigneth." "Lord God"–a title similar to this was used by the adherents to emperor worship when addressing or worshipping the monarch. Happenings just prior to the victorious phrase "the Lord God omnipotent reigneth," show the defeat of the whole blasphemous system of emperor worship. When that system collapsed, Christ the victor was still on the throne. Also ushered in by the final "alleluia" is another real cause for rejoicing–an announcement of "the marriage of the Lamb."

Oriental customs must be brought to mind if a proper understanding is to be had of "for the marriage of the Lamb is come, and his wife hath made herself ready" (Revelation 19:7). This seems to be more of an announcement of the engagement and coming marriage than a definite "now is the time of the marriage." Engagements were not entered into lightly; neither were they dissolved without legal action (either public or private) owing to the circumstances. Joseph's activity upon learning that Mary was pregnant before they had come together serves well to prove the point.

> Now the birth of Jesus Christ was on this wise: When as his mother Mary was espoused to Joseph, before they came together, she was found with child of the Holy Ghost. Then Joseph her husband, being a just man and not willing to make her a publick example, was minded to put her away privily. But while he thought on these things, behold, the angel of the Lord appeared unto him in a dream, saying, Joseph, thou son of David, fear not to take unto thee Mary thy wife: for that which is conceived in her is of the Holy Ghost.
>
> Matthew 1:18-20

Another thought that should be injected here is that John, as he did so often in his excitement, rushes himself and his readers on to a scene that shall be and declares it as though it is already. "Is come" could mean "is come into view." Whatever the meaning, anyone can plainly see that the marriage did not take place at that time but later. Twice in chapter twenty-one, verses 2 and 9, the student will take note that the "Lamb's wife" is still called "a bride" and "the bride." Just when the marriage is to take place is not spelled out specifically in the Scripture. Some would-be interpreters will speculate and some would even try to prove that the marriage took place when John announced "the marriage. . . is come," but a further study of verses 8 and 9 will prove them to be in error. That which transpires beginning with verse 10 brings a warrior on the scene, not a bridegroom. But just here, verses 7c, 8, and 9 must be explained. Christ's "bride" is called "his wife" at the announcement of the engagement. Recall that Mary was called Joseph's wife during the engagement period. Such is the case here. Engagements in those days, one must remember, were binding. When a man espoused a woman, she became known as his wife though she was not truly his wife until the marriage ceremony. All through the Old Testament the relationship between God and His people was often compared to that of husband and wife. In the New Testament similar language is employed to show the relationship between Christ and the church. After the announcement of the marriage, "the bride" was allowed a period of preparation for it is written, "to her was granted that she should be arrayed in fine linen, clean and white" (Revelation 19:8). Her attire (wedding gown) is "fine linen" (righteousness of the saints), "clean" (no defilement), and is "white" (signifying purity, a virgin). Since commentary is given on "fine linen" (righteousness of the saints), all doubt is erased in regard to the bride. All saints make up the bride of Christ. One need only read the writings of Paul to find apostolic agreement.

John was called upon to write a most blessed beatitude, "Blessed are they which are called unto the marriage supper of the Lamb." Other things in previous visions had been brought to view and dealt with briefly only to pass from the scene of action to be mentioned no more. Revelation does not reveal the wedding though perfect accord can be seen between Christ and the church in chapters twenty-one and twenty-two. Called to a wedding ceremony and then told that a blessing was involved was something new for the saints. To the Oriental a marriage was a joyous occasion, but public ceremonies had become so immoral and wicked the believer was not in attendance. Now, by divine invitation, they are beckoned to attend the marriage of the Lamb. Being told that the above things "are the true sayings of God," John falls at the feet of the messenger to worship him. Rebuked by the "fellowservant" of the "brethren" when attempting to worship him, the apostle is instructed to worship God "for the testimony of Jesus is the spirit of prophecy" (Revelation 19:10). Worship was in order, but the messenger wanted the worshiper to understand that the "spirit of prophecy" had made clear the revelation had come from God, and that He alone was the object of praise. Was John somewhat confused, or was he so overwhelmed with the knowledge that during the period of the bride's preparation many more would be called to the marriage, that he thoughtlessly fell to worship before his informer? And too, there were times when the voice that spoke or the person that appeared was not given clear identity. This could very well have been the case here. Before dealing too harshly with John, one needs to remember that the "voice came out of the throne" and until the act of worship no further identification is made known. One lesson at least is portrayed by the incident–man is not to worship angels or men, regardless of their importance or even when dispatched by the Lord.

"The testimony of Jesus" may carry with it the thought, "Keep on testifying for Jesus, for herein is the source of the prophecy spirit." His testimony for Jesus had brought him to the position that the spirit of prophecy was with him. It was in a one-man worship service that he "was in the spirit." That is how it began and that is how it would continue. Back in Asia Minor he had refused to worship a man. Because of that action he was exiled to Patmos for the testimony of Jesus. Worshiping God in spirit and in truth put him in the spirit. A continuation of not worshiping any other than God would assure him the spirit of prophecy.

Corrected and instructed, the Patmos seer saw the heavenly curtain drawn revealing "a white horse" (symbolic of victory) and a rider called "Faithful and True," "The Word of God," "KING OF KINGS, AND LORD OF LORDS." Christ is identified as the rider. Christ is further identified by "in righteousness he doth judge and make war," " His eyes were as a flame of fire," "on his head were many crowns," "out of his mouth goeth a sharp sword," "He shall rule them with a rod of iron," "He treadeth the winepress," and "His attire is a blood-sprinkled garment." The conflict is spiritual for it is stated, "in righteousness" by a "sharp sword . . . out of his mouth" (His Word), He makes war. Spiritual enemies are defeated in a spiritual battle by spiritual armament. Verse 14 reveals that the victorious armies that follow the warrior are the saints. They are not dressed in battle garb, but rather in righteousness–"the fine linen." They rode as victors coming home from a successful engagement in battle. Here the combined forces that were to defeat all wickedness are in grand review. One cannot help feel that this is a picture of the emerging forces of righteousness which have engaged in spiritual conflict with evil since the beginning of Christianity. Those slain by the sword of His mouth (His Word) He ruled, and those not slain by His Word He trod under foot. Thus, the two-way cutting of the two-edged sword (Hebrews 4:12) is made evident.

In the vision the prophet saw an angel standing with the radiance of the sun and heard him inviting with a loud voice the birds of prey to the great supper of God. Carnage from the successful conflict would be the feed for the birds invited. This is symbolism. There is no authority to switch from the spiritual to the literal. This is a war of righteousness versus evil. God had revealed the outcome of the war against the beast even before the battle. The angel made this all clear. Verse 19 relates that the beast and the kings of the earth moved to make war against Christ and His army. Only one kind of battle could be fought between these two opposing forces–spiritual. Nothing is said of Christ's army being equipped for mortal conflict. Neither is anything said of Christ being prepared for such a fray. A spiritual Being (Christ), leading a spiritual army (righteous saints), using only a spiritual sword (Word of His mouth); one can only conclude that it is spiritual warfare. How unlike the Lord who taught "put up thy sword" to take sword in hand, and in contradiction to His own teaching, lead those whom He had taught into a bloodbath battle! To teach that this conflict is literal is untenable to this writer. Such ascending to the throne would make the Lord no more than a dictator. He taught "if any man will come after me"–never did He teach a forced gospel! Man becomes a part of Christ's kingdom by the new birth (John 3:3 and 5), never by the pressure of brute force.

Casualties of the war are listed in verse 20–the beast (Roman emperor), the false prophet (Roman *concilia*), and worshipers of the beast. Both the beast and the false prophet were cast into the lake of fire. As had been predicted by Daniel (Daniel 2:45), the Roman Empire was destroyed by the Stone (Christ–His Word–His Kingdom) hewn out of the mountain. All of this serves to signify the final outcome of the conflict between good and evil.

Let it be noted once again that all of the slaying took place by the "sword which proceeded out of his mouth." There is no way this symbol can be interpreted to mean a literal sword. How absurd to even imply such! What an indictment against the Lord who taught turn the other cheek (Matthew 5:39).

Chapter twenty is the beginning point in Revelation for all second lieutenant interpreters. Almost without regard for chapters one through nineteen and what possible meaning the whole book held for the first century believers, they build schools of thought inconsistent with sound Biblical exegesis. Also characteristic of these is disregard for the background of the book, the circumstances of the day, and "this lone passage dealing with the millennium is couched in a book of the Bible literally filled with symbols, numerology, figures of speech, poetic language spiritual lessons couched in Old Testament terminology. . . ."[83] To attempt a sound interpretation of this chapter without some knowledge of apocalyptic literature would be an affront *extra ordinem* (Fr.). Remember that *apocalypse,* the first word in the original text, means "unveiling." But also call to mind that the unveiling (revelation) was shown ("to show unto his servants"), was sent ("things which must shortly come to pass . . . He sent"), and signified ("signified it by his angel") unto His servant John (Revelation 1:1). From the above, one gathers that the revelation was signified to John, by Christ, through the angels. The word "signified" means to show by signs (symbolism). Though this was pointed out somewhat in the beginning of this book, it needs to be stated here again. The nature of the book is made very clear. Revelation is an unveiling of God's message through symbols (signs). That message intended comes not through a literal understanding of its words, but rather through the interpretation of the symbols employed.

Beginning with chapter twelve, three enemies are seen tormenting the saints: the dragon (the devil), the first beast (Rome personified in the emperor–Domitian), and the second beast (the committee that enforced emperor worship–the false prophet). In several previous visions John saw and heard the defeat of all three and the triumph of Christ. But in chapter nineteen the seer saw the destruction of the beast and the false prophet in a vision. Now in chapter twenty he sees in a vision Christ binding Satan, the reign, the loosing of Satan, and the general judgment. John states,

> And I saw an angel come down from heaven, having the key of the bottomless pit and a great chain in his hand. And he laid hold on the dragon, that old serpent, which is the Devil, and Satan, and bound him a thousand years, And cast him into the bottomless pit, and shut him up, and set a seal upon him, that he should deceive the nations no more, till the thousand years should be fulfilled: and after that he must be loosed a little season.

Revelation 20:1-3

One central thought stands out in these three verses–the binding of the devil. Obvious to the student is the fact that the thought is conveyed by symbols. No one would contend that the key and chain are literal, for all know that you cannot bind a spiritual being with a literal chain, but rather with that which is spiritual. Figures of speech are seen in the key, the chain, the abyss, the binding, the sealing, and the thousand years. Christ is represented in the "angel come down from heaven," for He has "the key" (authority, power–Matthew 10:1; 28:18; Revelation 1:18; 9:1; Mark 6:7; Luke 10:19; and Isaiah 22:22). "All authority" rests with Him and is delegated to others (Matthew 16:19) only in the fact that they are given the privilege to preach His Truth which is the "power of God" (Romans 1:16). Christ, during His earthly, personal ministry, entered into the strong man's house and bound him (Matthew 12:22-29). This binding is seen to some degree in the work of the twelve (Matthew 10:1, " . . . his twelve disciples, he gave them power against unclean spirits, to cast them out . . ." and also in the ministry of the seventy [Luke 10:17-19], " . . . seventy returned . . . saying, Lord, even the devils are subject unto us through thy name. And he said . . . I beheld Satan as lightning fall . . . I give unto you power . . . over all the power of the enemy . . ."). Christ's statement, "I beheld Satan as lightning fall" is to be taken as a reference to Satan's defeat at the cross (Revelation 12:7-12). During His ministry, Christ referred to His crucifixion as the casting out of Satan (John 12:31-33). Genesis 3:15 is thus fulfilled, ". . . it shall bruise thy head. . . ." Hebrews 2:14 reveals "through death he might destroy him that had the power of death, that is, the devil." Christ won the victory at Calvary for it was there He shook the devil from His heel and stamped His foot upon the serpent's head. A deathblow was struck! John writes in 1 John 3:8, "For this purpose the Son of God was manifested, that he might destroy the works of the devil." Colossians 2:15 conveys the same thought for it states, "And having spoiled principalities and powers, he made a shew of them openly, triumphing over them in it." All of the foregoing gives conclusive evidence that Jesus bound Satan (set boundaries–limited his power) at the first advent. As "the stone cut out of the mountain" enlarged, that binding worked so effectually that Satan lost his power in deceiving the nations. For all those who would object that Satan is bound, and point to the Scripture that describes him "as a roaring lion," let it be said that John speaks of him as being imprisoned (not obliterated!). Thus, his power is limited. "To what extent was his power limited?" one may ask. After a careful reading of "that he should deceive the nations no more, till the thousand years should be fulfilled" (verse 3), and "Satan shall be loosed out of his prison, And shall go out to deceive the nations . . ." (verses 7b, 8a), one cannot help but understand that the binding has to do primarily with deception of the nations. This writer has consulted many scholars that hold to the same opinion. Satan is presently limited to the extent that he cannot marshal the forces of evil in outright physical war against the Christians. During his period of restraint he in fact may do many things and may go about as "a roaring lion seeking whom he may devour," but he is prevented from deceiving nations so as to gather them for battle.

Another thought imbedded in the statements dealing with the deception is that nations are no longer deceived into emperor worship as was the case in Rome. Through the spread of the gospel that practice was destroyed, and even the Roman government which martyred saints for not worshiping the emperor came in time to declare Christianity to be the State Religion. Both the Living Word and the Written Word play a significant role in the setting of limits to Satan's activity. God's Word is a linking chain from Genesis to Revelation. His Word cannot be broken (John 10:35). Individuals in nations are deceived, but not nations as such.

Futurists propound a scheme concerning verses 4-6 that is untenable to the conscientious Bible student. Such project these verses into the future, and though they claim for themselves untouchable exegesis, fallacies can be easily detected. According to their theory, Christ will come in the air to catch away His bride. The resurrection of the saints will take place when He comes in the air. Those resurrected are to be with Him for seven literal years. At the end of the seven years, Christ is to return to reign on the earth for one thousand literal years. When the thousand years are expired Satan shall be loosed a little season. Now please note that there are but one thousand years (interpreted literally by the futurist) between the resurrections. But how can that be? If the righteous dead is resurrected seven years before the start of the thousand years, and if there are but one thousand years between the resurrections, how can their theory stand? Remember, there are only one thousand literal years between the resurrections, according to them. But here in their theory one thousand and seven years are to be found. Besides that, the devil is to be loosed a little season at the expiration of the one thousand literal years, but prior to the resurrection of the unjust! If this writer's math is not completely haywire, it seems to add up: seven + one thousand + a little season. Now something is awry! Literalists are in trouble at this point. Some would object to the foregoing because of the injection of the seven years which are not mentioned. With that objection in mind, take another look at the verses and view them as absolute-literal, for that is how the futurist sees them. One thousand years are declared to be between the resurrections. It is not until the one thousand years are expired that Satan is loosed, yet that loosing must take place before the resurrection of the unjust. Here, without the seven years, one finds one thousand years and a little season between the resurrections, but there is to be only one thousand years between them. The dilemma for them is not improved. If the literalist holds to his theory in the light of this clear exposure, then he must admit that he does not see the one thousand as an exact literal one thousand years.

Admitting that the key, the chain, the binding, and the sealing are all symbolic terms, does it not seem only reasonable that the one thousand would likewise be symbolic? Authorities abound, and have since early church history, who hold that the one thousand is symbolic, representing that period in which Satan is restrained from "deceiving the nations" and when the saints reign with Christ. Without being too dogmatic and restrictive, Amillennialists contend that this represents the period of time between His first and second advents. One of the more outstanding authorities in the twentieth century was Dana, and he wrote the following,

> Everywhere else in Revelation numbers are clearly symbolic; consequently it is exceedingly doubtful that we should take this one number to be literal. It is exceedingly unwise to detach from its setting in this thoroughly and intensely apocalyptic book this one brief passage of three verses and insist upon taking it literally.[84]

Occupied thrones appeared before John and they that sat upon them were given judgment (Matthew 19:28; 1 Corinthians 6:2; Revelation 3:21). Locations of the thrones are not declared by the seer. Placing of them would only be speculation on the part of this writer or any other expositor. A quote from McDowell will help point this up.

> It would be well for us to observe carefully what these words say and what they do not say. First of all, it should be observed that they do not speak of the reign of the martyrs and saints as being upon earth . . . John states that he saw thrones; the implication is that these thrones are occupied by the martyrs and saints but whether these thrones are in heaven or upon the earth, he does not say.[85]

Buis simply stated, "there is not a word in this passage which mentions an earthly reign."[86] Since the term *thrones* would symbolize reign, and since it is pluralized, one could suppose that the prophet saw various ones reigning with Christ; some in the spiritual kingdom on earth (Revelation 1:6; 1 Corinthians 6:2; Ephesians 2:5 and 6) and some in Heaven with Him (Matthew 19:28). Both ideas are certainly suggested in Scripture. An added attraction claims the attention of the revelator, for he adds,

> I saw the souls of them that were beheaded for the witness of Jesus, and for the word of God, and which had not worshipped the beast, neither his image, neither had received his mark upon their foreheads, or in their hands; and they [they that sat upon the throne, the souls of them that were beheaded–martyrs, witnesses, and those which had not worshipped the beast] lived and reigned with Christ a thousand years.
>
> Revelation 20:4

How will all of this fit the statement, "this is the first resurrection"? Considering that Christ is called "firstfruits" in 1 Corinthians 15:20 and that the 144,000 are called "firstfruits" in Revelation 14:4, it is reasonable to believe that the 144,000 are those prophetically mentioned in Isaiah 26:19 and those resurrected with Christ in fulfillment of that Scripture (Matthew 27:52, 53). For that reason, the 144,000 must be linked to the "first resurrection." At the same time it must be pointed out that the "souls of the beheaded" figure also into the statement. Apostle John wanted his readers to know that the martyred saints were as much with the Lord and reigning as were the 144,000 (representative figure of all who died in faith before Christ's resurrection) who came forth at His resurrection. One can only conclude that every man resurrected in/with Christ has part in the first resurrection, for Christ is the first resurrection. To be dogmatic here is to lose the thought being symbolized–the saints have triumphed and are reigning with Christ. And too, those said to reign, reign with Christ

(Revelation 20:4-6). That within itself confirms the reign to be spiritual (Christ reigns now in Heaven on David's throne, Psalm 89:35-37; Isaiah 22:22; Luke 1:32, 33; Acts 2:30-34; Ephesians 1:19-23). For if they reign with Him, they must do it before He comes again, because when He comes again He will deliver up the kingdom (1 Corinthians 15:23b-28). When it is admitted that the 144,000 (symbolic number of all Old Testament saints) were resurrected with Christ (Isaiah 26:19; Matthew 27:53, 54) and are the first resurrection, it is not difficult to understand that the "rest of the dead" speaks of the then wicked dead who will be resurrected at the end of the reign when Christ comes again. But before the resurrection of the rest of the dead, Satan will "be loosed a little season . . . out of his prison." He was bound "that he should deceive the nations no more, till the thousand years should be fulfilled . . . ," and when he is loosed he "shall go out to deceive the nations which are in the four quarters of the earth, Gog and Magog, to gather them together to battle . . . ."

Gog and Magog are pictured as pagan enemies to God's people in Ezekiel 38 and 39; enemies who were to be destroyed by fire. "And I will send a fire on Magog, and among them that dwell carelessly in the isles: and they shall know that I am the LORD" (Ezekiel 39:6). This harmonizes with 2 Thessalonians 1:7b, 8a, " . . . when the Lord Jesus shall be revealed from heaven with his mighty angels, In flaming fire taking vengeance on them that know not God. . . ." God's fire will be a devouring force used of God when evil forces move against "the beloved City" and "the camp of the saints"–the True Church.

> But ye are come unto mount Sion, and unto the city of the living God, the heavenly Jerusalem, and to an innumerable company of angels, To the general assembly and church of the firstborn, which are written in heaven, and to God the Judge of all, and to the spirits of just men made perfect.
>
> Hebrews 12:22, 23

Satan is then cast into the lake of fire.

13

The Alleluia

1. The General Judgment, Revelation 20:11-15
   a. The Throne, 20:11a
   b. The Judge, 20:11b
   c. The Judged, 20:12, 13
   d. The Judgment, 20:14, 15
2. Heaven Characterized, Revelation 21:1—22:5
   a. The Tabernacle, 21:1-8
   b. The Holy City, 21:9-27
   c. The Garden, 22:1-5
3. The Epilogue, Revelation 22:6-21
   a. The Revelation Message Attested, 22:6-9
   b. The Revelation Message Pertinent, 22:10-15
   c. The Revelation Message Sacred, 22:16-19
   d. The Revelation Message Concluded, 22:20, 21

Study Text: Revelation 20:11—22:21

John, having observed the judgment of the devil, the beast, and the false prophet (Revelation 20:10), is caused to view the general judgment with its particular emphasis upon judgment of the wicked. Think it not strange that this writer would speak of the judgment as being general in nature. The Treatise under which he was ordained carries that very term and the present Treatise he embraces holds to the same principle. Note: "There will be a General Judgment, when time and man's probation will close forever. Then all men will be judged according to their works."[87] "There will be a judgment, when time and man's probation will close forever. Then all men will be judged according to their works."[88] And to this the Scriptures agree. There are many illustrations of judgment in the New Testament. There are, however, three basic pictures or concepts, and these three illustrations are but three ways of looking at the same judgment. They are: (1) the sheep and goat judgment, Matthew 25:31-46; (2) the judgment seat of Christ, Romans 14:10; 2 Corinthians 5:10; and (3) the great white throne judgment, Revelation 20:11-15. Acts 17:31 certainly conveys the idea of a general judgment, "Because he hath appointed a day, in the which he will judge the world in righteousness by that man whom he hath ordained." A general judgment of mankind is by no means necessary to the authority of the divine decision, in any individual case. Nor, is such a judgment necessary to secure a righteous sentence from the judge. Neither is a general judgment necessary to ascertain, to the individual judged, the character or the justice of the sentence awarded to him, whether of condemnation or approval, whether of weal or woe. But, a public adjudication, in the case of every individual to be judged, is necessary, that a manifestation of the righteousness of their fate may be made to their fellow creatures.

There are three basic reasons why God has designed a general judgment: (1) to prove His saints, Matthew 25:24; (2) to vindicate His Word, Matthew 5:18; and (3) to publicly condemn the sinner, Ecclesiastes 12:14. When one studies carefully Revelation 20:11-15 these reasons become manifestly clear. First Corinthians 4:5 throws even more light upon the subject for it states, "Therefore judge nothing before the time, until the Lord come, who both will bring to light the hidden things of darkness, and will make manifest the counsels of the hearts: and then shall every man have praise." Paul bore out the same thought again when he wrote, "I charge thee therefore before God, and the Lord Jesus Christ, who shall judge the quick and the dead at his appearing and his kingdom" (2 Timothy 4:1). Suffice it to say that Scriptural evidence supports the doctrine of the general judgment. In times of greater simplicity and of less intellectual hardihood than now, the bare announcement of the judgment text would have been quite sufficient to ward off all questions of the necessity or of the forthcoming of a general judgment of mankind, with a view to their final destiny. But, this age is so profoundly rational in its views, so confident in its keenness of judgment and so untrammeled by implicit deference to authority that in the face of the text, and many other clear Scriptural declarations to the same effect, there are many who querulously inquire what necessity there is for such a judgment. And others are somewhat more daring who roundly deny that there ever will be such a judgment; because, in their thinking no necessity exists that there should be one!

The seer writes, "And I saw a great white throne, and him that sat on it, from whose face the earth and the heaven fled away; and there was found no place for them." "Throne" is the emblem of supreme authority, dominion, and sovereignty. "White throne" indicates the gospel righteousness on which it is founded and the purity of Him that sits upon the throne. Dana suggests that "it is best to accept the white throne just as we do the beast or scarlet woman or white horse–as a symbol."[89]

Neither here nor elsewhere does John tell whether the One on the throne is God the Father, or Christ. In all probability the Father is meant here. Some Scriptures relate that Christ is to be the judge of all (Matthew 25:31; John 5:22), while the Apostle Paul speaks both of the judgment seat of Christ (2 Corinthians 5:10) and to that of God the Father (Romans 14:11, 12). It is to be understood that the Father is the judge, but He judges through Christ His Son. John wrote in John 5:22, "For the Father judgeth no man, but hath committed all judgment unto the Son." Also, Paul declared, " . . . He hath appointed a day, in the which he will judge the world . . . by that man whom he hath ordained . . . in that he hath raised him from the dead" (Acts 17:31).

"From whose face the earth and the heaven fled away; and there was found no place for them" calls to mind 2 Peter 3:10, "But the day of the Lord will come as a thief in the night; in the which the heavens shall pass away with a great noise, and the elements shall melt with fervent heat, the earth also and the works that are therein shall be burned up." Morris writes, "John invests the scene with the greatest solemnity. There was something so terrible in the demeanor of Him on the throne that earth and heaven themselves fled away from Him. There was found no place for them, i.e., they were completely destroyed."[90] The focal point is the throne and the main object to which the reader's attention is called is Him "from whose face the earth and the heaven fled."

The first act, in this "beyond measure" important and interesting transaction, is the opening of the books. St. John said, "And I saw the dead [all of the dead], small and great, stand before God; and the books were opened: and another book was opened, which is the book of life: and the dead were judged out of those things which were written in the books, according to their works" (Revelation 20:12). Scriptural commentary informs the reader that the other (another) book "is the book of life." But what about "the books" which were opened? What then should be understood by the books, and by their being opened? There is doubtless a reference to a practice (common–perhaps nearly universal) of producing in courts of law the laws governing the cases which are to be tried, and of explaining and showing the application of those laws. Thus, the Bible is considered to be one of the books opened. That the Bible will be present can be seen in Christ's statement, "Heaven and earth shall pass away, but my words shall not pass away" (Matthew 24:35), and in "and receiveth not my words . . . the same shall judge him in the last day" (John 12:48). The second volume of "the books" is a record of the "deeds of their lives." It would seem that the procedure would be: The Bible is opened, then the book of the deeds of one's life is opened. They then are laid side by side and a close check is made. After a comparison of the requirements and the works is made, the book of life (the Lamb's book of life) is opened that all may see what Heaven's register reveals in regard to the individual being judged. The judge knows the verdict from the beginning and so does the judged, but that all might know, the procedure is followed. "Books" suggest that the judge has the record before Him.

The dead of whatever stature stand before God and are judged out of those things which were written in the books, according to their works, whether good or bad. Prophet John saw all of the dead present. No matter from whence they came or what manner they had met death, they were present and they were judged. At this point death and Hell are cast into the lake of fire. This is declared to be the second death. Those whose names were not found written in the book of life (cf. Exodus 32:32, 33 and Luke 10:20) were cast into the lake of fire. But what about those whose names were found recorded? Chapters 21 and 22 tell well the destiny of the redeemed. Adams has said, "These chapters may be attempts to express the humanly inexpressable (sic) glory of the blessings which await Christ's own."[91] Paul said, "But as it is written, Eye hath not seen, nor ear heard, neither have entered into the heart of man, the things which God hath prepared for them that love him. But God hath revealed them unto us by his Spirit . . ." (1 Corinthians 2:9, 10a). The apostle at this juncture had already experienced that of which he wrote when in 2 Corinthians 12:2-4 he declared,

> I knew a man in Christ above fourteen years ago, (whether in the body, I cannot tell; or whether out of the body, I cannot tell: God knoweth;) such an one caught up to the third heaven. And I knew such a man, (whether in the body, or out of the body, I cannot tell: God knoweth;) How that he was caught up into paradise,

> and heard unspeakable words, which it is not lawful for a man to utter.

Man in his heart has been made to see the blessedness of the redeemed in eternity, but only John was given the privilege to see and then record. Just how literal or symbolic John's words are to be taken will never quite be settled this side of eternity. "Heaven will surely be worth it all!"

But what is one to understand when he reads chapters 21 and 22? Some would not dare make one word of John's description symbolic lest to do so might destroy an inherited, imaginative fantasy formed more from "song book theology" than from a true Scriptural concept. This writer holds that the eternal blessedness of the redeemed will be far beyond John's word description. The things that John's words symbolized meant (and yet mean) more to the redeemed than all the literalness one might desire. Heaven is characterized in three symbols that set forth its nature. They are the tabernacle of God (Revelation 21:3), the great city (Revelation 21:10), and the garden (Revelation 22:2, 3).

A new Heaven and a new earth came into John's view (2 Peter 3:13) for the first Heaven and the first earth had passed away (Revelation 20:11). "There was no more sea" harks back to Revelation 4:6 where it is stated, "and before the throne there was a sea of glass like unto crystal." Exiled, Pastor John had understood that expression to signify the transcendency of God.[92] On that Lord's Day morning the prophet longed to be in his pulpit back on the mainland. But he was separated from his people by the sea. Consolation came to him when he realized that as he was separated by the sea from his people, the crystal sea separated the transcendent God from His people. And as he longed to be at home with his people, God longed for His people to be at home with Him. Now there is "no more sea." In this, God assured the seer that He and His people would be in fellowship without any threat of separation. With that, the stage was set to show just how God would be with His people. When John saw the holy city (New Jerusalem) coming down in readiness, from God, as a bride adorned for her husband, he heard a great voice out of Heaven calling attention to the fact that the tabernacle of God is with men (Revelation 21:1-3). Not with men momentarily as was the tabernacle in the wilderness, but continually. "He will dwell with them." Further assurance came when the voice added, "And they shall be his people, and God himself shall be with them, and be their God." Three times in verse 3, the saints, who had been so despised and at times so devoid of fellowship, were promised God's immediate presence–"the tabernacle of God is with men," "he [God] will dwell with them" and "God himself shall be with them." Paraphrased, it reads, "God will pitch His tent with men. More than that, He will dwell with men and will actually be with them." Dwelling among them He will remove all cause for tears (the saints had known many; especially the original readers of Revelation), for all former things will pass, such as death, sorrow, and pain. Instructions to write the true and faithful words, "Behold, I make all things new" came from Him that sat upon the throne. Just as surely as He had made all things in the beginning (Genesis 1:1 and John 1:l-3), He would make all things new. God "tabernacling" among men was symbolic of perfect fellowship. John's readers and possibly John himself thought again of the words of Christ in John 14:3b, "that where I am, there ye may be also." Restrained in public worship and fellowship, the persecuted saints of Asia Minor took courage in the fact that one day He would dwell right among us. We shall have uninterrupted fellowship with Him. Even in this life, one of the sustaining forces is fellowship–as imperfect as it may be. A bit of eternity is the joy of the saint when he is made to sit in heavenly places (Ephesians 2:6). During such moments the angels encamp round about the saints. Once again it is said, "I started it (I am Alpha); I will finish it (Omega). It is done." Following that assuring announcement is an invitation to the thirsty, "I will give . . . of the fountain of the water of life." Thoughts of dwelling (tenting with the Lord) with the Lord are heightened when it is stated that "the fearful, and unbelieving, and the abominable, and murderers, and whoremongers, and sorcerers, and idolaters, and all liars, shall have their part in the lake which burneth with fire and brimstone: which is the second death."

As though dwelling with God is not enough, more is pledged, "He that overcometh shall inherit all things." Calvinists believe that the saved will overcome. Arminians believe that the saved must overcome. In both cases the belief is held that only the overcomers will make Heaven. Now note: According to verse 7, "He that overcometh shall inherit all things." Only overcomers make it to Heaven and the overcomers inherit all things. Where then is the doctrine of rewards as taught by some? There are those who would have one believe that it is possible to go beyond the call of duty in Christian warfare, but this is not true. They would also have one believe there is a special eternal reward for someone who goes beyond the call of duty. A man may go beyond the call of duty in any branch of the American military and receive a medal for such duty, but this is not true in spiritual battles of life with respect to rewards in eternity. To take such a stand as contended here is to buck stiff opposition, but the truth is worth more than all peace one may acquire through compromise. There is no example in all Scripture where a man was complimented by the Lord for going beyond the call of duty. There is no example in all Scripture where the Lord gave a man a medal for going beyond the call of duty. Notice what Christ had to say on the subject in Luke 17:7-9,

> But which of you, having a servant plowing or feeding cattle, will say unto him by and by, when he is come from the field, Go and sit down to meat? And will not rather say unto him, Make ready wherewith I may sup, and gird thyself, and serve me, till I have eaten and drunken; and afterward thou shalt eat and drink? Doth he thank that servant because he did the things that were commanded him? I trow not.

According to the Lord Jesus Christ, a man is but an unprofitable servant when he has done all the things that were commanded him. To do all that the Lord has commanded is but our duty according to Christ. How then can a man go beyond the call of duty? Christ tells us that the man who does all that is commanded is not thanked. In fact, Christ asked, "Doth he thank that servant because he did those things that were commanded him?'" He then answered, "I trow not.'" Some would have the student believe that just because one person must leave home, parents, brethren, wife, children, and land to do what God demands of him, he should have a greater reward than someone who may remain at home, with wife, children, brethren, parents, and land, though both are doing what God wants them to do. Since Christ is the authority, He should be consulted in this regard. In Luke 18:29, 30, He had this to say in answer to Peter's statement, "Lo, we have left all, and followed thee":

> Verily I say unto you, There is no man that hath left house, or parents, or brethren, or wife, or children, for the kingdom of God's sake, Who shall not receive manifold more in this present time, and in the world to come life everlasting.

Nothing is said of such a person having a greater reward in eternity, but "manifold more" here and now. With respect to eternity, Christ said, "in the world to come life everlasting." It is pointed out very clearly that in order for a man even to be a disciple he must forsake all that he has. "So likewise, whosoever he be of you that forsaketh not all that he hath, he cannot be my disciple" (Luke 14:33).

Every man has to forsake all, but not everyone has to move away from all. Some who move away from all have not necessarily forsaken all, whereas some who may be allowed to stay near all may have completely forsaken it. The point is this: The man who forsakes all is a disciple who will enjoy manifold more in this present time and will have everlasting life. Everlasting life is the promise of every disciple of the Lord Jesus. All shall receive a "penny a day'" (Matthew 20:1-16). No more or less is promised. The overcomer inherits all things. Differences in accomplishments may come as a result in a difference in abilities. Every man receives "according to his several ability" (Matthew 25:15), and God gives to every man severally as He will (1 Corinthians 12:11). And too, all good ground does not produce alike, but even so, it is called good (Mark 4:8). Every believer is an heir and a "joint-heir" (Romans 8:17). Prejudice and respect of persons will be no more for all shall share alike.

One of the seven vial-carrying messengers invited the revelator to a showing of the bride, the Lamb's wife. Accepting the invitation, he was conveyed to a high and lofty place where he saw the "great city, the holy Jerusalem." The city represented the protection that would belong to the saints when home–perfect protection. Early in this writer's ministry he declared that the holy city, New Jerusalem, would be the capital of the New Heaven and New Earth. Never did he look to Jerusalem in Palestine, nor does he now. Why? Because of that city, Paul has this to say in Galatians 4:22-26,

> For it is written, that Abraham had two sons, the one by a bondmaid, the other by a freewoman. But he who was of the bondwoman was born after the flesh; but he of the freewoman was by promise. Which things are an allegory: for these are the two covenants; the one from the mount Sinai, which gendereth to bondage, which is Agar. For this Agar is mount Sinai in Arabia, and answereth to Jerusalem which now is, and is in bondage with her children. But Jerusalem which is above is free, which is the mother of us all.

A distinction is made. Legitimate children hold to Jerusalem which is above (the one John saw coming down); bastard children hold to earthly Jerusalem. They that are Christ's are Abraham's seed, "and heirs according to the promise" (Galatians 3:29). Abraham "looked for a city which hath foundations. . ." (Hebrews 11:10) knowing that "here have we no continuing city" (Hebrews 13:14). The beauty of the city is expressed in the words, "Having the glory of God: and her light . . . like . . . a stone most precious . . ." (brilliant radiance). A continuing city (cf. Hebrews 13:14) is signified in the solidness of the foundation. An abundant entrance is the meaning of the three gates on either side (twelve in all) of the city. Also, call to mind Christ's statement, "And they shall come from the east, and from the west, and from the north, and from the south, and shall sit down in the kingdom of God" (Luke 13:29). Entrance by way of the triune God may also be signified in the gates. Christ was the manifestation of God (Colossians 2:9). He is the Pearl of Great Price (Revelation 21:21).

A great wall suggests protection, and "high wall" would signify perfect protection. The measured description of the city is given only that one might understand the perfection and the wonderful completeness of that city. Perfect room for all of the redeemed is seen in the multiple number, "12,000." Any attempt to make this into a literal number will certainly destroy the symbolism. John's word description, given in highly symbolic language, is intended to show a "room enough," perfect and glorious city where the redeemed saints will dwell with their God in perfect fellowship, well protected. Questions may arise about the stones (precious stones) in the walls and the street of pure gold. These terms are employed to show the wonderfulness of the City of God where divine protection for all eternity will be afforded God's people. To interpret each thing literally is to take away from the expectancy of it all. Dana stated, "The splendid furnishings and illumination of the city are symbolical of the glory of Heaven."[93]

No longer will there be a need for a temple for "the Lord God Almighty and the Lamb are the temple of it." On earth, God had met His people in the temple. It was at the temple that sacrifices were made. Also, intercession for sin was made at the temple. Such a temple is not needed in the New Jerusalem for "there shall in no wise enter into it any thing that defileth, neither whatsoever worketh abomination, or maketh a lie: but they which are written in the Lamb's book of life" (Revelation 21:27).

Thoughts of Eden come to mind when one reads, "And he shewed me a pure river of water of life, clear as crystal, proceeding out of the throne of God and of the Lamb" (Revelation 22:1). Here a garden is set forth to symbolize enjoyment and plenty. There was joy when God walked with Adam in the garden. That is, until sin entered. Now, with sin gone, the original joy would be experienced. Much significance may be attached to the statement, "and there shall be no more curse" (Revelation 22:3). The life-giving, life-sustaining tree of life on either side of the river of life was accessible. When man sinned in the garden, a flaming, rotating sword was so placed that man could not approach unto the tree of life (Genesis 3:24). Man is pictured as coming full circle. He began with his God in the garden. He has his eternity with his God in a garden. Having lost it all through sin in a garden, he gained it all in a garden through Christ.

Just a glimpse of Heaven's activity is seen in the expressions "and his servants shall serve him: And they shall see his face . . ." (Revelation 22:3c, 4a). Heaven will be perfect fellowship, perfect protection, and perfect enjoyment. What more could be asked?

Revelation 22:6, an attestation to the revelation message, is almost a restatement of Revelation 1:1. The great voice of Revelation 21:3 assures John that the message he had written was true and that the beginning of its fulfillment was soon. John, in verse 8, then speaks for himself and states, "I . . . saw these things, and heard them."

Pertinency of the message is shown in three statements: "things which must shortly be done" (verse 6), "Seal not the sayings of the . . . book" (verse l0a), and "for the time is at hand" (verse l0b).

Sacredness of the message is seen in the fact that it was to be read in all of the churches. Also, it contained an invitation to "come" and a solemn warning about tampering with its contents.

The conclusion is appropriate enough. It ends speaking of Christ's sudden return and with a blessed benediction. Not one hint of "signs of His coming" is given in the closing chapter, but "suddenness" of His coming occupies three verses: 7, 12, and 20. He speaks of His sudden coming and challenges to obedience in the light of it. He speaks of His sudden coming and declares His reward will be with Him. He speaks of His sudden coming and shouts, "Amen!"

John, lead us in prayer: "Even so, come, Lord Jesus."

Notes
for The Unsealed Book

[1]Damon C. Dodd, *The Book of Revelation, A Study Guide,* 111.

[2]Ray Summers, *Worthy Is the Lamb,* xiii.

[3]Jay E. Adams, *The Time Is At Hand,* vii.

[4]Ibid.

[5]Ibid.

[6]Leon Morris, *The Revelation of St. John, An Introduction and Commentary,* 13.

[7]Summers, 21.

[8]Harry Buis, *The Book of Revelation, A Simplified Commentary,* iii.

[9]C.F. Wishart, *The Book of Day,* quoted in Ray Summers' *Worthy Is the Lamb,* xv.

[10]Buis, 1.

[11]Summers, 98.

[12]Morris, 47.

[13]Summers, 107.

[14]Albertus Pieters, *Studies in The Revelation of St. John,* 83.

[15]Psalm 89:35-37; Acts 2:22-36; Acts 7:49.

[16]Philip Mauro, *Of Things Which Soon Must Come to Pass,* 61.

[17]Ibid., 62.

[18]Ibid.

[19]Summers, 105.

[20]Adams, 57.

[21]Pieters, 97.

[22]Ibid., 102

[23]Ibid., 102, 103.

[24]Summers, 108.

[25]Luther Poellot, *Revelation, The Last Book in the Bible,* 35.

[26]Robert Tuck, *The Preacher's Complete Homiletic Commentary on the General Epistles,* Vol. 31, p. 444.

[27]Morris, 68.

[28]Summers, 117.

[29]Edward A. McDowell, *The Meaning and Message of the Book of Revelation,* 53.

[30]Harvey J. S. Blaney, *The Wesleyan Bible Commentary,* Vol. VI, 436.

[31]McDowell, 53.

[32]Genesis 18:32.

[33]Morris, 77.

[34]Exodus 32:31-33.

[35]Summers, 124.

[36]Buis, 26.

[37]Summers, 136, 137.

[38]Poellot, 89.

[39]Ibid., 94.

[40]Pieters, 120.

[41]J. Marcellus Kik, *Matthew XXIV, An Exposition,* 69, 70.

[42]McDowell, 96.

[43]Poelott, 111.

[44]Summers, 155.

[45]Blaney, 455.

[46]Poellot, 120.

[47]Buis, 52.

[48]Summers, 157.

[49]Morris, 127.

[50]McDowell, 104.

[51]Buis, 53.

[52]Blaney, 458.

[53]Poellot, 123.

[54]Blaney, 458.

[55]Morris, 127.

[56]Ibid.

[57]Summers, 158.

[58]H.E. Dana, *The Epistles and Apocalypse of John, A Brief Commentary,* 127.

[59]Morris, 135.

[60]Summers, 159.

[61]Poellot, 131.

[62]Buis, 56.
[63]Dana, 123.
[64]Morris, 146.
[65]Blaney, 463.
[66]Summers, 165.
[67]Dana, 130.
[68]Morris, 165.
[69]McDowell, 139.
[70]Pieters, 241, 242.
[71]Dana, 138, 139.
[72]McDowell, 157.
[73]Summers, 186.
[74]Pieters, 243.
[75]Poellot, 199.
[76]Ibid.
[77]Blaney, 485.
[78]Pieters, 244.
[79]Dana, 143.
[80]Summers, 192.
[81]Dana, 145.
[82]Ibid., 147.
[83]William E. Cox, *Biblical Studies in Final Things,* 158.
[84]Dana, 150.
[85]McDowell, 191.
[86]Buis, 109.
[87]*A Treatise of the Faith and Practices of the Original Free Will Baptists,* 1940 Revision, 35.
[88]*A Treatise of the Faith and Practices of the Original Free Will Baptists,* 1974 Revision, 40.
[89]Dana, 152.
[90]Morris, 240.
[91]Adams, 95.
[92]Summers, 132.
[93]Dana, 154.

Printed in the United States
205138BV00002B/157-162/A